Picture Yourself Creating

with Photoshop® Elements 5.0

Diane Koers

THOMSON
™
COURSE TECHNOLOGY

Professional ■ Technical ■ Reference

ISBN-10: 1-59863-350-3

ISBN-13: 978-1-59863-350-4

Library of Congress Catalog Card Number: 2006907916

Printed in the United States of America

07 08 09 10 11 BU 10 9 8 7 6 5 4 3 2 1

Thomson Course Technology PTR,
a division of Thomson Learning Inc.
25 Thomson Place
Boston, MA 02210
http://www.courseptr.com

THOMSON

COURSE TECHNOLOGY

Professional ■ Technical ■ Reference

Publisher and General Manager, Thomson Course Technology PTR:
Stacy L. Hiquet

Associate Director of Marketing:
Sarah O'Donnell

Manager of Editorial Services:
Heather Talbot

Marketing Manager:
Heather Hurley

Senior Acquisitions Editor:
Emi Smith

Marketing Coordinator:
Adena Flitt

Project and Copy Editor:
Marta Justak

Technical Reviewer:
Dave Rivers

PTR Editorial Services Coordinator:
Erin Johnson

Interior Layout:
Shawn Morningstar

CD-ROM Producer:
Brandon Penticuff

Cover Designer:
Mike Tanamachi

Indexer:
Larry Sweazy

Proofreader:
Kezia Endsley

To Vern

*For your continual encouragement during the
writing of this book, all while going through tough times yourself.
You are truly unique and incredibly special.*

Acknowledgments

IN A BOOK SUCH AS THIS ONE, it's hard to know where to start. There are so many people working behind the scenes, each one as valuable as the next. First, I'd like to thank Emi Smith for believing in me enough to let me write this book. To Marta Justak, whose patience and sense of humor (not to mention her wonderful grammatical skills) kept me going through the process. To David Rivers, who used his incredible knowledge of Photoshop Elements to keep me on track. To Shawn Morningstar, for exercising all her layout talents in making this a beautiful book. To Kezia Endsley and Larry Sweazy, and all the others working madly behind the scenes to get this book into print. To all of you, thank you from the bottom of my heart.

There were a number of people who provided the photographs you see in this book. It was often difficult for all of them because I frequently needed "less than perfect" images to work, which sometimes is easier said than done. A special thank you to all photograph and creation contributors:

Hossley Partington
Griffing Partington
Paul Koers
Tresee Koers
Lois Van Ackern
ScrapGirls, LLC

And finally, a huge note of appreciation goes to my husband of 38 years. Vern, thank you for your patience and understanding of the *many* late night hours, for fending for yourself or both of us at supper time, and for keeping me encouraged and supplied with Diet Coke and working chocolate. I love you.

About the Author

DIANE KOERS owns and operates All Business Service, a software training and consulting business formed in 1988 that services the central Indiana area. Her area of expertise has long been in the word-processing, spreadsheet, and graphics areas of computing. In addition, she provides training and support for Peachtree Accounting Software. Diane's authoring experience includes over 35 books on topics such as PC Security, Microsoft Windows, Microsoft Office, Microsoft Works, WordPerfect, Photoshop Elements, Lotus SmartSuite, Quicken, Microsoft Money, and Peachtree Accounting, many of which have been translated into other languages such as Dutch, Bulgarian, French, Spanish, and Greek. She has also developed and written numerous training manuals for her clients.

Diane and her husband enjoy spending their free time RVing around the United States and playing with their four grandsons and their Yorkshire terrier.

Author Competence

You'll quickly determine, as you delve into this book, that I'm not a professional photographer. Even calling me an amateur would require a large stretch of the imagination. I am, however, a teacher and a writer, a computer geek, and a Photoshop Elements enthusiast. With those tools and a lot of help and research, I have written this book with the intention of helping you get the most you can out of Photoshop Elements. I hope you enjoy learning from it as much as I've enjoyed writing it.

If you have any comments about this book, please feel free to contact me at diane@thepeachtreelady.com.

Diane Koers

Table of Contents

Introduction

Designed for anyone interested in photography or photographic creations, this book came into existence to show you how you can put the incredible power of Photoshop Elements into play with your images. This book cuts right to the chase of the Photoshop Elements tools that are best used when working with photographs. You will learn about photographs and how to correct and enhance them, making them better than they appeared out of your camera. There's even a chapter dedicated just to color and understanding how it works.

You'll learn about using layers to make adjustments, such as brightness, hue, color contrast, and many others. This book covers the often-misunderstood topic of resolution and how it applies to your monitor, your images, and your prints.

It's not all work, though. You'll also learn about many of the fun things you can do with your photographs, such as creating greeting cards and digital scrapbook pages with them. You'll discover how you can make composite images, retouch and repair damaged photographs, and how you can create works of art with the special effects provided with Photoshop Elements.

The best way to absorb a feature is to jump in and try it. Taste is relative. What you like about an image may be completely different than the person next to you. We are confident that as you make your way through this book, you will gain a good feel for the awesome power of Photoshop Elements.

Assumptions

We make a couple of assumptions about our readers in this book. First, and most obviously, since you're reading this right now, we assume that you want to know more. So we are going to try and fill you with knowledge. Secondly, we assume that you know the basics of working with a computer, such as using the mouse, making menu selections, and opening, saving, and closing a file. If you know those basics, you can find your way around Photoshop Elements.

Book Structure

This book is divided into 10 chapters, which fall into three main sections. Chapters 1-3 get you acquainted with the basic tools available in Photoshop Elements. Chapters 4-8 show you how to work with managing and manipulating photographs, including adding filters and working with the various output functions. Chapters 9 and 10 are where you put all the tools and photographs together to make fantastic fun items, such as scrapbook pages, postage stamps, photo albums, and greeting cards.

Throughout the book, you'll also see various tips and notes designed to alert you to special considerations. Attached to the back of this book, you'll find a CD filled with hundreds of useful items, including graphics, photographs, fonts, and lots of other free, fun stuff. You'll also find a variety of demo programs you can install to try some of the Photoshop Element add-on filters.

Getting *Acquainted*

Photographer:
Jonathan Hawkins

PICTURE yourself viewing a colony of artists: artists who draw, artists who paint, artists who photograph. Visualize them standing outside in the sunlight with their sketchpads, easels, and cameras— all of them enjoying the serene beauty of nature. Now picture yourself in the midst of them. Do you see it?

If you cannot see yourself in their company because you don't draw, paint, or photograph, don't give up hope. There's another artists' colony around, and you can, with the aid of the fabulous Adobe Photoshop Elements software program, join right in—even if you're allergic to sunlight. This colony consists of artists all using Photoshop Elements where you can create electronic works of art from your digital photographs.

This chapter shows you the basic instructions for maneuvering around in Photoshop Elements, as well as introduces you to the various screen elements and tools. You probably already know about opening and saving files, but we'll review those features and perhaps show you a few shortcuts along the way.

This is a great time in our history to work with digital images. Relax. You're just a few mouse clicks away from releasing your inner creativity.

Just What Is Photoshop Elements?

PHOTOSHOP ELEMENTS is an unparalleled image editor and organizer software package, designed to give you the wide range of features required when working with digital images. Its abundance of impressive features allows you to easily share, organize, and edit your digital photos. Do you want to learn how to build amazing slide shows or get into digital scrapbooking? How about organizing the thousands of digital images stored on your computer hard drive, camera, or memory card? To accomplish those tasks, you need software like Photoshop Elements. Let's take a brief look at some of the specific things you can do with Photoshop Elements:

► Fix common photographic flaws such as red eye, scratches, color, contrast, or lighting.

► Crop unwanted image areas, allowing you to zoom in on the subject of interest.

► Convert your favorite color image to black and white or sepia to give it an old-fashioned appearance.

► Twist, warp, or stretch your images to create surreal scenes.

► Imitate painting with realistic paintbrush effects to simulate oils, watercolors, charcoals, pastels, and different canvas textures.

► Stylize your photos with special effects and combine elements from different photos on multiple layers to create artistic composites or panoramas.

► Change or erase photo backgrounds or remove unwanted portions (such as your ex-brother-in-law).

► Allow your images to tell a story in colorful decorative scrapbook pages, calendars, greeting cards, and more by adding text and shapes. Go one step further and add sound and transitions to create dynamic slide shows you can view on your computer or television.

► Organize your digital photos by grouping them by event, date, keywords, and more. Using face recognition technology, you can, with a single click, locate all images of a specified person.

Launching Photoshop Elements

Photoshop Elements is as an image-editing package, which is designed specifically for amateur photographers, hobbyists, and business users. Originally released in 2001, Photoshop Elements 1 was touted as the consumer version of Adobe Photoshop, which was, and still is, the granddaddy of all image editing software. Five years later comes Photoshop Elements 5.0 with more features than most of us will ever use.

If you're ready, let's take a look at Photoshop Elements. Launch Photoshop Element by double-clicking the desktop icon or by Choosing Start > All Programs > Adobe Photoshop Elements 5.0.

When you first launch Photoshop Elements, the entire application doesn't load into your computer memory; just a portion of it does. The Welcome screen appears, providing a number of options, many of which will launch other parts of the Photoshop Elements program. From the Welcome screen, you select an option to get you into a Photoshop Elements workspace. Let's begin by taking a look at Figure 1-1 and the Welcome screen options:

Across the top of the Welcome screen, you see five buttons. The Product Overview button is really a form of advertising Photoshop Elements, listing a few of the things you can do. For example, if you click the View and Organize photos button, Adobe launches the Organizer workspace where you can organize all your digital images. In Chapter 4, we'll extensively review the Organizer and all its great features.

The third and fourth buttons, Quickly Fix Photos and Edit and Enhance Photos, launch the Editor workspace where you do repairs, modifications, and drawings. It's also where we'll spend most of our time in this book.

The fifth button, Make Photo Creations, also launches the Editor, as well as guides you into the creative side of Photoshop Elements. From this button, you can begin to make special items such as greeting cards, calendars, and slide shows, as well as designing unique photo layouts.

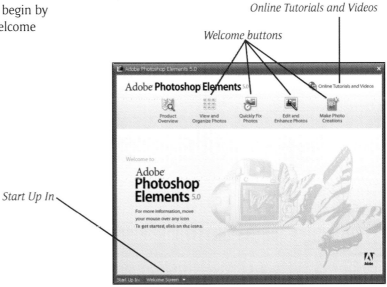

Figure 1-1
The Photoshop Elements Welcome screen.

The nice thing to remember is that, even if you pick the wrong button and launch the Organizer instead of the Editor, or open the Editor when you intended to open the Organizer, you can switch back and forth between the two windows.

In the Welcome screen top-right corner, notice the link to Online Tutorials and Videos. Clicking this link launches your Web browser and connects you to an Adobe Web site where you'll find an abundance of helpful tutorials like the ones you see in Figure 1-2, each designed with a specific outcome.

Finally, look in the lower-left corner of the Welcome screen. You can see an arrow. If you click the arrow, you'll see the options that determine how the Photoshop Elements program starts up. Options are the Welcome Screen, the Editor, or the Organizer. If you primarily use the Editor or Organizer workspace, choose it from here and skip the Welcome screen.

Since, during the course of this book, we'll spend most of our time in the Editor workspace, let's examine that window and the elements that appear in it. Click the Edit and Enhance Photos button to launch the Editor workspace.

Tutorial link

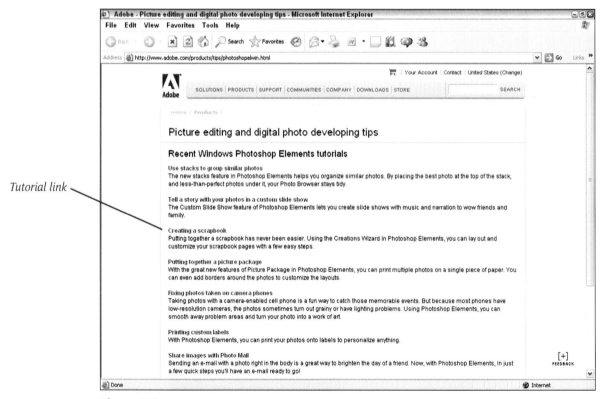

Figure 1-2
Online Photoshop Elements tutorial links.

Introducing the Editor Window

The Editor window has a well put-together interface and an extraordinary collection of tools. It's a busy screen with lots of buttons and options, all of which are designed to help you work quickly on your photograph. Figure 1-3 illustrates the Editor workspace with an image already loaded into it. Later in this chapter, I'll show you how to load an image.

Full Edit Tab

There are two tabs across the top. When you want to do major image manipulation, you should use the Full Edit tab. The Quick Fix tab is for those situations when you just need some minor adjusting. Each tab has its own set of features. Let's start with the Full Edit tab.

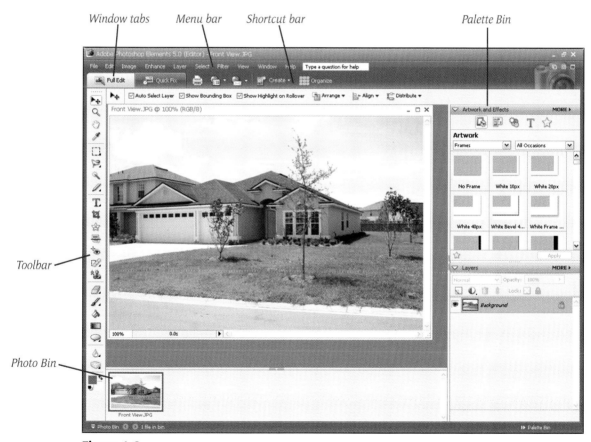

Figure 1-3
The Editor workspace.

Menu Bar

Traditional to Windows programs, you'll see the menu bar across the top. Every feature available in the Photoshop Elements program is accessible through the Menu bar. When a menu feature has an arrow next to it (such as the New option in Figure 1-4), choosing that feature opens another submenu from which you can choose. Some features, like the Page Setup feature, has an ellipsis (three dots) after it, which means that if you select that feature, Photoshop Elements opens a dialog box prompting you for further instructions.

Also note that next to many choices are shortcut keys. If you prefer using the keyboard instead of the mouse, you can press the key combinations shown to access those features. For example, pressing Ctrl+P opens the Print dialog box.

Figure 1-4

The File menu.

Key Oddity

Different than many Windows applications, pressing the Alt key does not open the menu; however, pressing the Escape key is still a keyboard method to close a menu.

Shortcuts Bar

Next to the Full Edit and Quick Fix tabs, you can see several icons that Photoshop Elements calls the Shortcuts bar. The icons are quick ways to get to several key features including printing and switching to the Organizer workspace. As you'll discover, when you get into the Organizer workspace, the Shortcut bar buttons will change to provide quick tool access for Organizer tools.

Toolbar

Along the left side of the screen is the Photoshop Elements toolbar, also known as the Tools palette. Each tool has a different use and Chapter 2 shows you how to use each of the tools in the toolbar. You access tools by either clicking the button with the mouse or pressing the shortcut key assigned to each tool. As you suspend your mouse over the individual buttons, a tool tip appears with the tool name and its shortcut key. Figure 1-5 also shows you the toolbar and each associated shortcut key. If you click the tool tip, Photoshop Elements launches the Adobe Help Center with hints and information about the selected tool.

Some tools, such as the Magnetic Lasso, Eraser, and Brush tools display a small arrow on the button. Called a tool group, the arrow indicates there are more tools nested within that tool button. Right-click a tool to display the additional tools. In Figure 1-6, you see the nested menu for the Brush tool.

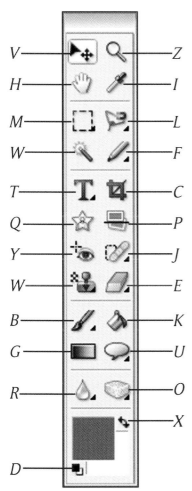

Figure 1-5
The Editor toolbar and its shortcut keys.

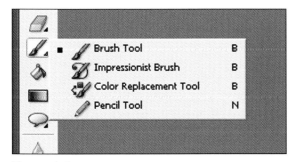

Figure 1-6
Right-click a tool to see additional tool choices.

Options Bar

Many of the toolbar tools have additional options. For example, if you want to use the Brush tool, you need to tell Photoshop Elements what style of brush you want to use—the thickness, opacity, and mode. The Options bar is located near the top of the window under the Shortcuts bar. As you select different tools, the Options bar changes to display the selected tool options.

Palette Bin

On the right side of the screen is the essential Palette Bin. Both the Editor and Organizer work-spaces have a Palette Bin, but the contents and functions are different. Basically, palettes are small windows that help you manage, monitor, and modify your images. Where the toolbar contains the program's main tools, the palettes display the options. In the Editor, by default, Photoshop Elements displays the Artwork and Effects palette and the Layers palette. Other palettes available in Editor are the Color Swatches, Histogram, How to, Info, Navigator, and Undo History palettes. Throughout the course of this book, you will become acquainted with many of the different palettes and their uses. You can display and hide individual palettes through the Window menu where each click turns a selected palette on or off.

Any palette can be located in the Palette Bin, or it can be opened anywhere on the workspace. If you have all the available palettes open, but don't store them in the Palette Bin, your workspace can get very cluttered and messy, as you see in Figure 1-7.

Hide/Display Palette Bin button

Palette Bin

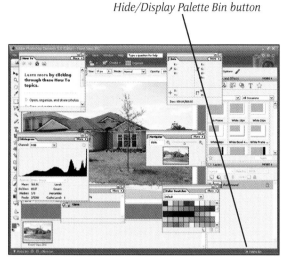

Figure 1-7
Having all palettes open can make it difficult to work.

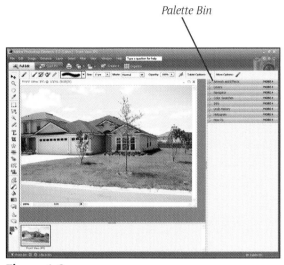

Figure 1-8
Storing the palettes in the Palette Bin.

Instead, you can park any of the palettes in the Palette Bin. On any palette you want to park in the Palette Bin, follow these steps:

1. Click the More button. A list of options appears.

2. Choose Place in Palette Bin when Closed.

3. Click the Palette Close button. The palette is stored in the Palette Bin.

Figure 1-8 shows how much cleaner and neater the workspace looks with the palettes stored in the Bin.

Here are a couple of things you should know about working with the different palettes:

▶ **Open and close any palette by clicking the triangle next to the palette name. When the palette is open, the triangle points downward and the palette options appear. When closed, the triangle points right.**

▶ **To move a palette off the Palette Bin, drag the palette title bar to a different spot in the workspace. Drag it back into the Palette Bin to put it back.**

▶ **To rearrange the palettes, drag the palette's title bar to a new location.**

▶ **Resize a palette by dragging any corner of the palette. This only works when the palette is not stored in the bin.**

▶ **To hide or display the entire Palette Bin, click the word Palette Bin in the bottom-right corner of the Photoshop Elements window.**

▶ **To reset palettes to their default positions, choose Windows > Reset Palette Locations.**

Palette Preferences

When you reopen Photoshop Elements, the palettes appear in the location they were in when you last exited Photoshop Elements. To have the palettes always open in the default locations, choose Edit > Preferences > General. Deselect the Save Palette Locations option.

File Information

Right-click any open photo in the Photo Bin and select File Info. An information box appears that tells you the file name, file format, the type of camera used, F-stop, flash information, copyright data, and lots of other image data.

Photo Bin

Along the bottom of the screen is the Photo Bin, which displays thumbnails of all open images. Use the Photo Bin to switch quickly between the different images. Next and Previous controls are included in the Photo Bin to assist you in managing the images (see Figure 1-9). If you don't want to see the Photo Bin, you can close it with the close Photo Bin button.

Hide/Display Photo Bin   *Open Images*
                Next and Previous

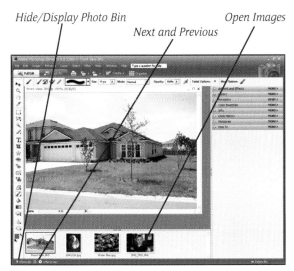

Figure 1-9
Open images in the Photo Bin.

Image Window

The main part of the screen, where you see your photograph, is the Image window. It has Minimize, Maximize, and Close buttons along the top right, and scroll bars along the right side and bottom. Across the title bar, you also see the image file name, current magnification percentage, and color mode.

Along the bottom of the window, as noted in Figure 1-10, you'll see other useful tools, including the Size handle, which you can drag to manually resize the window, and the Magnification box, where you can enter a percentage amount to zoom in and out of the image. You'll soon discover Photoshop Elements includes a much easier tool for zooming.

Title bar   *Information box*

Magnification box   *Size handle*

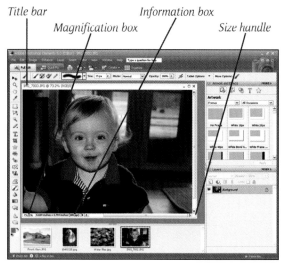

Figure 1-10
The Image window with an open file.

One other important piece of information along the window bottom is the Information box. By default, the Information box displays your image dimensions and resolution. While this is certainly critical information when working on an image, you can click the arrow to the right of the box to change the display options. Information display options include:

▶ **Document Sizes:** Displays the saved file size.

▶ **Document Profile:** Displays the color scheme used.

▶ **Document Dimensions:** Displays the image dimensions and resolution.

▶ **Scratch Sizes:** Displays the amount of RAM memory used by all open Photoshop Elements images. If your images use more than your RAM memory, Photoshop Elements creates virtual memory by using your hard disk.

▶ **Efficiency:** Displays whether Photoshop Elements is using the standard RAM memory or the Scratch disk memory. If at 100% you are still using RAM, but if below 100%, Photoshop Elements is using scratch memory.

▶ **Timing:** Displays the amount of time Photoshop Elements took to complete the last operation you requested.

▶ **Current Tool:** Displays the currently selected tool on the Toolbar.

Rulers and Grids

By default, neither the rulers nor the grids display in the workspace; however, as you get into the intricate details of image manipulation, you may want to precisely position the cursor or an object on the screen. Using the rulers and grids can help. Both items are located under the View menu. Choose View > Rulers to display a horizontal (Y axis) and vertical (X axis) ruler, as you see in Figure 1-11, and choose View > Grid to display a nonprinting positioning grid. Choose the options again to turn the feature off.

Vertical Ruler   *Horizontal Ruler*

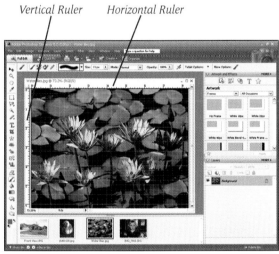

Figure 1-11
Use the ruler for positioning items or aligning brush strokes.

Units of Measurement

By default, the ruler and most Photoshop Elements measurements are in inches. To change the unit of measure, choose Edit > Preferences > Units & Rulers. Change the grid color, line style, and spacing by choosing Edit > Preferences > Grid.

Quick Fix Tab

If you click the Quick Fix tab shown in Figure 1-12, you'll see many of the same items that are in the Full Edit tab. However, the toolbar contains fewer tools, and the Palette Bin contains different items, typically those that apply to adjusting image color and lighting.

Toolbar   *Palette Bin*

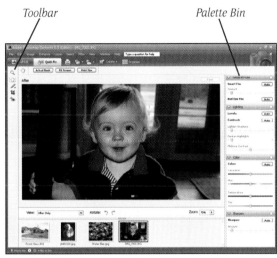

Figure 1-12
The Quick Fix window with an open file.

Reviewing File Basics

MOST OF THIS SECTION may be a review for you since Photoshop Elements handles files similarly to other software packages you may have used. However, since PE works with images instead of documents, you may notice some slight differences. Let's take a quick look at opening, saving, closing, and creating a file.

Open an Existing Image

Photoshop Elements has three different Open commands where you will retrieve an image already saved to a disk—whether it is from your hard disk, your camera media, or a CD or DVD. You can have as many files open at the same time as your computer memory will allow. As you open an image, a thumbnail image is added to the Photo Bin located at the bottom of the windows. The image windows are stacked with the most recently opened image on top.

Open

The following steps show you how to open an existing image:

1. Choose File > Open or press Ctrl+O. Photoshop Elements displays the Open dialog box you see in Figure 1-13. Notice the Preview window at the bottom of the dialog box.

2. Click the Look in drop-down list to select the drive and folder where the image is located. By default, Photoshop Elements looks in the My Documents folder, but if you change the folder location, the next time you use Photoshop Elements, it remembers to look first in the new folder location.

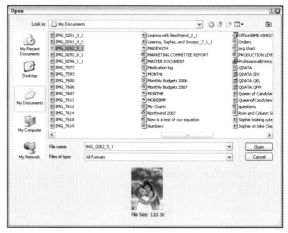

Figure 1-13
Open an image.

Select File Type

Click the Files of Type drop-down arrow to filter from a list of selected file types.

3. Click the image name you want; then click the Open button. The image appears in the window ready for you to modify.

Open As

The Open As command allows you to open a file in any of many different file formats, such as JPG or GIF, but open it in an entirely different format, such as TIFF or PNG. By default, Photoshop Elements expects you to open it in the native Photoshop Elements format. Photoshop Elements files end in a .PSD or .PDD extension.

You open a file in a different format by choosing File > Open As; then select the file you want and the format you want to use.

Comparing File Formats

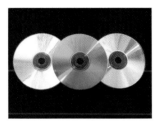

In the film world, format refers to the size of the film you use, such as 35mm or APS. In the digital realm, there are many format types. A digital format refers to the way digital images are stored on the disk. File formats are identified by the three-letter extension at the end of the identifying file name: filename.ext . Each format has its own characteristics, advantages, and disadvantages. Many digital cameras offer several different save file formats. Here are some of the more popular formats:

▶ **JPEG (Joint Photographic Experts Group) is one of the most common file formats. JPEG files can be used on both Mac and PC computers and are most commonly used for images on Web pages or in e-mail. JPEG uses a lossy compression scheme, which means it throws away some of the graphic data every time you save your file using the JPEG format. There are varying levels of compression with varying loss of detail. With a higher compression, a number of unwanted noise artifacts begin to appear on the image, giving a substantial loss of quality. At the highest compression (lowest quality), it can reduce files sizes to about 5% of their normal size. Merely opening a JPEG file, as on the Internet, does not result in any loss of data.**

▶ **PNG (Portable Networks Graphic) is a format similar to a JPEG file, but produces higher quality pictures and supports transparency and other features. PNG is still a relatively new format and if you are putting a PNG image on a Web site, the visitor must have a newer Web browser. Also, PNG files are typically a little larger in file size. Like a JPEG, PNG formats use a lossy data compression for color images with varying levels of compression and with varying loss of detail.**

▶ **TIFF (Tagged Image File Format) is another widely supported file format for storing images on a computer (both PCs and Macs). TIFF graphics can be any resolution, and they can be black and white, grayscale, or color. Additionally, TIFF files use a nonlossy format so that no data is lost when you save and resave files in a TIFF format. Files in TIFF format end with a .TIF extension.**

Comparing File Formats *(continued)*

▶ **GIF** (Graphics Interchange Format) is a Web standard file format that typically is small in file size and usually quick to load. GIF images also support transparency. GIF files use a lossless compression scheme and retain all the image information, but they only store 256 colors so the prints might look rough, blotchy, jagged, or banded because they don't include enough shades of color to accurately reproduce an image. A GIF format is not a good choice for color photographs.

▶ **RAW** file format, while the largest in file size, includes all information regarding a photograph, sort of a "digital negative" containing all the original information gathered by your camera with no compression or other processing. While every camera takes an image in a RAW format, you might need special software from your camera vendor to save an image in RAW format. Although RAW files are the largest in size, they are the most accurate representation of your image, in terms of white balance, color, sharpening, and so forth.

▶ **BMP** (Bitmap) files consist of rows and columns of dots. The value of each dot (whether it is filled in or not) is stored in one or more bits of data. For simple monochrome images, one bit is sufficient to represent each dot, but for colors and shades of gray, each dot requires more than one bit of data. The more bits used to represent a dot, the more colors and shades of gray that can be represented. The density of the dots, known as the resolution, determines how sharply the image is represented. This is often expressed in dots per inch (dpi) or simply by the number of rows and columns, such as 640 by 480. To display a bitmapped image on a monitor or to print it on a printer, the computer translates the bitmap into pixels (for display screens) or ink dots (for printers). Bitmapped graphics are often referred to as raster graphics. Bitmapped graphics become ragged when you shrink or enlarge them, and they are not a good choice for photographs or Web graphics.

▶ **PSD or PDD** (Photoshop) are proprietary formats native to Photoshop and its subsidiaries (such as Photoshop Elements). While you can open, save, and close the PSD or PDD file without losing any special features, the file can only be opened with the Photoshop or Photoshop Elements program. Therefore, it probably won't be the final format in which you save your file, but it's a great format to use while working on an image, especially since the image can contain layers in which you can continue to work.

Open a Recently Edited File

Photoshop Elements also includes a list of the recent file names you worked with in Photoshop Elements. This is especially time saving if you want to work with a file that is buried many layers deep in your hard drive, or you can't remember where the image is located. Choose File > Open Recently Edited File, which then displays a drop-down list of your recent images. Click the image you want to work with.

Previously Opened File

By default, the Recent File list includes the last 10 files. To change the number of listed files, go to Edit > Preferences > Saving Files. From there, you can set a value between 0 and 30.

Duplicate an Image

If you are going to do image editing to protect your original image, you should open the image and then duplicate it. Do the work on the duplicate, and you can compare the original to the modified to see if you really like the changes. When you are finished, you can save it over the original image if you want. Or you can keep both. Open the image using one of the above methods; then choose File > Duplicate. Photoshop Elements prompts you for an image name, although by default it takes the original name and adds copy to the end of it. Both images appear in the Photo Bin.

Close an Image

When you are finished working with an image, you can free your computer memory by closing it. Photoshop Elements offers two different options:

Close and Close All. The Close command simply closes the current image and Close All closes all open images. For the Close commands, choose File > Close or File > Close All. Both options prompt you to save your file if unsaved changes exist (see Figure 1-14).

Close Box

Optionally, click the image Close box.

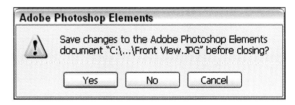

Figure 1-14
When closing a file, Photoshop Elements may prompt you to save it.

Save an Image

Photoshop Elements provides three variations for saving your file.

Quality Loss

Use caution when resaving an image as a JPG file. Each time you save it, it has the potential for losing a little more of its quality. If you are going to continue working on the image, you should save it as a PSD file until you are completely finished working on it.

Save

The Save command simply resaves your file in the exact same format and location, and with the same file name as when you opened it. To save a file, choose File > Save or press Ctrl+S. If you are working with a new file without a name, Photoshop Elements automatically displays the Save As dialog box where you can enter a different file name, format, or location.

Save Often

To avoid loss of work due to a power outage or software hiccup, it's a good idea to save your work every few minutes.

Save As

The Save As command prompts Photoshop Elements to stop and ask you for a file name, format, and location. Follow these steps for the Save As command:

1. Choose File > Save As to display the Save As dialog box (see Figure 1-15). It's very similar to other Save As dialog boxes you've used in other programs.

Save As

Optionally, press Ctrl+Shift+S to open the Save As dialog box.

2. Select a location. Either accept the default My Documents folder or choose a different folder from the My Places bar on the left or from the Save in drop-down list.

Figure 1-15
The Save As dialog box.

3. Enter a file name.

4. Select a file format from the Format drop-down list. The options that appear along the bottom of the dialog box will vary depending on the file format you are using.

5. Click Save. Again, depending on the file format you chose, you may be prompted for more information.

Save for Web

The third save option, File > Save for Web, allows you to see your image as it would look with optimization options as required for processing the image to a Web site. Because Web surfers generally don't want to wait for an image to load, you need for your image to appear quickly, so you should use compression, but you don't want to lose too much quality either. Through the Save for Web dialog box, you can experiment with different compression techniques to find the right combination for your image.

As shown in Figure 1-16, you'll see the original image on the left and a preview of the optimized image on the right. Controls also exist on the far right side from which you can choose different file formats and compression options. Under the preview image, you'll see the file type and other statistics, including approximate loading time.

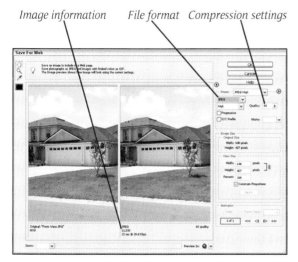

Figure 1-16
Preview an image as it will look on a Web page.

After you determine which compression settings you want, click the OK button. Photoshop Elements displays the Save Optimized As dialog box, where you can specify a file name and location.

Create a New Image

While a lot of the time you spend in Photoshop Elements will be working with photographs, you can start with a blank canvas and create your own graphic or logo.

As you've already seen, unlike some programs you use, Photoshop Elements doesn't automatically open with a blank canvas for you. If you want to

create an image from scratch, Photoshop Elements first requires several key pieces of information. Choose File > New > Blank File or press Ctrl+N to display the New dialog box you see in Figure 1-17.

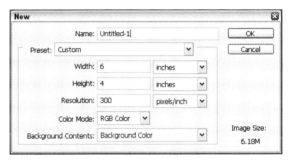

Figure 1-17
Create a new blank canvas.

Size

Photoshop Elements requires you to predetermine the size of the new image. You can declare the image measurements in a variety of different units, but the default unit is in inches. Another common unit of measurement is pixels, which stands for picture element. Pixels are the individual square or dots of light that are used to make up an image. In terms of measurement, a pixel is the smallest element that can be assigned a color.

Resolution

The second element Photoshop Elements requires is resolution. Resolution measures the number of pixels in a specific unit of measurement. With a higher resolution, more detail is displayed. The resolution you need depends on the purpose of the image. Most Web browsers and e-mail applications use a resolution of 72 pixels per inch. If you're going to print the image, go with a higher resolution, such as 600 pixels per inch or 1200 pixels per inch, depending on your printer's capabilities. Be aware though that large dimension sizes combined with high resolutions can result in very large file sizes.

Color Mode

Color modes are typically chosen based upon the output you'll want for your image. See Chapter 5 for more details about color and color modes. Photoshop Elements provides three color modes:

▶ **RGB (which stands for Red Green Blue) color mode is what you use if you're going to print the image on a color printer or send it to a photo service center.**

▶ **Bitmap mode is common when creating line art such as illustrations. Typically, bitmap modes have two colors—black and white.**

▶ **Grayscale mode is also black and white along with any of 256 shades of gray.**

Photoshop Elements does not support CYMK (Cyan Magenta Yellow Black) color mode. CYMK is typically used in commercial printing.

Background

The background simply determines the basic starting color on the canvas. You can start with white and fill it later with any color you choose, or you can begin with a color. You can also select a transparent background. Click the Background Contents drop-down arrow to make your selection. In most cases, you'll select the White background and take it from there.

Looking for Help

ALTHOUGH I HOPE you get much of your information from this book, there are times you will be stuck understanding a concept or how a feature works. There's a wealth of knowledge at your fingertips, and we're going to take a quick look at some of that information.

Photoshop Elements provides a number of different ways to access its built-in help system. You've already seen how you can get help on a specific toolbar tool by pausing your mouse over the tool and clicking the tool tip link. The Photoshop Elements help system loads with specific details about the tool you selected.

A second method is the Search box along the menu, just to the right of the Help menu. Type a word or phrase into the Search box and press the Enter key. Photoshop Elements searches through its help system for the words you entered. Take a look at Figure 1-18 where the words "file formats" was typed in the Search box and the Adobe Help Center window appeared with a lengthy article about the various file formats for saving.

Search box   Print button   More Resources

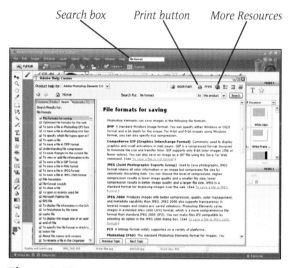

Figure 1-18
Help results from the Search box.

On the left side of the Adobe Help Center window, you see several tabs, two of which are invaluable when you need assistance. The Contents tab lists the available topics. Most topics have subtopics available, which are indicated by a triangle next to the topic title. Click the triangle to expand the list of subtopics; then click the subtopic you want to review. Note that some subtopics have their own subtopics to choose from. The second tab is the Index tab, which lists the help topics in alphabetical order.

You can print the current topic by clicking the Print button, or click the More Resources button to access Adobe's Support knowledgebase from the Internet.

Another option is to select a menu command from the Help menu:

▶ **Photoshop Elements Help:** Choose this to launch the Adobe Help Center window as seen previously.

▶ **Glossary of Terms:** Choose this to view definitions of Photoshop Elements terms, as well as photography and image editing terms.

▶ **Tutorials:** Choose this to select from a number of different tutorials designed to help you through image editing tasks.

▶ **Online Support:** Just like the More Resources button in the Adobe Help Center, this option takes you to the Adobe Support Internet knowledgebase.

Help Option

One other method to activate the Adobe Help Center is to press F1 at any time.

Photographer: Hossley Partington

2

Using the Photoshop
Element Tools

**Photographer:
Jonathan Hawkins**

PICTURE YOURSELF a skilled craftsperson—a carpenter, for example. Whether you're building a bird house or a beach house, you know you need to use the right tools to get the job done. So it is with Photoshop Elements. Different tasks require different tools and it's important to use the right tool for the job.

In Chapter 1, I mentioned the Photoshop Elements toolbar. By default, the toolbar is located on the left side of the screen and contains 47 tools, each designed to accomplish a different task. Each time you select a tool, options for that specific tool appear on the Options bar. The general flow is that you select the tool you need for the job and then you determine the necessary options.

In this chapter, we're going to take a peek at each tool's mission. As you work with Photoshop Elements, you may find you use some of the tools a lot and other tools very seldom. As you proceed through the next several chapters in this book, when you start working directly with images, I'm sure you'll find yourself looking at one of your photographs and thinking "Aha! I can use the (*xxx*) tool to accomplish this." Let's take a look at some of those tools.

Viewing Tools

I T'S ALL IN YOUR perspective, right? When you're working creatively, sometimes you need to see the finest detail, and sometimes you need to stand back and check out the overall look. Well, two of the first three toolbar tools are used to change the way you look at your image. The Zoom and Hand tools both pertain to how and what you see on your screen. Neither of these tools actually physically modifies your image in any form; they only change how you view it on the screen.

Zoom

The Zoom tool increases or decreases image magnification. When you select the Zoom tool, the Options bar you see in Figure 2-1 appears. By default, each time you click on the image, it zooms in for greater intensification, allowing you to perform close-up detail work. You can continue to zoom in until you get to a pixel-by-pixel depiction of the image at 1600% of the normal 100% view. Likewise, you can zoom out until the image is only 1% of the 100% normal view.

The Options bar shows the magnifying glass with a plus in it—that's for zooming in. The magnifying glass with the minus in it is for zooming out. You can switch between the two icons as often as you want. Optionally, to the right of the two magnifying glasses is a zoom slider. Click the arrow to display a zoom slider you can drag left or right to decrease or increase the zoom level. You'll use the Zoom tool quite a bit.

Notice that after you select the Zoom tool, your mouse pointer looks like a magnifying glass, and the Options bar changes to include the following:

▶ **Resize Window to Fit: Choosing this option causes the window itself to enlarge or shrink as you modify the zoom percentage. When not selected, the window stays the same size and just the image perspective changes.**

▶ **Zoom All Windows: Zooms all open images the same proportional percentage.**

▶ **Actual Pixels: Quickly returns the image to 100% zoom.**

▶ **Fit Screen: Zooms the image to the maximum screen size.**

▶ **Print Size: Zooms the current window to printing resolution.**

Use the Mouse Scroll Wheel

Optionally, if your mouse has a scroll wheel, you can roll the scroll wheel forward on the image to zoom in and roll the scroll wheel backwards to zoom out.

Figure 2-1

Zoom tool's options.

Hand

Sometimes called a *Pan tool*, when you select this tool, your mouse pointer turns into a small hand. Use the hand to click and drag to view different areas of your image. It's especially helpful to use when you are zoomed in or working with a large image. You can zoom to a high percentage, yet still see other areas easily. It's similar to using the horizontal or vertical scroll bars.

Navigator Palette

Although it's not actually a tool on the toolbar, the Navigator palette seen in Figure 2-2, provides you with the best of both worlds. You can zoom tightly on the image detail and still see the image in its entirety on the Navigator palette. Turn the Navigator on by choosing Window > Navigator. You can move it to the Palette Bin or let it float on the window, whichever is easiest for you. To move from one area of your image to another quickly, zoom in on the image and drag the rectangle in the Navigator to the area you want to view.

Navigator

Figure 2-2
Zoom tool options.

Selection Tools

BEFORE YOU CAN make changes to a portion of an image, whether the image is one you create, a photograph, or other type of artwork, you need to indicate to Photoshop Elements which portion you want to change. Called making a selection, you can then make your change to the isolated area without affecting the rest of the image. You also need to select an area if you want to copy or cut it to the Windows Clipboard for use in other programs or images. Photoshop Elements includes a variety of selection tools you can use to select those areas.

Choose Another Tool

If the tool you want is included in a tool group (such as with the Lasso, Magnetic Lasso or Polygonal Lasso), you can also choose the specific tool from the Options bar.

Marquee

When selecting an area, Photoshop Elements shows the selection boundaries with a marquee that looks like marching ants around the area. This marquee allows you to visually see the area marked for change. Photoshop Elements includes two marquee tools—one for selecting rectangular or square areas and the other for selecting elliptical or circular areas. Marquee selection options include the selection type, feathering, anti-alias, and mode.

Select the tool you want; then click and drag in the image to create the selection area. If you want to constrain the selection to a perfectly square area, choose the Rectangle tool; then hold down the Shift key before you click and drag over the image area. For perfect circles, choose the Ellipse tool and drag with the Shift key held down. Be sure to release the mouse button *before* you release the Shift key.

Cancel Selection

To cancel any selection area, press the Escape key, Ctrl+D, or choose Select > Deselect.

Selection Type

With the Marquee selection tool, four different selection types are offered. Selection types are primarily used when you need to make multiple selections on the same image. In fact, most of the other selection tools include these same options:

▶ **New Selection: With this option selected, each time you click and drag in the image, it creates a brand new selection. If there is a previous selection still highlighted, the previous one is replaced with the new one.**

▶ **Add to a Selection: Used when there is already a selection on the screen; with this option, each time you click and drag in the image, it adds to the current selection. It only works outside an existing selection. In Figure 2-3, you see two separate areas selected, both surrounded by the marquee.**

Selection types

Figure 2-3
Determine how you want multiple selections.

▶ **Subtract from a Selection**: Used when there is already a selection on the screen; with this option, each time you click and drag in the image, it takes away from the current selection. It only works inside an existing selection.

▶ **Select an Area Intersected by Other Selections**: Use this option when you already have two or more selected areas. By dragging the mouse across the two (or more) areas, it only leaves that area selected and removes the remainder of the selection area.

Feathering

Feathering is part of the selection process that expands your selection boundaries and softens the edges of the selection area. Specified by width in pixels from 0 to 250, feathering determines how much of the selection is faded along the edges.

When you move or paste the selection, feathering helps blend the selection into the surrounding area and makes it appear more natural. The default feathering of 0 creates a sharp selection with very distinct edges, so the higher the feather value, the softer the edges. You'll find feathering in most selection tool options.

Anti-alias

When you select an area using a rectangular or square selection, all you have are straight lines selected. If you select an area with a curve, such as an elliptical or circular shape, the edges become jagged. The anti-alias feature is designed to help with the smoothing and blending of selection pixel edges to help eliminate those jagged edges. The Options bar has a check box where you turn anti-alias on or off. Anti-alias is available in many of the selection tool options.

Mode

Three different selection modes appear. Normal mode, which is the default, allows you to visually set the selection size and proportions by clicking and dragging the mouse. Fixed Aspect Ratio mode is where you set a width to height ratio. For example, if you set width at 2 and height at 1, for every two inches wide you make your selection, the height will only be half that at 1 inch. The third mode is Fixed Size, where you set the selection size you want.

Move Selection Marquee

To move the selection marquee, with the Marquee tool still selected, drag the selection to a different location.

Lasso

The Lasso selection tools allow you freehand access for selecting boundaries. Each of the three tools (Lasso, Magnetic Lasso, and Polygonal Lasso) has a distinctly different purpose. The Lasso tool options include Mode, Feathering, and Anti-Alias.

Lasso

The Lasso tool lets you draw the selection area freehand. When you select the Lasso tool, your mouse pointer looks like a small lasso. Often used when you are zoomed into your image, you can click and drag around the area you want to select, using the tip of the lasso as your guide. When you release your mouse, the area is selected and, if you did not complete a selection area returning to the starting point, Photoshop Elements automatically adds a straight line selection from the point you released the mouse to the starting point. If you didn't get the selection area just where you wanted it, remember you can use the Add to Selection or the Subtract from Selection options to modify your selection area. Lasso tool options include Selection type, Feather, and Anti-alias.

While lasso selections are more precise than rectangular or elliptical selections, they are still often hard to control. See Figure 2-4 for an example of a Lasso selection.

Add to or Subtract from Selection

While making a selection, hold down the Shift key to add to the selection, or hold down the Alt key and subtract from the selection.

Figure 2-4
Make loose selections with the Lasso tool.

Magnetic Lasso

The Magnetic Lasso is very similar to the Lasso tool; however, it allows you to draw a selection border freehand with the magnetic snap that searches out edges in the image. It's slightly more precise than the standard Lasso tool. The Magnetic Lasso is helpful if your hands are a little shaky or if your image has very distinctive edges. To use the Magnetic Lasso, select the tool and either click various points along the edge of the image object you want to select, or drag along the edge. Figure 2-5 illustrates an image with an area selected using the Magnetic Lasso.

Magnetic Lasso options include Selection type, Feather, Anti-alias, and a few additional special options:

▶ **Width: With a value between 1 and 256, measured in pixels, the width determines how close the edges are to the mouse pointer.**

▶ **Edge Contrast**: Use this tool to specify the tool's sensitivity to edges. Use a value between 1 and 100 where a higher value picks up only the edges that contrast sharply with the areas around it.

▶ **Frequency**: Used when dragging across the area, frequency determines the rate the tool uses to set how often fastening points are added to the selection area path. Enter a value between 1 and 100. The higher the value, the closer together the points will be.

▶ **Pen Pressure**: Used with pressure sensitive drawing tablets, this option uses the tablet pressure to determine the pen's width.

Figure 2-5
Make very precise edge selections with the Magnetic Lasso.

Polygonal Lasso

The Polygonal Lasso selects areas in straight line segments. You click where you want the first segment and then click where you want the next segment to begin and continue until you select the area you want. There's no magnetic snap to edges, so it's basically a freehand selection tool with exclusively multiple straight lines. Options include the Selection type, Feather, and Anti-alias.

Magic Wand

The Magic Wand selection tool works differently from the other selection tools. The Marquee and Lasso tools both work by selecting an area of the image, regardless of the content, but the Magic Wand works by selecting pixels of equal or similar colors. Through the options, you control which type of pixels you want the Magic Wand to select.

When you select the Magic Wand tool, your mouse pointer looks like your fairy godmother's favorite wand. (What do you mean you don't have a fairy godmother?) Options include the standard four selection types: New Selection, Add to a Selection, Subtract from a Selection, and Select an Area Intersected by other Selections. Along with an Anti-alias option, you see Tolerance option, which controls how closely the selected pixels must match the initial pixel you selected. With a range from 0 to 255, at higher settings, the Magic Wand tool selects a wider range of pixels. Figure 2-6 illustrates an image with the entire leaf selected by two clicks of the Magic Wand.

The Contiguous option, if selected, tells Photoshop Elements to select only matching pixels that connect to your original pixel. When unchecked, this option selects any image pixel meeting the criteria you've specified. Finally, the Sample All Layers option, unchecked by default, tells Photoshop Elements whether to extract the color from only the current layer or to include other layers in the image. You'll learn more about layers in Chapter 3.

Figure 2-6
Using the Magic Wand selection tool.

Selection Brushes

A long time ago, there was a science fiction movie, maybe it was a *Twilight Zone* episode, where an artist was angry with someone so she just painted them out of a painting and they disappeared from real life. Every time I use the selection brushes, I think of that old show. The Selection Brush tools let you virtually paint the area you want to select either by an area with the standard Selection brush, or by color with the Magic Selection brush. Like most selections, once the area is selected, you can delete it, move it, copy it, or just change it.

Selection Brush

One nice thing about the Selection brush is that you can paint the areas you *want to change,* or you can paint the areas you *don't want to change.* You can also make a basic selection using a different tool such as the Rectangle or Lasso and then fine-tune the selection with the Selection brush.

1. Using a Marquee or Lasso tool, select the general area you want to work with.

2. Choose the Selection brush from the Toolbar.

3. Choose whether you want to add to the selection or remove some of the selection.

4. Select a brush setting. There's a drop-down list of preset brushes from which you can choose. Double-click the brush setting you want.

5. Specify your brush size. Brush sizes are measured in pixels from 1 to 2500 with 1 being a *very* tiny brush. You can type a size, or use the slide to select it.

6. Choose Selection or Mask mode. You use Selection mode to pick the area you want to select, and you use Mask mode to select the areas you want to protect (or not select). If you choose Mask mode, you can also choose a color and opacity for the mask. Selection mode doesn't use color. It looks like a regular selection with a marquee around it.

Opacity Description

Opacity is the density of a brush stroke. A higher value applies a more solid color effect, whereas a lower value results in more transparent color. Opacity is measured in percentages from 1 to 100.

7. Paint over the area you want to select, or if you are in Mask mode, paint over the area you do *not* want to select. Each brush stroke adds to the selection, but you can switch the selection type from add to subtract. Figure 2-7 illustrates an image with the little girl masked out. If I were to press the Delete key on this image, everything but the little girl would be deleted.

Figure 2-7
Making masked selections with the Selection brush tool.

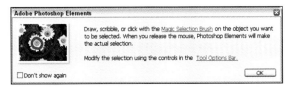

Figure 2-8
The Magic Selection brush instructional message box.

Magic Selection Brush

Used like a paintbrush, the Magic Selection brush lets you paint what you want to select, but instead of selecting based on a physical area, the Magic Selection brush bases the selection on the color and texture in the painted area.

When you click the Magic Selection brush, you see the message box in Figure 2-8 instructing you on the use of the Magic Selection brush. Optionally, click the Don't Show Again option before clicking the OK button. When using the Magic Selection brush, your mouse pointer looks like a paintbrush, and you can select the brush size and color from the Options bar. You can also start with an existing selection and add or subtract to the selection using the Selection Type options. The Magic Selection Brush tool uses an algorithm based on the area you paint over, to determine what pixels to select. It's similar to the Magic Wand, but much more accurate if you take the time to select a good representation of the pixels you want to select.

Invert a Selection

Sometimes, the easiest way to select a complex portion of an image is to select the part of the image that you don't want to edit and then invert the selection. For example, if you have a picture of a tree silhouetted against a blue sky, you could use the Magic Wand to select the blue sky and then reverse the selection to select the tree. Reverse a selection area by choosing Select > Inverse.

Magic Extractor

One more tool that is used for selections is the Magic Extractor. While this tool is not located on the toolbar with the rest of the selection tools, it has a unique purpose. You use the Magic Extractor to make selections based upon the foreground and background areas in your image.

Often, the Magic Extractor is used to select people or objects from your image so you can use them in composites with other images. It works similarly to the Magic Brush Selection tool in that you dab the brush tool to select the image areas you want.

The Magic Extractor is located under the Image menu, so to launch it, you choose Image > Magic Extractor. The Magic Extractor dialog box seen in Figure 2-9 appears.

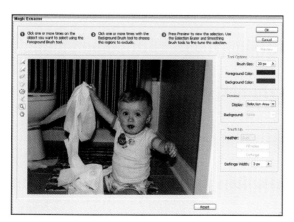

Figure 2-9
The Magic Extractor dialog box.

This is a large dialog box, so let's take a few minutes to explore the dialog box itself. On the left side is a toolbar with the following tools:

▶ **Foreground Brush Tool**: Use this brush to select the portions of the image you want to select. The shortcut key for this tool is B.

▶ **Background Brush Tool**: Use this brush to select the portions of the image you *do not* want to select. The shortcut key for this tool is P.

▶ **Point Eraser Tool**: Use this tool to click and clear selected points you created with the Foreground Brush tool or the Background Brush tool. The shortcut key for this tool is E.

▶ **Add to Selection Tool**: Use this tool to add additional selection areas. The shortcut key for this tool is A.

▶ **Remove from Selection Tool**: Use this tool to remove portions of the selection areas. The shortcut key for this tool is D.

▶ **Smoothing Brush Tool**: Use this tool after you preview your selections to smooth out edges the extractor missed or picked up. The shortcut key for this tool is J.

▶ **Zoom Tool**: Use this tool to zoom in on your image to work with fine detail. Use this tool and the Alt key to zoom out of your image. The shortcut key for this tool is Z.

▶ **Hand Tool**: Use this tool to move around and view different areas in your image. The shortcut key for this tool is H.

As with most toolbars, you click the tool to activate it.

On the right side of the dialog box are the options. Depending on the detail size you are selecting, you may need to increase or decrease the brush size. The mouse pointer, which looks like a circle, indicates your current brush size. The Foreground Color and Background Color indicate the color of "paint" the brushes will use. Click on either color box to change the color, although unless your image has lots of bright red or bright blue in it, you probably won't need to change the colors.

The middle area, the Preview section, doesn't really matter until you make your selections and preview them. After you choose to preview your selection, Photoshop Elements makes the background area disappear. Once you preview your selection area, you can switch back and forth between the Original area with the background still showing, or the Selection area with just the foreground area displaying. If you choose to preview the Selection area, then the next option, Background, becomes available. By default, the background area is transparent, but you can click the Background drop-down list and select a different background fill such as black, white, or gray. Sometimes, using a background color helps you determine the selection detail better.

The bottom area, the Touch Up section, provides a few options for working with the image selection detail. Set a value in the Feather box to soften the edges of your selection. Click the Fill Holes button for Photoshop Elements to remove extraneous selection holes left in the selection area. The Fringe button represents those pesky little pixels that get left between the foreground and background. The Defringe button removes the fringe. You can set a defringe value from 0 to 50 in the Defringe Width box.

To use the Magic Extractor, follow these steps.

1. Click the foreground brush; then click or brush over the general area you want to select. Red circles appear where you click. In Figure 2-10, I have selected the baby.

2. Click the background brush, and click or brush over the general area you want to eliminate. Green circles appear where you click. Again, refer to Figure 2-10 to see the background filled with green dots. Notice that the background color in this example is black.

3. Click the Preview button. The Magic Extractor processes the image and shows you what your selection looks like. (See Figure 2-11, which shows the extraction against a black matte background.)

4. Use any of the touch-up tools or options to further your selection.

Background selection   *Foreground selection*

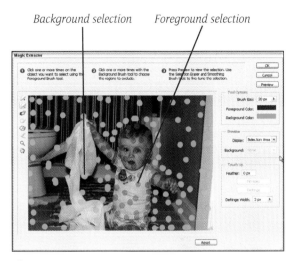

Figure 2-10
The image with Magic Extractor points indicated.

Select background

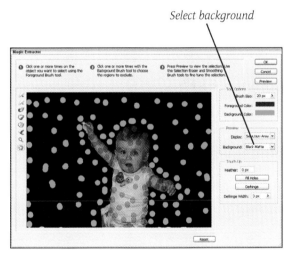

Figure 2-11
The previewed image after using the Magic Extractor.

5. When you are finished, click the OK button. The Magic Extractor window will close, and your modified image will be redisplayed in the Editor window.

Move

You've spent a lot of time learning how to select desired areas of your image. Now the question remains as to what to do with the selection. One thing you can do is delete a selected area by pressing the Delete key. Later in this chapter, you'll discover how you can modify the selection by changing its color or adding blur to it. You'll discover in later chapters how you can perform a myriad of other actions on a selected image area. But one thing you frequently need to do is move a selected area. You may want to move the selection to a different layer, which you will see in Chapter 3. Perhaps you want to move the selected area on top of another area, to another image, or to a different layer. Photoshop Elements provides the Move tool to accomplish these action types.

The Move tool is the first tool on the Photoshop Elements toolbar. When you select the Move tool, your mouse pointer looks just like the Move tool icon. While there are a number of options available for the Move tool, most of them pertain to working with layers. (We'll discuss those options in Chapter 3.) Most people use the Move tool to move a selected area to a different location. After you make your selection and click the Move tool, the selected area displays eight small sizing handles, a plus shape in the center that serves as a move point, and a rotation handle as you see in Figure 2-12.

Move point   Rotation handle   Sizing handles

Figure 2-12
A selected area after choosing the Move tool.

▶ **Move Point:** Position the mouse pointer over the move point and drag the selected area pixels to a different location.

▶ **Sizing Handles:** As you place your mouse pointer over a sizing handle, the pointer changes to a double-headed arrow. Drag a handle to make the selected image portion larger or smaller. This is not simply changing the size of the selection, but also changing the image itself. After you resize the area, the Commit and Cancel buttons appear. Click the Commit button or press the Enter key. You'll use the Commit and Cancel buttons quite often when working with Photoshop Elements image changes.

▶ **Rotation Handle:** As you place your mouse pointer over the rotation handle, the mouse pointer turns into a circle of arrows. Drag the rotation handle until the selection is turned the way you want it. After you rotate the area, the Commit and Cancel buttons appear. Click the Commit button or press the Enter key.

Color Tools

SCIENTISTS SAY DOGS can only see in black and white while we are fortunate enough to see all the colors in the rainbow. Photoshop Elements provides every color imaginable for you to use in your images. The program breaks the color down into two distinct areas: background and foreground. Some tools use the foreground color exclusively and others use the background color exclusively. The Gradient tool uses a blend of both foreground and background colors.

Color Swatches

The current foreground and background colors are displayed at the bottom of the toolbar, in the two small overlapping color samples or *swatches*. There are also two other items to note around the color swatches.

Foreground

Considered the primary color, the foreground color is what Photoshop Elements uses when you use the Type tools, the Brush tool, or to fill the interior of a shape. The default foreground color is black. Of the two linked color swatch icons, click the one on the front to change the foreground color with the Color Picker.

Background

The background is often known as the canvas color or *base color*. When you use the Eraser tool, Photoshop Elements fills the erased area with the background color. The default background color is white. Of the two linked color swatch icons, click the one on the bottom to change the background color with the Color Picker.

Color Picker

The Color Picker is part of the color swatches that lets you select from millions of colors. Follow these steps to use the Color Picker:

1. Click the foreground color swatch if you want to change the foreground color or click the background color swatch if you want to change the background color. The Color Picker dialog box you see in Figure 2-13 appears.

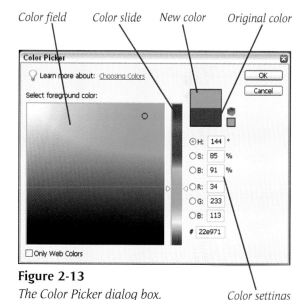

Color field   Color slide   New color   Original color

Figure 2-13
The Color Picker dialog box.   *Color settings*

2. Drag the color slider to get into the general color range you want, such as blues, yellows, or reds.

3. Click in the color field to choose the exact shade you want. The color you choose appears in the New color box. Since colors are based on a number of elements, notice how the color settings values change as you select different colors. (See Chapter 5 for more information about color detail.)

4. Click OK when you are satisfied with the color you chose. The new color appears in the Color Swatches.

Switch Between Foreground and Background

To quickly reverse the foreground and background colors, click the small arrows next to the Color Swatch tool.

Change to Default Colors

If, after picking colors, you don't want them and would rather have the default black and white colors back, press the letter D or click the small black-and-white box by the Color Swatch tool.

Eyedropper

Photographs can contain millions of colors and shades and picking the exact shade from the Color Picker dialog box can be difficult. Because of this, Photoshop Elements includes the Eyedropper tool, which you can use to pick up any specific color from your image. There's only one Eyedropper tool option and that pertains to how large of a sample you want the Eyedropper to select. If you select

Point Sample, it picks up the color of the pixel you click on. If you select 3×3 Average or 5×5 Average, Photoshop Elements select colors in a 3×3 (or a 5×5) pixel grid, and then it comes up with a color that is the average of those 9 or 25 pixels.

Click the Eyedropper tool from the toolbar. After determining the sample size, click in your image where you want to pick up the color. Clicking on the color selects the foreground color and if you hold down the Alt key before you click, you can choose the background color. Also, you can choose the color from any open image in your Photo Bin. Take a look at Figure 2-14. The color of the flower was picked up and used to draw a heart.

Color swatches   Switch Colors   Default Colors

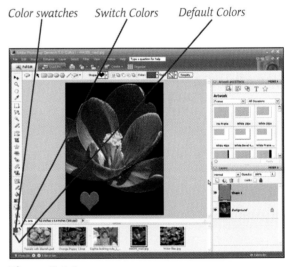

Figure 2-14
Use the Eyedropper tool to select foreground and background colors from your image.

If you're using many of the other tools, such as the Brush, Pencil, or Shape tools, and you need to pick a different foreground color, hold down the Alt key, which temporarily switches to the Eyedropper tool, pick your color, and release the Alt key. The tool you were using resumes control.

Color Swatches Palette

One of my favorite ways to pick a color, although not on the toolbar, is from the Color palette. Just as an artist holds his or her color palette close by while painting, having the Photoshop Elements Color palette is quite handy. First, choose Window > Color Swatches to turn on the palette. Then you can drag the Color Swatches title bar to move the palette wherever you want on the screen, or click the More button and select Place in Palette Bin when closed. Click the X (Close button) on the palette and Photoshop Elements places it in your Palette Bin, as you see in Figure 2-15.

To select a new foreground color, just click the color you want. To pick a different background color, hold down the Ctrl key and click the color you want. As you select a new foreground or background color, the new colors appear in the toolbar Color Swatches.

Here are a few options you can use with the Color Swatches palette:

▶ **The collection of colors you see is called the *Default library*. Click the drop-down arrow next to Default to display various other libraries, such as libraries with colors specific to Web graphics, Photo filters, Mac operating systems, and Windows operating systems.**

▶ **Click the More button to change the way you see the color samples, such as with large samples instead of small samples, or in a list that includes the color name.**

▶ **If you already have a unique foreground color, perhaps one you selected from your image with the Eyedropper tool, click the Create New Color Swatch of Foreground Color icon, which is located at the palette bottom.**

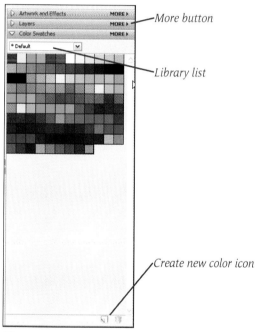

—More button

—Library list

Create new color icon

Figure 2-15
The Color Swatches palette placed in the Palette Bin.

Drawing Tools

PHOTOSHOP ELEMENTS provides wonderful features you can use to correct or enhance your photographs. But sometimes you want to make a manual modification, such as adding shapes or text to an image. Or perhaps you just want to fill in a blank area with a little matching color. Any of these things are possible with the drawing tools included in Photoshop Elements.

Undo

To reverse a step you take, choose Edit > Undo or press Ctrl+Z.

Brush

Bring out your inner creativity with the brush tools! A couple of different brushes exist for your drawing or painting convenience. Whether you're creating your own masterpiece or editing an existing image, you use brushes to apply color or style to your image.

Brush or Pencil

Drawing with the Brush tool creates soft feathered edges around the brush strokes and even automatically uses anti-aliasing, while the Pencil tool provides a harder, crisper edge. Because these two tools are very similar, Photoshop Elements considers them both a brush. The following steps show you how to work with the Brush or Pencil tools:

1. Select the Brush tool or the Pencil tool.

Create Separate Layers

If you want to be able to adjust your opacity and blend mode after you draw, put your brush and pencil strokes on a separate layer (see Chapter 3).

2. Decide on a brush tip style, such as rounded or squared. Be sure to scroll down the list, as there are some very creative brush tip styles farther down the list.

3. Select a brush size. Sizes range from 1 to 2500 with a higher value resulting in a larger wider brush stroke.

4. Pick a blending mode. See Chapter 3 for a description of each blending mode.

5. Make a choice for the brush opacity. Remember that opacity is the density of the brush stroke, and the lower the percentage, the more background that shows through your brush strokes.

6. Choose a paint color foreground color.

7. If you're using the Brush tool, you may want to select options from the More Options menu. Click the Brush next to More Options to display the menu like the one you see in Figure 2-16.

Figure 2-16
More Brush and Pencil options.

▶ **Spacing**: Determines the distance between brush strokes. A higher value decreases the frequency of the drops of paint as the brush tip touches the image, whereas a lower value produces a smoother and denser effect. Step ranges are from 1%–1000%.

▶ **Hardness**: Defines the brush center size using values between 0 and 100%, .

▶ **Angle**: Sets the brush angle from minus 180 degrees to plus 180 degrees. Used with the roundness figure, when you have an elliptical shaped brush.

▶ **Roundness**: Ties together with the brush shape. Sets a value from 0–100% with 100% being perfectly round. Lower values result in a more elliptical shape.

8. Click and drag the mouse across the canvas. You will see the strokes from the color and brush style you selected appear on the canvas.

Airbrush Mode

One additional choice on the Brush options is the Airbrush mode. Select this choice to apply paint as though you were using an airbrush or spray can. Just like a real spray can, the longer you hold down the mouse button, the more paint comes out.

Drawing Straight Lines

Hold down the Shift key to draw straight lines with either the Brush or Pencil tools. Release the mouse before you release the Shift key.

9. Release the mouse button.

▶ **Fade**: The lower the value, the sooner the brush fades the color out. Values range from 0 to 9999.

▶ **Hue Jitter**: Varies the stroke color between the foreground and background color. With values between 0–100%, choosing a lower value retains the foreground color and higher values using the background color.

▶ **Scatter**: Pertains to the number of brush marks and how close together they are. Values run from 0–100% with lower values producing a denser brush stroke with less splattering.

Impressionist Brush

Impressionist art is a style in which the artist captures the image of an object as people would see it if they had just caught a glimpse of it. Impressionist art usually contains lots of color, but without a lot of detail. If you're a fan of Impressionist art, you'll like the Impressionist Brush tool. Remember the artist colony I mentioned in Chapter 1? Well, here's your chance. With the Impressionist Brush tool, you can pretend you're the next Monet, Degas, or Renoir and turn a photograph into a painting.

Select the Impressionist Brush tool and select from the options. Options include the Brush Tip style, Brush Size, Mode, and Opacity. (See Chapter 3 for an understanding of Blending Modes.) Even more brush control options exist if you select the More Options button. Brush away to your heart's content!

Take a look at Figure 2-17. On the left, you can see the original photograph—a sharp photographic image of a home and an outdoor floral garden. On the right, you can see the same photograph after brushing it with the Impressionist Brush.

Color Replacement Brush

The third brush in the Brush list is the Color Replacement brush. You use it like a regular brush in the sense that you paint over an area, but the Color Replacement brush picks up colors and tones from your image and replaces only those colors with your current foreground color. Select the Color Replacement brush and choose a brush tip size.

There are several different modes the Color Replacement brush uses to pick color samples from the image. Available modes include Color, Hue, Saturation, and Luminosity. The most commonly used option is Color.

Next, you can determine the method the Color Replacement brush should use when picking up colors (sampling) from the image:

▶ **Continuous: Samples and replaces color continually as you drag across the area with your mouse.**

▶ **Once: Replaces the color only in areas containing the color you first clicked.**

▶ **Background Swatch: Replaces colors only in areas containing your current background color.**

Figure 2-17
An image before and after using the Impressionist Brush.

The Limits options are Contiguous and Discontiguous. Contiguous means the Color Replacement brush will replace all similarly colored pixels that are adjacent to the point you click. If you select Discontiguous, it will replace the similarly colored pixels elsewhere in the image.

The Tolerance value determines how similar the colors must be when compared to the pixel colors under the hot spot. A higher value includes a wider range of colors, where a lower value restricts the color range. Values range from 1 to 100 percent.

After setting any desired options, choose the foreground color you want to use to replace the unwanted color. Then, in the image, click the color you want to replace. Drag in the image to replace the color. Take a look at the image in Figure 2-18. The brown frame around the outside is being replaced along the top edge with an orange shade picked up from the flower. The gray and white portions of the frame are not being touched.

Figure 2-18
Replacing one color with another.

Erasers

When you are practicing your drawing techniques, you might decide that it would be easier to start over. You can close the current file without saving it and start again with a new file, but you can also erase your canvas and start over. Of course, most of the time you won't be drawing in Photoshop Elements, but working with photographs; however, Photoshop Elements also has erasers for working with photo images. Photoshop Elements includes three different eraser tools: the standard Eraser, the Background Eraser, and the Magic Eraser.

Eraser

The Eraser tool works similarly to a regular pencil eraser, except that you have options from which you can select. Eraser options are similar to the Brush options you discovered earlier in this chapter. The Eraser works by changing the pixels in the image as you drag through them. If you are working with a background layer, the Eraser changes the pixels you erase over with the current background color. If you erase from a layer other than the background layer, Photoshop Elements replaces the erased pixels with transparency.

Follow these steps to use the Eraser tool:

1. Select the Eraser. (Don't pick up the Background Eraser or the Magic Eraser just yet.)

2. From the Options toolbar, select a brush tip style and thickness.

3. Select a Mode: Brush, Pencil, or Block. The choice you pick determines the shape and hardness of the eraser. Brush mode gives you soft-edged erasing while Pencil mode gives hard-edged erasing. Block mode uses a 16-pixel hard square and disables all other erase options.

4. Select the Opacity at which you want to erase. The default is 100 percent, which means a total erase of an area. If you set the opacity low, say at 15 percent, the area will be only lightly erased.

5. If you are erasing on a background layer, choose a background color.

6. Click and drag the mouse pointer over the area you want to erase. The erased area is replaced with the background color. In Figure 2-19, you see the original image on top and the image with an erased area on the bottom. The background color is white so the erased area is filled with white also.

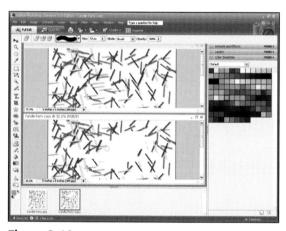

Figure 2-19
Erase an unwanted area.

Restrict Erasure Area

To restrict the eraser to a specific area, select the area before you use the Eraser tool.

Background Eraser

The Background Eraser, while similar to the regular Eraser and often used in conjunction with the regular Eraser, works more from the center of the brush, resulting in softer edges. The tool works best on images with higher contrast between the background and the foreground. For example, if you have a picture of a poppy growing wild in the grass, and you want just the flower, the Background Eraser is the tool you want to use. It makes the erased pixels transparent. When you have the Background Eraser selected, your mouse pointer becomes a circle with crosshairs in it. The crosshair (called the *hot spot*) is a key element in how the tool works. The Background Eraser determines which pixels to erase by finding similarly colored pixels under the hot spot.

If you use the Background Eraser on a background layer, Photoshop Elements automatically converts the background layer to a standard layer. The Background Eraser contains the following options:

▶ **Size: Use this selection to determine an eraser size and eraser brush tip. This option also contains settings for use with pressure sensitive drawing tablets.**

▶ **Limits: Contiguous means the eraser will erase all similarly colored pixels that are adjacent to the hot spot. If you select Discontiguous, it will erase the similarly colored pixels elsewhere in the image.**

▶ **Tolerance: This value determines how similar the colors must be when compared to the pixel colors under the hot spot. A higher value includes a wider range of colors, whereas a lower value restricts the color range. Values range from 1 to 100 percent.**

Figure 2-20 illustrates an image with some of the background removed by the Background Eraser.

Figure 2-20
Erasing a background area.

Magic Eraser

The Magic Eraser works like the Magic Wand in that it picks up similarly colored pixels. Instead of just selecting them as the Magic Wand does, however, the Magic Eraser selects them and erases them at the same time, converting the erased pixels to a transparency. Just a simple click selects the pixels within the range you determine. Look at Figure 2-21. You can see where the sky was erased, and the erasure occurred with just a single mouse click with the Magic Eraser tool.

Figure 2-21
Use the Magic Eraser tool to remove large areas with a single click.

Let's take a quick look at the options.

▶ **Tolerance:** The Tolerance value determines how similar the colors must be when compared to the selected pixels. A higher value includes a wider range of colors; a lower value restricts the color range. Values range from 0 to 255.

▶ **Anti-alias:** Discussed earlier in this chapter, it provides smoother edges around the erased areas.

▶ **Contiguous:** The Contiguous option, if selected, lets Photoshop Elements select only matching pixels that connect to your original pixel. When unchecked, this option selects any image pixel meeting the criteria you've specified.

▶ **Sample All Layers:** When checked, this option picks up colors from all layers, but only erases on the active layer.

▶ **Opacity:** This option selects the density of the erasure. The default is 100 percent, which means a complete erasure of an area. If you set the opacity low, say at 15 percent, the area will be only lightly erased.

Paint Bucket

The Paint Bucket tool floods an area with the selected foreground color or a pattern. The area it fills can be a selection you specify, or it can be the interior of a closed shape. It could even be the entire canvas. The tool uses pixels to determine where it fills. At the point where you click the mouse pointer on the image, Photoshop Elements looks for matching pixels. The tool options determine exactly which pixels it matches.

First, you select your Foreground color; then you select the Paint Bucket tool. When the tool is selected, your mouse pointer looks like a bucket of paint. Set any desired options and click in the area you want to fill.

Paint Bucket tool options include:

▶ **Fill:** Choose Foreground if you only want a solid color or choose Pattern if you want to fill the area with a pattern.

▶ **Pattern:** Choose a pattern for the fill. Click the arrow to the right to display a list of other pattern categories and options (see Figure 2-22).

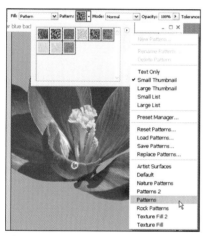

Figure 2-22
Pattern options.

▶ **Mode:** Specify the blend mode.

▶ **Opacity:** Specify the density of the fill.

▶ **Tolerance:** Specify how close the color pixels must match before Photoshop Elements fills the area with the selected color.

▶ **Anti-alias:** Smoothes the edges of the filled selection if it has other than straight edges.

▶ **Contiguous:** If checked, selects only matching pixels (within your tolerance settings) that connect to your original pixel.

▶ **Use All Layers:** If checked, Photoshop Elements fills the color from all layers instead of only the current layer.

Figure 2-23 shows a photograph where the background in the photograph is being changed from a solid black to a bubble pattern using the Paint Bucket tool.

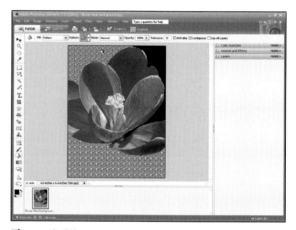

Figure 2-23
Quickly fill large areas with the Paint Bucket.

Gradient

Gradients are color blends in a variegated pattern. The Gradient tool works similarly to the Paint Bucket tool in that it fills in an area, but you use it in a slightly different manner. It either fills in a selection area or the entire canvas. When working with gradients, you can choose from one supplied with Photoshop Elements, or you can create your own gradient.

1. Select the area you want to fill. For best results, make the selection on a new layer. You can also apply gradients to text. Select the text on its layer before proceeding.

2. Click the Gradient tool.

3. On the Options bar, choose a preset gradient from the gradient drop-down list. Click the arrow to the right to display more gradient categories and gradient options.

New Gradient

Click the New button to define and name a new gradient.

4. Choose a Gradient type. The different types determine where the gradient shades begin, such as a straight line for a Linear gradient or counterclockwise for an Angle gradient.

5. Select a blending mode and opacity setting along with any other desired option. For example, if you click the Reverse option, the gradient starting color begins in an opposite manner. If you have a blue into yellow gradient, it becomes a yellow into blue gradient, or if you have a light green to dark green, it will begin with dark green and end with light green. Selecting the Dither option creates a smoother blend of colors.

6. Click and drag the mouse in the selection area or on the canvas. Where you begin the drag is where the starting color will begin, and where you release the mouse is where the ending color. A longer drag provides more restrained transitions between the color variations while a shorter drag gives sharp sudden evolutions. In Figure 2-24, you can see an arrow filled with a yellow to red gradient.

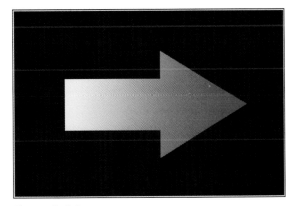

Figure 2-24
Using gradient fills.

Constrain the Gradient

To constrain the gradient to a 45-degree angle, hold down the Shift key as you drag the mouse.

Shape

Lines and boxes and shapes, oh my! Photoshop Elements provides a large variety of shapes you can use in your images. Some of the shapes are standard shapes, such as rectangles, ellipses, and polygons. But there are hundreds of unusual custom shapes, such as hearts, leaves, animals, and food. Lines are a shape, too—straight lines, angled lines, or funny looking lines.

Photoshop Elements creates shapes as a particular type of graphic called a *vector graphic*. Up until this point, you've been working with raster graphics. Let's take a look at the difference. Raster graphics, sometimes called *bitmap images*, are composed of individual pixels such as those you see in a photograph. Vector graphics, however, are distinct objects that Photoshop Elements creates using mathematics, more specifically, geometry. Both have advantages and disadvantages. One advantage of a vector graphic is that you can easily edit, move, or resize it.

By default, Photoshop Elements creates each shape on its own individual layer, and you cannot combine raster graphics and vector graphics on the same layer. Therefore, if you try to add a raster graphic, such as a paintbrush line, to an image that has a vector shape (perhaps a rectangle), Photoshop Elements will prompt you to convert the vector layer to a raster layer through a process it calls "simplify." Once you simplify the layer, the vector graphics are no longer easily edited.

Standard Shapes

Standard shapes include square cornered rectangles and squares, rounded corner rectangles and squares, ovals and circles, and multisided polygons.

Select the Shapes tool and from the Options bar, select what shape you want to use. The options available depend on which tool you select. For example, with the Rounded Rectangle tool, you can choose the radius for the corners; with the Polygon tool, you can determine how many sides you want on the polygon. Other options include the fill color, which has a drop-down color palette from which you can choose. From the Style drop-down list, you can determine the edge of the shape, such as whether it should include a bevel or not. For specific options to the tool you select, click the drop-down arrow next to the Custom Shape tool.

There's a section on the Options bar that determines how Photoshop Elements should handle multiple shapes on the same layer.

▶ **New: Creates the additional shape on its own new layer.**

▶ **Add: Adds the additional shape to the existing shape layer. The shapes can be intersecting, or they can be independent. If they intersect, they become one big shape. Both shape objects are on the same layer.**

▶ **Subtract: Subtracts from the existing shape. This option only works if you draw one shape on top of another. Both of the actual original shape boundaries show on the screen (they don't print), but only the remaining area has the fill color and other options. Both shape objects are on the same layer.**

▶ **Intersect: Leaves only the area that intersects between the first and second objects. Both of the original shape boundaries show on-screen, but only the intersected area has the fill color and other options. Both shape objects are on the same layer.**

▶ **Exclude:** Leaves only the areas that don't intersect between two objects. The original shape boundaries show on-screen, but only the excluded area has the fill color and other options. Both shape objects are on the same layer.

Click and drag the mouse to draw the shapes such as the ones you see in Figure 2-25.

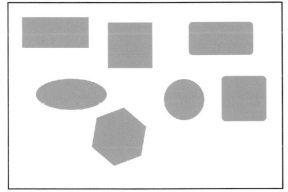

Figure 2-25
Draw various shapes with Photoshop Elements.

Line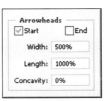

Photoshop Elements includes a Line tool with which you can create straight lines, thin lines, thick lines, and even lines with beveled edges or arrowheads. The Line tool is a vector object, just like the other shapes. In fact, you select the Line tool from the Shapes button. Choose the Line tool and then specify its options.

If you want arrowheads at the beginning, end, or both ends, you must click the down arrow next to the Custom Shapes tool (see Figure 2-26). Choose the options you want from the Arrowhead box. The Width and Length options refer to the arrowhead as a percentage of the line weight. The Concavity option refers to how much curve you want at the

back end—the widest part of the arrowhead. A 0% curve provides a straight arrowhead, a 50% curve provides quite a bit of turn, and a minus 50% makes the arrowhead look more like a spearhead. Figure 2-27 shows three different arrowheads with different concavity options. Values from –50% to +50% are permitted.

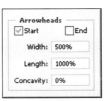

Figure 2-26
Set arrowhead options.

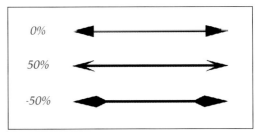

Figure 2-27
Adjust arrowhead concavity settings.

Weight refers to how thick the line should be, ranging from .014 inches, which is 1 pixel, to 13.889 inches. The line type options are the same options as the standard shapes as to how Photoshop Elements should handle multiple line objects, such as whether to put them on a new layer or add them to the existing layer.

The next option is the Color option. Click the drop-down arrow and select one of the many colors listed from the displayed color palette, or click the More Colors button, which displays the Color Picker from which you can choose a color. Another set of options appears if you click the Options button on the color palette (see Figure 2-28).

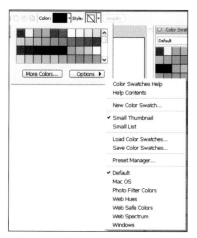

Figure 2-28
Line color options.

From the Style drop-down list, you can determine the edge of the shape, such as whether it should include a bevel or not, although for a standard line typically you use the default style of None.

Click and drag to draw the line. If you want a perfectly straight horizontal or vertical line, click where you want the line to begin, hold down the Shift key, and draw the rest of the line. Be sure to release the mouse button before you release the Shift key.

Custom Shape

Custom shapes are just plain fun. With hundreds of shapes to select from, you can create impressive borders around your photographs or use them with or around other drawn objects you've created. Again, they are part of the Shapes category so they are a vector graphic and appear on their own layer or on a layer with other vector graphic shapes. The following steps show you how to work with the Custom Shape tool:

1. Choose the Custom Shape tool, which is the one that looks like a talk balloon.

2. Click the down arrow next to the Custom Shapes tool. Custom Shape options appear:

   ▶ **Unconstrained**: This option allows you to freely draw the shape on your image.

   ▶ **Defined Proportions**: This option enables you to keep the height and width ratio proportional.

   ▶ **Defined Size**: This option crops the image shape to the original size of the Cookie Cutter tool. Usually, these are pretty small, and this option is not often used.

   ▶ **Fixed Size**: This option has you enter your own height and width. It measures in inches.

   ▶ **From Center**: This option, when checked, draws the shape from the center out instead of the outside to the inside.

3. Click the Shapes down arrow. If you don't see a shape you want to use in the default gallery, click the arrow next to the gallery. A menu of options appears, like the ones you see in Figure 2-29.

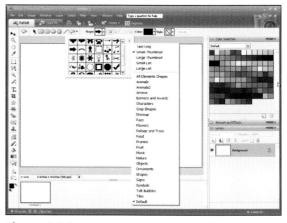

Figure 2-29
Draw any of hundreds of different shapes.

4. Select the shape you want to use.

5. Select the additional Shape Options you want. Options include New, Add, Subtract, Intersect, and Exclude. (See the earlier section "Standard Shapes" for information on these options.)

6. Click the drop-down arrow and from the displayed color palette, select one of the many colors listed, or click the More Colors button.

7. Select an edge style from the Style drop-down list.

8. Click and drag to draw your custom shape. If you are drawing over a photograph, you can use one of the Frame shapes to apply a quick frame to your image. See Figure 2-30 for a sample of some of the many custom shapes included with Photoshop Elements.

Figure 2-30
Sample shapes in Photoshop Elements.

Shape Selection Tool

The Shape Selection tool looks like an arrow and is located with the Shape tools. You click the tool and then click the shape you want to modify. A selected vector shape has eight selection handles surrounding it (see Figure 2-31). You can drag a selection handle (the mouse pointer changes to a double-headed arrow) to resize the shape, or you can position the mouse in the middle of the object and drag it to a different area on the layer.

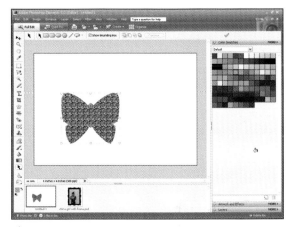

Figure 2-31
Shape with selection handles.

> **Delete a Shape**
>
> Press the Delete key to delete a selected shape.

Text Type Tools

WE'VE BEEN TOLD that a picture is worth a thousand words, and Photoshop Elements has certainly proved that statement to be true over and over again. However, sometimes you just *have* to spell it out. If you've used a word processing program such as Microsoft Word, then you're used to working with text. You might use text in Photoshop Elements when creating scrapbook pages, calendars, greeting cards, brochures, posters, or DVD labels.

Horizontal and Vertical Type

You create text with the Photoshop Elements Type feature. Photoshop Elements uses the terms *Type* and *Text* interchangeably to indicate letters and words. There are two main types of text: Horizontal Type and Vertical Type. The majority of what you create will use the Horizontal Type since it runs left to right, just as we are used to reading. Vertical type runs up and down, and while there will be special occasions to use it, many people find it difficult and unnatural to read.

Using the following steps to add text to your image:

1. Select the Horizontal or Vertical Type tool.

2. Select a font name. The default font is Times New Roman, but from the Set the Font Family drop-down list, you can choose from any font installed on your computer.

3. From the Set the Font Style drop-down list, select a font style. Styles include Regular, Italic, Bold, and Bold Italic. Figure 2-32 illustrates samples of each style used with the default Times New Roman font. Not every font has the Bold or Italic style available, but you can use the Faux Bold and Faux Italic options you'll see in step 6.

Times New Roman Regular

Times New Roman Bold

Times New Roman Italic

Times New Roman Bold Italic

Figure 2-32
Font styles.

4. From the Set the Font Size drop-down list, choose a font size. As a general rule of thumb, when printing, a 72-point font is approximately one-inch tall, but when viewing text on a computer screen, the sizes vary depending on the screen resolution.

5. If you want to turn off the anti-alias feature, click the Anti-aliased option, but your text will look much crisper if you leave the option on. In Figure 2-33, you can see that the character on the left is much smoother than the character on the right, which does not have anti-aliasing applied.

Figure 2-33
Curved edges are much smoother with Anti-alias.

6. The next two options, Faux Bold and Faux Italics, apply a bold or italic style if your font doesn't provide bold or italics in the Style option.

7. Choose an Alignment option. Alignment options apply when you have multiple lines of text. In Left-aligned text, the left edges of each text line align together. With Center-aligned text, each line centers to the one above it, and with Right-aligned text the right edges of each text align together (see Figure 2-34).

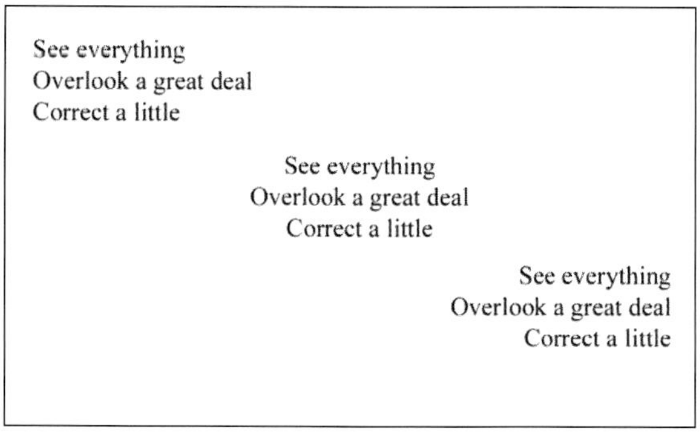

See everything
Overlook a great deal
Correct a little

      See everything
      Overlook a great deal
      Correct a little

            See everything
            Overlook a great deal
            Correct a little

Figure 2-34
Text alignment.

8. Set the desired amount of Leading. Leading (pronounced like *sledding* without the s) refers to the space between lines of text. Leading takes effect when you have multiple lines of text.

9. Pick a text color. By default, the text color is the current foreground color. If the color you want is not displayed, you can select it by clicking the More Colors button.

10. Optionally, pick a style from the Style Picker. These styles apply to the edges of the text such as shadows, beveling, or embossing.

Additional Styles

To select from a large variety of really cool styles, click the More button and choose one of the other style categories, such as Glass Buttons or Wow Neon. To remove a style, click the More button and choose Remove Style.

11. Click in the image and type the text you want. Press Enter if you want the text to go to another line.

12. Click the Commit button (the green check mark) located at the end of the Options bar (see Figure 2-35).

Text as a Vector Graphic

Photoshop Elements treats text as a vector graphic and places text on its own layer.

Figure 2-35
Add style and pizzazz to your text.

Edit Text

Since Photoshop Elements places the text on its own layer, it makes it very easy to modify. Refer to Chapter 3 about working with layers.

▶ **To change a text option, make sure that the text layer you want to change is the current layer and select a Type tool. All you have to do to change the text style or attributes is to select the change on the Options bar. If you only want to change the options for a portion of the text, drag the mouse over the section you want to change before you change the options.**

▶ **To move the text, make sure you have the text layer active and click the Move tool. Position the mouse pointer over the move point and drag the text to a different location.**

▶ **To edit the actual text, with the text layer active, select a Type tool and drag over the text you want to change. Retype the corrected text.**

Select Specific Selections

Another method to select portions of the text is to double-click to select a single work and triple-click to select an entire line of text.

Type Masks

Think of Type Masks as reverse text. With regular text type, you add letters on top of your image. With a Type Mask, you create the letters you type *from* your image. As with standard text, you have a Horizontal and a Vertical option to control the direction of the text.

1. Select the Horizontal Type Mask tool or the Vertical Type Mask tool.

2. From the Options bar, select a font name, font style, and font size.

Type Masks

Type Masks works best if you use very large size characters and uppercase letters.

3. Select any other desired options, which are the same options as for adding regular type. The color selection defaults to white, and even though you can select a different color, Type Masks ignores the color choice.

4. Click in your image. As soon as you click, a red mask coveres the entire image.

5. Type your text using the edit and format options you used with regular type.

6. Click the Commit button. Pressing Enter doesn't work because it creates a new line of text. You see a marquee surrounding your text like the one in Figure 2-36.

Figure 2-36
Creating text masks.

7. Choose Edit > Copy or press Ctrl+C, which copies the selection to the Windows Clipboard. Now you need to get the selection to the image you want to place it on.

8. If you want it on another image, make sure that the image is open and active. If you want it on a new canvas, create a new canvas by choosing File > New and clicking OK.

9. Choose Edit > Paste or press Ctrl+V. Take a look at Figure 2-37.

Use Other Applications

You could also paste the selection into Microsoft Word or other applications.

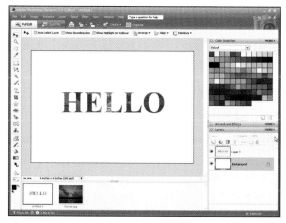

Figure 2-37
Create a new image from the masked text.

Warp Text

Twist and distort your text in distinct patterns, such as a wave, flag, or an arch. While you cannot warp specific characters or words in your text (you must warp all text on the layer), you can create different text on different text layers and warp the layer of your choice. Also, warping must be applied as an edit to text after you create it.

Text Warping

Text warping doesn't work on text with the Faux Bold option applied.

Select the layer containing the text you want to warp and click the Warp Text button on the far right side of the Options bar. You will see the Warp text dialog box (see Figure 2-38). Click the Style drop-down list and choose a warp style. The Warp Text dialog box has additional options to control the warp motion. Click OK to apply the warp to your text.

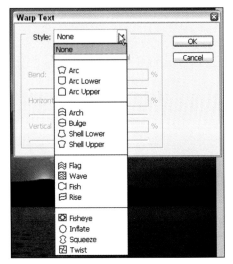

Figure 2-38
Choose from a number of Warp text styles.

Figure 2-39 shows some text with the Flag warp style applied.

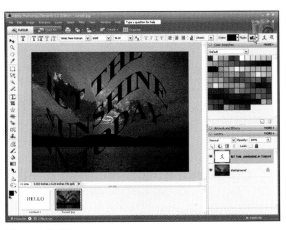

Figure 2-39
Let the sunshine in today!

Tools for Retouches

WHEN YOU JUST NEED to make minor retouches to selected areas of your photograph, you can often use a series of Photoshop Elements tools designed just for retouching.

Retouch Brushes

Some of the brushes (Blur, Sharpen, and Smudge) bring out or change the focus of the image, while other brushes (Sponge, Dodge, and Burn) change exposure limits through the saturation or hue in your image. These brushes take time and practice to master, but they are definitely worth the effort. Select the brush, select your options, and then brush over the area you want to retouch (see Figure 2-40). Notice how the bunny on the right is much darker after using the Burn tool on it.

Figure 2-40
Use the retouch tools to bring out or change image focus.

Table 2-1 lists the various retouch brushes and their functions.

Table 2-1 Photoshop Elements retouch brushes

Icon	Brush Name	Function
	Blur	Smoothes and reduces contrast on the edges, making them blend better into the background. It's a good tool to use for the edges of pasted areas.
	Sharpen	Brings an area into better focus by heightening the edges and creating greater contrast.
	Smudge	Intermingles colors as if you were running your finger through wet paint by spreading the color and details from the starting point.
	Sponge	Increases or decreases color brightness or contrast by adding more light or darkness to an area.
	Dodge	Lightens shadowed areas to bring out more details.
	Burn	Darkens light areas it passes over and is commonly used to add depth to an image, as well as darkening light spots.

Similar to the other painting and drawing tools, these brushes also include brush tip and size options, along with a number of other options. Note that not all tools have all options:

▶ **Brush:** Specifies the brush tip style, such as rounded or squared. But, remember, there are some very creative brush tip styles farther down the list.

▶ **Size:** Specifies the brush size.

▶ **Mode:** Specifies how the changes blend with existing pixels in the image (see Chapter 3). The Blur, Sharpen, and Smudge options are Normal, Darken, Lighten, Hue, Saturation, Color, and Luminosity. Sponge tool options are Saturate and Desaturate, and the Dodge and Burn tools list Shadows, Midtones, and Highlights.

▶ **Strength:** Specifies the amount of blurring, sharpening, and so forth that occurs with each brush stroke.

▶ **Sample All Layers:** Tells Photoshop Elements whether to extract the color, brightness, or other attribute from only the current layer or to include other layers in the image (unchecked by default).

▶ **Finger Painting:** *(Smudge brush only)* Smears the foreground color at the beginning of each stroke. If deselected, Photoshop Elements uses the color under the pointer at the beginning of each stroke (see Figure 2-41).

▶ **Flow:** *(Sponge tool only)* Determines how much the saturation should change with a value from 1 to 100%.

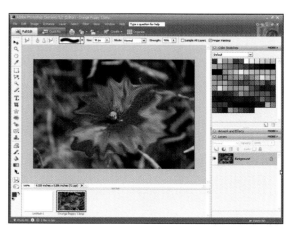

Figure 2-41
Pretend you're five years old and finger paint away!

▶ **Range:** *(Dodge and Burn tools only)* Determines the range of tones you want to adjust. Shadows change the dark areas; Midtones change the middle ranges; and Highlight changes the lighter areas.

▶ **Exposure:** *(Dodge and Burn tools only)* Sets the effect of each stroke. A high percentage increases the effect.

Conceal Retouching

Less is more when using many of the retouch brushes. Make smaller repeated changes and use lower settings as you work to make the changes less obvious.

Other Retouch Tools

Retouching tools are most commonly used for subtle alterations to an image, such as adding highlights or removing blemishes and other unwanted items in an image. Photoshop Elements contains several tools used for retouching your photographs.

Red-Eye Removal

We've all seen it. You snap a picture of friends, loved ones, or even your dog only to find that their eyes have taken on an eerie red glow. Red eye is a basic fact of human biology because the pupils expand and contract in response to light exposure. In bright light, the pupils are small; in low light, they can get very big. When a camera flash erupts, it travels through the dilated pupil and reflects light off the blood vessels behind the retina inside the eye. The camera picks it up as a distracting red spot.

Photoshop Elements Organizer mode automatically tries to remove photo red eye when you bring the images into the Organizer. And while most of the time it does a very good job, occasionally it misses its mark. For those times when you need to work on the red-eye problem, Photoshop Elements includes a tool for that too!

Zoom in the area of the image containing the red eye. Select the Red Eye tool. Then click the area where the red eye exists. Photoshop Elements looks for the unnatural pixels and removes the red hues. In Figure 2-42, you can see a little girl with red eye. The eye on the left was fixed by clicking in it with the Red-Eye Removal tool.

About Red Eye

The term red eye is particularly appropriate for people. The lighter the eye color, the more pronounced the effect can be. The red-eye effect can have a different appearance with animals. Many animals have a reflective layer in the back of their eyes that enhances their night vision. Studies have shown that the color of the reflective layer varies to some extent with the animal's coat color. For example, a black dog will have a green layer, producing a vivid green-eye effect. No matter what the color, it still makes the person or animal look possessed by a demon.

The best thing you can do is to prevent red eye from happening when you take the photo. Here are a couple of tips:

▶ **Move the flash away from the lens altogether.**

▶ **Use the red-eye reduction feature on your camera, which fires a few quick bursts of light that cause the pupil to react before the real camera flash goes off.**

▶ **Turn on a light or move the subject to a brighter area. The pupils become smaller, and the red-eye reaction is reduced.**

▶ **Have the subject look away from the lens, either above the camera or to the side opposite the flash, to reduce the reflection.**

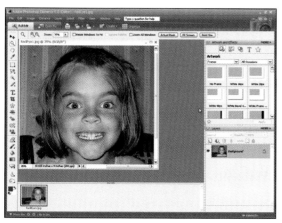

Figure 2-42
Quickly and easily remove red eye.

Clone Stamp

The Clone Stamp tool is another one of those really fun tools provided with Photoshop Elements. With it, you can duplicate areas in your image. You can also use it to remove unwanted objects in an image. The tool works by using other parts of the image as a paint source. When you use the Clone Stamp, although really it's a type of a brush, you also get the color and texture in the area you select.

Here's how it works: You choose a source location somewhere in the picture. The source location can be part of the same image layer, another layer in the image, or an area from another open image. You select the source location by holding down the Alt key and clicking the mouse. Then you paint over the area where you want the section cloned. Take a look at Figure 2-43. In the first image, a lone solitary bunny rabbit suddenly multiplies into three rabbits in the second image.

Author's Confession

Okay, I have to fess up that I cheated a little on this one. In the image on the right, the second bunny is an exact clone of the first, but the bunny on the right, I cloned to its own layer and then flipped the layer.

Figure 2-43
One bunny, two bunnies, three bunnies.

Most of the Clone Stamp options are the same as you've seen in previous tools, such as selecting a Brush tip Style and Size, Mode, Opacity, and Sample All Layers. However, the Aligned option is new. When selected, the sampled area moves with your mouse pointer whenever you stop and resume painting. If it's deselected, and you stop and resume cloning, it continues from the same spot where you originally sampled.

Pattern Stamp

Use the Pattern Stamp to copy a selected pattern over an image or just a selected image area. Just follow these steps:

1. Select the Pattern Stamp tool.

2. Choose a Brush tip style, Brush Size, Mode, and Opacity.

3. Optionally, select or deselect Aligned, which, if selected, repeats the pattern in a contiguous uniform design. If not selected, the pattern starts again each time you stop and restart the painting

4. Optionally, select Impressionist if you want to turn your brush into an impressionist brush that blurs and dabs the pattern instead of smoothly painting it.

5. Click the Pattern drop-down list and select a pattern. Click the More button for an entire list of patterns by categories.

6. Brush over the area you want to fill with the pattern. Figure 2-44 began as a simple yellow daisy, but now the petals are filled with a pattern.

Figure 2-44
Use the Pattern Stamp brush to fill an area with your favorite pattern.

Create Your Own Pattern

Use your favorite photo or portion of a photo to create your own pattern. It's best to have a very small image, so you might have to resize the image (Image > Resize > Image Size) to make sure that it's very tiny. Then save the image or selected portion of the image as a pattern. Choose Edit > Define Pattern or Define Pattern from Selection and give the pattern a name (Bob, kids, leaves, etc.). Click OK and when you select from the Pattern drop-down list again, you'll see your custom pattern.

Create a New Layer

For better opacity control and placement, create a new layer and brush the pattern on the new layer.

Spot Healing Brush

The Spot Healing brush can remove blemishes. either on a person's face or on any object, such as the dirt on the tomato you see in Figure 2-45.

Simply choose the Spot Healing brush tool and select a brush size. It's best to make the brush slightly larger than the area you want to fix. Choose a Type option and click the area you want to fix in the image. That's it.

Type options are:

▶ **Proximity Match**: Only uses pixels around the selection edge as a match.

▶ **Create Texture**: Uses all the pixels in a selection as a match.

Remove Wrinkles

Use the Spot Healing brush to remove wrinkles around lips and eyes. Your family and friends will love you for it!

Figure 2-45
Before and after—removing blemishes with the Spot Healing brush.

Healing Brush

This brush is similar in nature to the Clone Stamp tool, in that the Healing brush copies pixels from one area of the image into another. The Healing brush has a great advantage over the Clone Stamp because it not only picks up the pixel colors, but it also picks up the surrounding texture and high-lights. It actually uses the texture from the source location and applies it by using the colors surrounding the brush stoke as you paint over the destination area. This makes the repair more realistic and natural looking.

Copy Pixels Between Images

One thing to remember is that if you are going to select pixels from one image and apply them to another image, both images must be in the same color mode, unless one of the images is in grayscale.

The photograph in Figure 2-46 was taken with the date stamp inadvertently left on. The Healing brush tool makes it easy to remove. Just follow these steps:

1. Select the Healing brush tool.

2. Select any desired options. Options include Brush tip style, Brush size, Mode, Source, Aligned, and Sample All Layers.

3. Alt-click the area containing the "good" pixels; in other words, the pixels you want to use to fix the flaw.

4. Drag the mouse pointer over the flawed area to replace it with the pixels you picked up in step 3.

Figure 2-46
The Healing brush copied pixels from one area of the image to another and successfully removed the date stamp.

Modification Tools

Some of the modification tools make changes to the physical size of your image. These tools include the Crop, Cookie Cutter, and Straighten tools. Other tools help correct flaws or imperfections, such as removing red eye or facial blemishes.

Crop

Cropping an image allows you to cut away pieces of the image you don't want. When you use the Crop tool, you select a rectangular shape area of the image that you want to keep and the extra area outside the selection darkens. This way, you can easily see if you have the right area selected. When you commit the change, Photoshop Elements deletes the darker area outside the rectangle. Several crop options appear on the Options bar, all of which pertain to the image size and resolution.

By default, Photoshop Elements preserves the image's original resolution. Let's say, for example, that you have a 4" x 6" photograph you want to crop and that photo is at 180 ppi (pixels per inch). If you cut off 1 inch from the left side of the image, the photograph becomes a 4" x 5" photograph, but it's still at 180 ppi. By setting certain Aspect Ratio options, you can still crop away part of the image but only in proportional width and height increments. This retains the perspective so the image will not distort when you print it as a 4" x 6" photograph. If you're going to resize the image, it's important that the image has sufficient resolution to handle the "stretching." If not, your cropped and resized image will not be as crisp and sharp as the original. For more information about resolution, see Chapter 5.

Use these steps to crop away a portion of your image:

1. Select the Crop tool.

2. Specify an Aspect Ratio option. Choose No Restriction to freely crop the image to a new size, or choose Photo Ratio or Preset Sizes if you want to keep a specific size ratio.

3. Drag the mouse selection box around the portion of the image you want to keep. Similar to other selection tools, you can move the selection box, or you can resize it by using one of the sizing handles.

4. Press Enter or click the Commit button. In Figure 2-47, you can see an image in its original state, an image being cropped, and the same image after cropping.

Figure 2-47
Images showing the cropping process.

Cookie Cutter

Real cookie cutters come in a variety of shapes from ABC's to animals to airplanes to gingerbread men. When you use a real cookie cutter, you have a flat base of rolled out cookie dough, and you press down on the cookie cutter and end up with a cookie shaped like your cutter. The Photoshop Elements Cookie Cutter tool works in a similar way. The Cookie Cutter tool crops or removes outside edges of your image. However, when cropping, you can only make straight edge adjustments, whereas with the Cookie Cutter you can crop the image to hundreds of shapes. Adding feathering softens the edges of the crop and provides a smoother transition between the shape and the background.

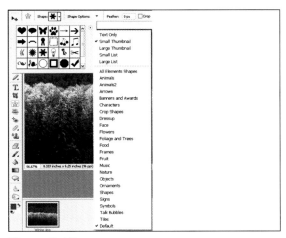

Figure 2-48
Cookie Cutter categories.

Use the Cookie Cutter Tool in Scrapbooking

The Cookie Cutter tool is one of my favorites and great to use in scrapbooking. See Chapter 10.

The following steps show you how to use the Cookie Cutter tool:

1. Choose the Cookie Cutter tool from the toolbar.

2. From the Options bar, click the Shape dropdown arrow. You see a gallery of about 30 shapes.

3. If you don't see a shape you want to use in the default gallery, click the arrow next to the gallery. A menu of options like the ones you see in Figure 2-48 appears.

4. Select the shape category you want to use or choose the All Elements Shapes option to see the entire shape gallery.

Change Icon Size

By default, Photoshop Elements displays the cookie cutter icons as small thumbnails. If you have trouble seeing the icons, click the triangle next to the Shape gallery and select Large Thumbnail.

5. Select the shape you want to use.

6. Select the Shape options. Shape options are similar to the Mode options you discovered with the Marquee selection tools. Options include Unconstrained, Defined Proportions, Defined Size, Fixed Size, and From Center. See the earlier section "Custom Shape" for an explanation of these options.

7. Select the amount of feathering you want, if any.

8. Choose if you want to crop the image into the shape.

9. Drag the mouse across the image until the image is the shape and size you want and release the mouse button. Figure 2-49 shows a winter scene cropped into the shape of a snowflake.

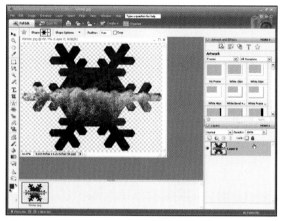

Figure 2-49
Crop your image into a variety of unusual shapes.

Resize or Move the Selection

If you need to resize the selection boundaries, drag one of the corner handles around the selection. If you need to move the selection position, position your mouse pointer into the center of the selection and drag it until it's in the position you want.

---

10. Press Enter or click the Commit button to accept the change.

Straighten

Most people find crooked photos extremely distracting. These photos commonly occur in actions shots where the camera may not have been sitting level with the horizon. Sometimes, you can just retake the photo but if that's not an option, you can use the Photoshop Elements Straighten tool. The Straighten tool works best when the image has a strong vertical or horizontal feature, such as a building or a horizon.

Select the Straighten tool and then select a Canvas option:

▶ **Grow or Shrink Canvas: Since straightening an image causes portions to fall outside the original canvas area, choosing this option forces the canvas to get a little larger (or smaller) to handle the rotated image edges.**

▶ **Crop to Remove Background: Choose this option to trim off some of the canvas where there is white area around the image and remove pixels that hang over the canvas.**

▶ **Crop to Original Size: Selecting this option has the canvas retain its original size, and removes pixels from the area that hangs over the canvas.**

When selected, the Rotate All Layers option straightens all the image layers.

Straighten Options

Photoshop Elements also includes two automatic straightening options. Choose Image > Rotate > Straighten Image or Image > Rotate > Straighten and Crop Image.

To illustrate the Straighten tool, take a look at the house in Figure 2-50, which needs a very obvious straightening. Drag the straightening line to the area on which you want it to align. In this example, I wanted to straighten it to the bottom of the porch, so I'll drag the straighten line under the porch. Click and drag the line to align it with the portion of the image you want to straighten.

Figure 2-51 shows the same picture after using the Straighten tool and selecting the Crop to Remove Background option.

Vertical Straighten

If you want to straighten the image vertically, hold down the Ctrl key and draw the vertical edge.

Straightening line

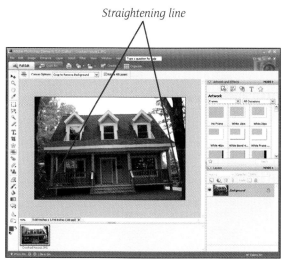

Figure 2-50
Before straightening.

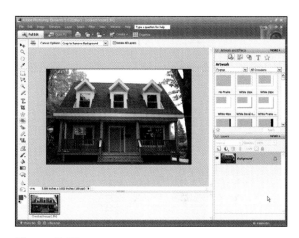

Figure 2-51
After straightening.

3

Working with *Layers*

PICTURE YOURSELF OUTSIDE on a blustery rainy cold day. You're all bundled up. Closest to your skin you might have a t-shirt and a sweater over the shirt. Next, you don your jacket and a neck scarf and then finally a raincoat to keep you dry. Now imagine you live in the Midwest, where the weather changes rapidly. It stopped raining so you peel off the raincoat. The wind dies down so you don't need the neck scarf and later you don't even need the jacket.

Hikers, bikers, walkers, and even little children dress in layers. When dressing in layers, it's helpful to remember that each layer must perform a specific task. One layer is to keep you comfortable, another to keep you warm, and yet another to keep you dry. Each layer has its own purpose, and you can easily remove or shift the layers as necessary. So what does this have to do with a computer software program?

Photoshop Elements has layers. Just like clothing layers, each Photoshop Elements layer can have its own use, and you can easily move the layers around or delete them if unwanted. This chapter discusses layers and how you use them. It also considers blending and blend modes, which is how multiple layers interact with each other.

Understanding Layers

L AYERS ARE ONE OF THE BEST features of Photoshop Elements and once you start using them, you'll never want to be without them. Think of Photoshop Elements layering as putting each portion of your graphics image on a separate transparent sheet of paper, such as tracing paper. Layering makes it much easier to edit or move a particular portion of the image, because as you edit one portion of the image, you won't disturb the other portions. Then you can shuffle the order of the layers (sheets). If you are making composite images, you'll find layers particularly helpful.

All images have at least one layer. When you open a digital photograph or a scanned image in Photoshop Elements, the image is on the background layer. For most photographic enhancements, such as cropping, correcting colors, or retouching, you can work on this background layer without ever adding another layer. However, there are many ways to use layers with your photographic images to make changes easier and create interesting effects, especially when you intend to do more complex work, such as adding elements to the image, creating photo compositions, adding text and other effects, and so forth. Figure 3-1 illustrates an image on the left, which when combined with several other image layers, becomes the image on the right.

Figure 3-1
Blending three images to make one image.

Layer Types

PHOTOSHOP ELEMENTS SUPPORTS many different layer types, and the layer type you use depends on your needs. Layer types include Background, Image, Adjustment, Fill, Shape, and Type. For example, often when working with photographs, you'll use adjustment layers, which enable you to make easily changeable modifications to your photographs. Photoshop Elements supports up to 8,000 layers, but most likely, your computer memory won't fully support that many layers, each with its own settings. Most images use only a few layers. Let's take a look at the different layer types.

Background Layers

Every image has at least one layer, appropriately called the *background layer,* and it is the bottom layer in an image. Background layers are a type of raster layer in that they contain raster data, but background layers have some limitations to them that regular raster layers do not. For example, you cannot change the background layer order in the stack since it's always on the bottom, and you cannot change a background layer blend mode or opacity. For protection, background layers are always locked. You can, however, change a background layer to a regular layer and then make any desired adjustments.

Image

Image layers, or regular layers, are layers with only raster data, which is made up of individual pixels such as photographs. You can use raster layers for painting, retouching, and other tools, but not for shapes or text.

Fill Layers

Fill layers are typically filled with solid colors, patterns, or gradients, and they do not affect layers below them, only the ones above them.

Simplify Layers

If you want to paint or use a retouch tool on a fill layer, you must simplify it to a regular image first.

Adjustment Layers

Photoshop Elements provides adjustment layers to make color and tonal corrections instead of changing the image directly. Adjustment layers are non-destructive correction layers that modify an image color or tone, but place the changes on individual layers instead of the original layer. You can place each correction type on its own layer to test various color corrections or to see how several corrections look when you combine them.

Layer Masks

Adjustment layers also use layer masks. See "Masking with Layers" later in this chapter.

Shape Layers

Shape layers are layers with only vector objects that are composed of geometric characteristics, such as lines and shapes. When you edit vector objects, you edit these lines and curves, rather than editing individual pixels like you do on raster layers. Vector graphics maintain their clarity and detail when scaled to any size, making them easy to edit. Before you can add filters to a vector layer, you must first perform a step called *Simplify*, which converts the vector layer into a raster layer. See Chapter 7 to learn about applying filters. Figure 3-2 illustrates a photograph of a butterfly with several circle shapes added.

Type Layers

Type layers are very similar to shape layers in that Type layers only contain vector objects. When you edit vector text, instead of editing individual pixels, you edit the lines and curves that make up the letter. Also, like Shape layers, before you can add filters, you must first simplify the layer.

Figure 3-2
Adding shapes creates new layers.

Using the Layers Palette

THE EASIEST AND FASTEST METHOD to layer management is through the Layers palette, although you could also accomplish layer tasks through the Layer menu. Displayed on the right side of your screen, in the Palette Bin, the Layers palette shows you all the information about each layer in your image, as well as providing a place to create, delete, rename, hide, group, and generally manage your image layers. Let's take a closer look at a Layers palette of an image with multiple layers (see Figure 3-3).

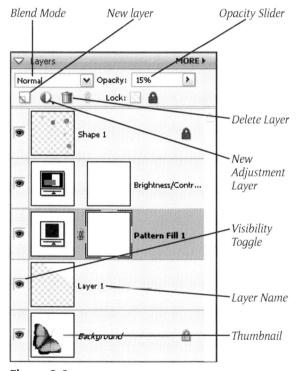

Blend Mode   New layer   Opacity Slider

Delete Layer

New Adjustment Layer

Visibility Toggle

Layer Name

Thumbnail

Figure 3-3
The Layers palette.

View the Layers Palette

If you don't see the Layers palette, choose Window > Layers.

The following list describes the icons you see on a layer:

▶ **Visibility Toggle: The eye icon indicates that the layer is visible. On occasion, you might want to hide one or more layers so that you can more easily view and edit objects on the remaining layers. Click the visibility icon to hide or display the selected layer.**

▶ **Layer Thumbnail: Small images that represent the layer contents.**

▶ **Layer Name: When you start adding lots of layers, you'll want to give each layer a unique name to identify quickly what each layer holds.**

▶ **Blend Mode: This feature displays a combination of pixels of the current layer with the pixels of all the underlying layers; however, it is for display only— the layers are not actually combined.**

▶ **Opacity: Opacity measures how much an object blocks light transmission (the opposite of transparency). When the opacity is lower, the resulting image is more transparent. Background layers do not have opacity control.**

▶ **New Layer: Click this button to auto- matically create a new transparent regular image layer.**

▶ **New Adjustment Layer:** This option has a drop-down menu where you can select the type of adjustment or fill layer you want.

▶ **Delete Layer:** This option allows you to delete a selected layer.

▶ **Link Layers:** This option allows you to collectively group a combination of layers as a single unit. This feature allows for easier editing because any action to take to one layer applies to all layers that are linked together.

▶ **Lock Transparent Pixels:** This option lets you locks transparent pixels in an image so that only the nontransparent pixels can be edited.

▶ **Lock All:** This option not only locks the transparent pixels, but also locks the layer in its entirety so you cannot add to it, move it, or delete it unless you unlock it.

Changing Layers Palette Options

Photoshop Elements includes a way you can modify the way the layers appear in the Layers palette. You can change the size of the thumbnail images, or you can choose not to display them at all. Follow these steps to change the options:

1. In the Layers palette, click the More button. A submenu of layer options appears.

2. Choose Palette Options. You see the Layers Palette Options dialog box seen in Figure 3-4.

3. Choose a thumbnail size. Photoshop Elements uses the middle size as a default.

4. Click the OK button.

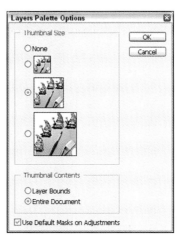

Figure 3-4
Layers palette options.

Creating Layers

Photoshop Elements provides several methods to add new layers. The three common layer types (Image, Fill, or Adjustment) can be added by clicking one of the two Add layer icons on the Layers palette. You can also add any layer type, including Adjustment layers, through the Layers menu. When you add any new layer, Photoshop Elements names it sequentially, such as Layer 2 or Layer 3. If you created the new layer by using the icons on the Layers palette, the layer is created without any questions; however, if you add the layer from the menu (Layer > New > Layer), you see the dialog box in Figure 3-5. From this dialog box, you can give your layer a name, select a blend mode, opacity, and group the layer with another layer. Photoshop Elements places new layers above the layer that was last selected. The new layer also becomes the active layer.

If you want to move a selected part of an image to its own layer, choose Layer > New > Layer Via Cut. Photoshop Elements pastes the selected area into a new layer in the same position relative to the image boundaries.

Figure 3-5
New Layer dialog box.

Duplicate Selection

Choose Layer > New > Layer Via Copy if you want to duplicate the selection instead of moving it.

Photoshop Elements creates some layers automatically. For example, if you paste a selection from the current image or a different image, Photoshop Elements automatically places the selection on to its own new layer. If you create a shape or text, Photoshop Elements also automatically puts them on their own layer. You can then decide whether you want additional shapes or additional text on the same shape or text layer or another new one.

Selecting Layers

In order to make changes to a specific layer, you need to select it first. If you want to apply identical changes to multiple layers, you can select all the desired layers and make the changes once, which affects all the selected layers. The following list shows you how easy it is to select the layers you want to change:

▶ **To select a single layer, click the layer name or thumbnail image. Photoshop Elements shows the active layer with gray shading around it.**

▶ **To select multiple adjacent layers, click on the first layer you want; then hold down the Shift key and click the last layer you want. The beginning and ending layers are selected, as well as all layers in between them.**

▶ **To select multiple nonadjacent layers, click on the first layer you want; then hold down the Ctrl key and click each subsequent you want. Only the layers you actually Ctrl-click are selected. Figure 3-6 shows the Layers palette with the Background layer, Layer 4, and Layer 5 selected.**

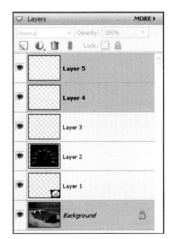

Figure 3-6
Selected layers.

▶ **To select all layers of the same type, click on the first layer you want; then choose Select > Similar Layers.**

▶ **To select all layers, choose Select > All Layers.**

▶ **To deselect layers, choose Select > Deselect Layers.**

Select the Correct Layer

A common mistake is *not* to have the right layer selected. If you choose a command and nothing seems to happen, make sure that you've selected the right layer.

Specifying Layer Opacity

In Chapter 2, you read that opacity is the density of a brush stroke and that a higher value applies a more solid color effect and a lower value results in more transparent color. Layers also have an opacity setting that determines the density or sheerness of the current layer, which determines how much of a lower layer is allowed to show through.

You can adjust the opacity of the current layer by clicking the Opacity arrow and dragging the Opacity slider to the left to decrease the current layer density or to the right to increase the density. Take a look at Figure 3-7. There are actually two photograph layers, with the bottom layer being a statue from the Women in WWII memorial and the top layer being the United States flag. But all you see is the flag top layer because the opacity is at 100% and isn't allowing any of the lower layer to peek through. On the right, you see the same image, but now with the opacity of the top layer set to a much lower 40%, you can see some of the statue in the underlying layer.

Naming Layers

As you add more layers, you can identify more easily what each layer represents by using the Rename feature to name each layer clearly. Background layers are already named, so you cannot rename a Background layer, unless you convert it first to a normal layer, but to rename other layers, choose Layer > Rename Layer. The Layer Properties dialog box appears displaying the existing layer name. You can just type over the existing name with a new descriptive name and click the OK button.

Rename Layer

Optionally, right-click the layer name and select Rename Layer or simply double-click the layer name and type a new one.

Figure 3-7
Adjusting opacity.

Duplicating Layers

For most simple image retouches and corrections, you do not have to add any layers. However, you can duplicate the layer before applying actions such as the photo correction commands. By applying any changes to the duplicated layer, you'll always preserve the original image on its own layer. Another example might be if you created a layer just the way you want it, and you need another similar layer; then you can duplicate the existing layer and modify the new one rather than recreating the layer. Either right-click the layer you want to duplicate or click the Layers menu and choose Duplicate Layer. The Duplicate Layer dialog box seen in Figure 3-8 appears. By default, Photoshop Elements names the duplicated layer with the original layer name and the word *copy* after it. Optionally, type in a new name.

Destination drop-down

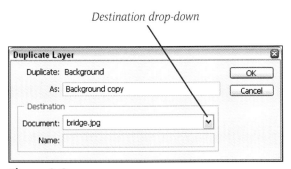

Figure 3-8
Duplicate Layer dialog box.

The Destination section assumes that you want to duplicate the layer to the current image file, but you can click the drop-down arrow and select from any other open image, or click the New option where you'll deposit the layer on a new image. If you select a new image destination, the Name text box becomes available where you can name your new image.

If you duplicate the layer to a different image, and the pixel dimensions of the two images are not the same, you may see the duplicated layer appear smaller or larger than you expect.

Skip Dialog Box

To bypass the Duplicate Layer dialog box, from the Layers palette, drag the layer you want to duplicate until it is on top of the New layer icon at the top of the Layers palette. Release the mouse button and Photoshop Elements creates a copy of the layer in the current image.

Reordering Layers

Photoshop Elements displays layers based on how they are stacked in the Layers palette, with the layer name on top being the top layer of your image. If your layers are stacked differently than you want, you can change their order with the exception of the background layer, which is always the lowest layer. You can move layers up or down one layer at a time, or you can move a layer to the top or bottom of the stack. Reordering layers is an option under the Layers > Arrange menu, or you can simply place your mouse pointer on the Layers palette, on the layer name you want to move, and drag it to the desired stacking order. The options under the Layers > Arrange menu are the following:

► **Bring to Front**: Moves the layer to the top of the layers.

► **Bring Forward**: Moves the layer up one level in the Layer palette.

► **Send Backward**: Moves the layer down one in the Layer palette.

► **Send to Back:** Moves the layer so it's directly above the background layer. If there is no background layer, it moves the selected layer to the bottom layer.

► **Reverse:** Use this feature with two or more layers, and it reverses their order in the stack. For example, if you have Layer 1 and Layer 3 selected, with Layer 3 being the top layer, then with the Reverse command, Layer 1 becomes the top layer.

As an example, take a look at Figure 3-9. You see a background and two layers with the top layer (Layer 2) on the left being some highway signs. After sending Layer 2 backward, Layer 1 (the car) becomes the top layer.

Moving Layers

If a particular layer isn't displaying the portion of the image where you want it, you can slide the layer into a different position. We're not talking about changing the stack order, but actually moving the entire layer content into a new position.

From the Layers palette, click the layer name you want to move; then click the Move tool on the toolbar. When the Move tool is selected, the mouse pointer turns into a four-headed arrow and the current layer is displayed. Drag the layer and its contents around until it's in the position you want and then click the Commit button. In Figure 3-10, you see a palm tree layer that was originally in the middle of the image, moved to the right.

Figure 3-10
Move layer elements for better positioning.

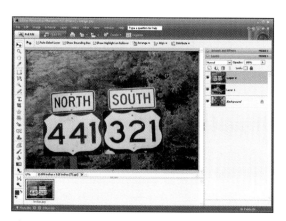

Figure 3-9
Changing layer order.

You cannot move Fill layers or Background layers. If you want to move something residing on a Background layer, select the object and place it on its own layer or convert the Background layer to a regular layer. If you need to adjust the fill layer, you can mask out a portion of it. See "Masking with Layers" later in this chapter.

Deleting Layers

If you've created a layer you no longer want, you can easily delete it from the Layers palette. If you delete the Background layer, the background of the image becomes transparent.

Like other Layer commands, you can access the Delete command from the Layers menu, or by right-clicking on the layer you want to delete and selecting Delete. A third method is to select the layer you want to delete and click the Delete button on the Layers palette. It's the one that looks like a trash can. Whichever method you choose, Photoshop Elements confirms that you're deleting a layer, but you can turn off the confirmation message if desired by clicking the "Don't show again" check box in the Delete dialog box.

Use the Undo Function

If you delete a layer in error, don't forget that you can click Edit, Undo (or press Ctrl+Z) to reverse your last action.

Hiding Layers

On the Layers palette, you see an eye icon, called the *Visibility icon*, next to each layer. When you see the eye, it means that you see the layer in the

editing screen. If you want to work on an image without seeing the effects of a particular layer, you can hide it by clicking the Visibility icon. The icon disappears, and your image does not display the layer results. Click the gray area where the visibility icon was to redisplay the selected layer. Hiding layers is especially helpful when you are working with adjustment layers and don't want the distraction of the adjustment on your screen. Technically, you can hide all layers in your image, but then you would have nothing but a transparency on your screen.

Let's take a look at another image with layers. Figure 3-11 shows an image of an aquarium, which is the background layer, but I've added two new regular layers, which I've called *Tiger* and *Baboon*. The image on the top shows all the layers being visible, but in the image on the bottom, by clicking the visibility toggle, you see only the Tiger layer because the Baboon layer and the Background layer are hidden.

Hidden Layers

Hidden layers do not print.

Figure 3-11
Hide and display layers as needed.

Locking Layers

After spending time working on your images, sometimes you can get a little tired and careless. To protect your layers against accidental changes, you can lock them. When a layer is locked, a lock icon appears to the right of the layer name, and the layer cannot be deleted. Except for the background layer, you can still move locked layers to different locations in the stacking order of the Layers palette. Click the layer you want to lock and click the Lock All icon. Click the Lock All icon again to unlock a layer.

If you only want to protect any transparent areas in a layer against accidental drawing or painting, you can choose the Lock Transparency icon instead.

Linking Layers

After you merge layers, which you'll learn about shortly, the elements are on a single layer and cannot be manipulated individually. Instead of merging the layers, you might want to link them. For example, you might want to link layers if you want to move items on one layer and want the items on some of the other layers to move along also. You can also copy, paste, merge, and apply transformations to all linked layers simultaneously. Think of linking as a temporary way of merging layers.

Obviously, linking doesn't work with just a single layer, so you'll need at least two layers to link. In the example you see in Figure 3-12, by linking the Tiger and the Baboon layers together, if I move the Tiger layer to the top of the image, the Baboon layer moves also.

To link multiple layers, from the Layers palette, select two or more layers you want to link; then click the Link Layer icon at the top of the Layers palette. If you want to edit the layers individually, click the Link icon on the linked layer, which then unlinks them.

Figure 3-12
Linking layers.

Being Creative with Layers

NOW THAT YOU'VE GOT a good grasp of what regular layers can do for you and how they operate, let's put it to some practical photographical use. In this example, by using layers, you see how you can convert a color image like the one shown in Figure 3-13 into one that is a combination of color and grayscale. Let's use the Eraser tool, which erases pixels and makes them transparent.

Figure 3-13
Original image.

The following steps walk you through the process of creating the combination image.

1. To begin this project, you'll need two copies of the same image. You'll need to change one of the copies to a grayscale image, so you can't just duplicate the layer—you need to duplicate the image. Click the File menu and select Duplicate to duplicate the open image.

2. Next, take the duplicate image and change its color range to grayscale. You'll learn more about working with grayscale images in Chapter 5, but for now, make sure the duplicate image is the active window, click the Image menu, choose Mode, and select Grayscale. A message box will appear asking if you want to discard the color information. Click OK.

3. Now you're going to take the grayscale image and make it a layer in the original image. First, click the Select menu and choose All (or press Ctrl+A). Notice the marquee that appears around the entire image. Click the Edit menu and select Copy (or press Ctrl+C). It doesn't look like anything happened, but it did. Windows and Photoshop Elements are keeping track of your steps.

4. Activate the original image, click the Edit menu, and select Paste (or press Ctrl+V). The grayscale image appears as a new layer on the Layers palette. Your original image may look grayscale, too, but that's because the grayscale layer is on top of the background layer. That's OK, and as it should be. (You can now close the copy of the original window if you want.)

5. Now choose your favorite selection tool (mine is the Magnetic Lasso tool) and select the part of the image you want to be in color (see Figure 3-14).

Figure 3-14
Select the image portion you want to color.

Erased transparent pixels

Figure 3-15
Finished image.

6. Click the Eraser tool from the toolbar. From the Tool Options palette, make sure that the opacity is 100%. Make the size large enough so that you don't have to spend too much time uncovering your colored image.

7. Using your mouse pointer, erase the complete area within the selection boundary. You don't have to worry about staying in the lines, because you selected the area you want to erase, and the eraser will not go beyond those boundary lines. As you run the eraser over the image, Photoshop Elements replaces the gray pixels with transparent pixels, and the color from the background layer begins to show through.

8. Deselect your selection boundary by pressing Ctrl+D or choosing Select, Deselect. Take a look at the finished image in Figure 3-15.

Save as a PSD File

Remember that if you save the image as anything other than a Photoshop Elements proprietary format, Photoshop Elements will merge the layers, and you won't be able to come back and easily bring out other colors in the image. You should save the image first as a Photoshop Elements image and then save it as another format, such as a TIF or JPG.

Working with Background Layers

AS YOU'VE SEEN SO FAR, a background layer, created when you open a new image with a nontransparent background, is a little different from the other layers. First, it is always the lowest layer in the stack. Second, it does not have opacity control like the other layers. If you want to control the opacity or transparency of the background layer, you must first promote it to a regular layer. Choose Layer > New > Layer from Background. The New Layer dialog box appears where you can assign a new name to the former background layer. From that point on, you can apply blends, filters, change the stacking order, or do anything with it you do with a standard raster layer.

Just the opposite of promoting the background layer to a regular layer is to change a regular or vector layer into a background layer. Choose Layer > New > Background from Layer. All the attributes of a background layer are applied, including the layer lock. If the original layer had any transparent areas, those areas become filled with the current background color.

Only One Background Layer

Each image is only allowed one background layer. If the image already has a background layer, you must first promote the existing background layer to a regular layer.

Using the Background Eraser on a Background Layer

If you drag the Background Eraser tool on the Background layer, Photoshop Elements automatically promotes the background layer to a regular layer, and erased areas become transparent.

Simplifying and Merging Layers

SIMPLIFYING TURNS NONRASTER layers into raster layers. Layer types, such as vector layers with shapes or type and fill layers with solid colors, gradients, or patterns, require that you simplify the layer before you can further process them with painting tools or filters. Once you simplify a vector layer, however, you can no longer select the vector object and edit it with the shape tools. After simplifying, you select and manipulate the layer objects as you would any raster area, such as with the Marquee or Lasso Selection tools.

Many times, Photoshop Elements will prompt you to simplify the layer with the dialog box you see in Figure 3-16. To manually simplify a layer, right-click the layer or choose Layer from the Layer menu and then select Simplify Layer.

After you get your images in the correct position on their individual layers, you might want to merge the layers. When you create multilayered images, you must save them in Photoshop Elements' native format to maintain all layer information. When you save to most other file types, such as .JPG, .GIF, or .PNG, Photoshop Elements tells you that all layers are merged into one background layer, since these formats only allow for a single layer.

Figure 3-16
Simplify a layer.

Photoshop Elements provides several types of merging:

▶ **Merge Down: Takes the current active layer and combines it with the layer beneath it. The merged layer retains the name of the lower level.**

▶ **Merge Layers: Selectively combines two or more layers. The layers need not be adjacent to each other. The merged layer retains the name of the topmost layer and contains images from all selected layers. You must select all the layers you want to merge before choosing this command.**

▶ **Merge Visible: Merges all nonhidden layers into a single layer, but leaves any hidden layers separate. This is helpful if you want to pick and choose which layers you want to merge because the layers don't need to be adjacent to each other. The selected unhidden layers must include the background layer.**

▶ **Flatten: When you merge (flatten) all the layers, the image becomes nonlayered. If you have transparent areas in the image, Photoshop Elements fills them with white, and the image consists of a single background layer with all the components.**

Save Before Merging

After you flatten and merge your layers, other than using the Undo command, you cannot restore the individual layers. You might want to keep a copy of your images with all the layers. Save a copy of the file as a Photoshop Elements file before you merge the layers.

Adding Adjustment Layers

EARLIER IN THIS CHAPTER, I mentioned that the type of layer used most often by photographers is an adjustment layer. What are adjustment layers? Although similar to regular layers, adjustment layers are correction layers that modify an image color or tone without directly modifying the image pixels. You can't paint or add anything to an adjustment layer, but you can intensify or lessen its effect by adjusting its opacity or blend modes. (You'll learn more about blend modes in the next section.). You can also mask out areas of the layer you don't want to adjust. (See "Masking with Layers" later in this chapter.)

Layers Beneath Adjustment Layers

Adjustment layers affect all layers that are under them.

You can, and should, place each correction type on its own layer to test various color corrections or to see how several corrections look when you combine them. Falling into three main types of corrections, Photoshop Elements provides eight different types of Adjustment layers. When you opt to add an Adjustment layer by clicking Layers > New Adjustment Layer, a submenu appears with the eight choices.

- ▶ **Levels:** Via a histogram, allows you to adjust image tones and color casts by manipulating the actual image color channels.

- ▶ **Brightness/Contrast:** Lightens or darkens the image by controlling the lightness and number of color shades in the image.

- ▶ **Hue/Saturation:** Manipulates the image colors. Saturation is the color strength. Hue represents the color reflection.

- ▶ **Gradient Map:** Takes the grayscale area of an image to a gradient pattern of your selection.

- ▶ **Photo Filter:** Mimics using a colored filter in front of the camera lens to adjust color temperatures and color balance.

- ▶ **Invert:** Creates a negative of the image based on brightness values.

- ▶ **Threshold:** Displays the image in true black and true white, which helps you locate the lightest and darkest areas.

- ▶ **Posterize:** Gives a flat posterlike appearance by reducing the number of brightness values, thus reducing the number of colors.

Follow these steps to add an adjustment layer to your image:

1. Select the layer on which you want to place the adjustment layer.

2. Choose Layer > New Adjustment Layer.

3. Select the type of adjustment layer you want. The New Layer dialog box appears.

Change Layer Type

After you've created an adjustment layer, if you need to change the adjustment layer type, choose Layer > Change Layer Content and select a different type.

Practice, Practice, Practice

In reality, modifying an image takes a lot of trial and error. Try a setting and see if you like it. If not, then undo it or delete the layer. You'll find yourself doing a lot of "what-if" scenarios, and working with each correction on its own adjustment layer makes trying the "what-if" issue much easier.

4. Optionally, enter a different name for the layer and select a blend mode and opacity setting. Remember you can change these settings any time after you create the adjustment layer.

5. Click the OK button. A dialog box appears with settings appropriate to the layer type you chose. In Figure 3-17, you see the Brightness/Contrast dialog box.

Figure 3-18 shows an image that was originally very dark as you see on the top, but on the bottom, after adding three adjustment layers: Hue/Saturation, Brightness/Contrast, and Levels, you can see the subject more clearly.

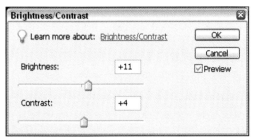

Figure 3-17
Adjustment filter options.

6. Select any desired settings; then click the OK button. The new layer appears on the Layers palette, along with a second thumbnail to the right of the adjustment or fill layer icon. The second thumbnail is for the layer mask, which you'll learn about shortly.

Figure 3-18
A too dark image after adding adjustment layers.

Adding Fill Layers

FILL LAYERS COME IN THREE FLAVORS: Solid color, Gradient, and Pattern. Similar to adjustment layers, you can adjust the blend mode and the opacity of a fill layer, but you cannot change its size.

To create a fill layer, follow these steps:

1. Choose Layer > New Fill Layer. A menu of fill layer choices appears.

2. Select which type of fill layer you want. A New Layer dialog box appears.

3. Optionally, enter a different name for the layer and select a blend mode and opacity setting. You can change these settings any time after you create the fill layer.

4. Click OK. Depending on your fill layer type, a dialog box appears.

   ▶ **If you selected a Solid color fill layer, the Color Picker dialog box appears, and you can select the color you want for the fill.**

   ▶ **If you selected a Gradient fill layer, the Gradient fill dialog box you see in Figure 3-19 appears. Select the gradient colors, style, and angle.**

   ▶ **If you selected a Pattern fill layer, the Pattern Fill dialog box appears, and you can select the pattern you want to use.**

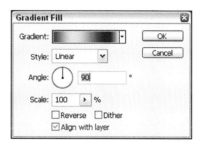

Figure 3-19
Creating a gradient fill layer.

When you add a fill layer, you'll notice a second thumbnail to the right of the fill layer icon. You can mask out areas of a fill layer that you don't want reflected in the layers above it. See the next section for information about masking.

Simplify the Layer First

Before applying any paint or other raster feature to a fill layer, you must first simplify it.

Masking with Layers

W E USE MASKS IN A LOT OF PLACES. Obviously, at Halloween, you see masks that hide the face, but still allow the eyes and mouth to show through. When you use a stencil to spray paint some letters onto a sign, you are using a mask. When you paint your living room and you don't want to get paint on the woodwork, you use masking tape around the areas that you want to protect. In the art world, water-color artists use a masking product to keep washes of color from bleeding into particular areas of a painting.

Similarly, Photoshop Elements supports masks, which are linked to the fill or adjustment layers. Masks allow you to hide portions of a layer without actually deleting it or modifying it. You can use mask layers to hide and show parts of a layer, create a fade between layers, and create other special effects by either completely masking an area or covering portions of the layer with varying levels of opacity.

Because the mask is a portion of the fill or adjust-ment layer, when you save the image in a Photoshop Elements format, the mask is saved as well; however, if you save your image in another format such as JPEG or TIFF, Photoshop Elements flattens the image and merges all layers together, including the mask.

All it takes to create a mask is the Paint Brush tool and black, white, or gray color paint. Choose the Paint Brush tool and then select the appropriate color:

▶ **Use black if you want to block certain areas from the adjustment effect or fill.**

▶ **Use white if you want to add back in areas from the adjustment or fill layer. For example, you painted black to mask an area that you've now decided you didn't want to mask.**

▶ **Use gray if you only want to tone down (not completely mask) the adjustment effect or fill so that it shows in various levels of transparency. The shade of gray you select determines how much is toned down. Darker gray shades result in more transparency, while using a lighter gray leaves more of the adjust-ment or fill layers effect.**

Make sure the adjustment or fill layer is active and paint over the area you want to mask or unmask. Take a look at the Layers palette. As you paint over the area you want to modify, the areas you are masking out with the Paint Brush appear on the second (masking) thumbnail (see Figure 3-20).

Turn Off Masking

If you want to temporarily turn off the masking, hold down the Shift key and click the Mask thumbnail. Shift-click the thumbnail again to reactivate the mask.

Mask layer thumbnail

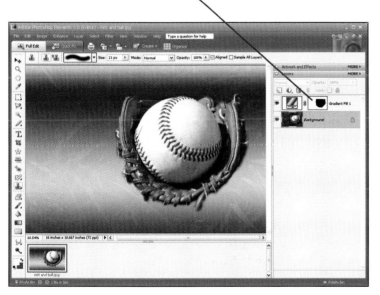

Figure 3-20
Use masking to display areas under a layer.

You can't delete a mask without deleting the actual adjustment or fill layer. What you can do, however, is fill in the image mask with white, which in effect, erases the mask.

Blending Layers

MANY PHOTOSHOP ELEMENTS features request that you select a blending mode. By blending layers, you can change the mood of a photograph or create very interesting abstract images. Just as the name implies, blends result from mixing. Mixing, in this case, refers to two or more layers together. Blend modes allow you to control how colors in one layer affect the underlying layers because the blend layer's pixels are blended into underlying layers without actually combining the layers. The way the pixels blend together depends on which blend mode you apply.

Photoshop Elements includes a large variety of blend modes. Table 3-1 illustrates an example image of a colorful parrot with a solid teal layer set at 60% opacity. You can see the image layers using each blend mode and a description of its effect. The blend modes are listed in alphabetical order.

Select a Blend Mode

With many Photoshop Elements tools, the Options bar provides a list from which you can select a blend mode. You can click the drop-down arrow to select an option, but you can also use the keyboard. To cycle through all of the blend modes quickly, use Shift-+ (plus) to change to the next mode, and Shift-– (minus) to change to the previous mode.

Layer Order

In most cases, the order of the layers becomes an important issue, because Photoshop Elements blends the pixels of the selected layer with all the underlying layers.

Table 3-1 Blend Modes

Sample	Blend Name	Effect
	None	Original image with no layer blending.
	Color	Without affecting the lightness, color applies the hue and saturation of the selected layer to the underlying layers, preserving the gray levels.
	Color Burn	Creates a darkening effect by looking at the color information in the layers and darkening the image, which creates a contrasting effect.
	Color Dodge	Creates a lightening effect by looking at the color information in the layers and brightening the base color to reflect the blend color (similar to bleaching). No changes occur to black color.
	Darken	Creates a darkening effect by displaying pixels in the selected layer that are darker than the underlying pixels. Pixels lighter than the blend color are replaced with the darker pixels, and pixels darker than the blend color do not change. Darken is the opposite of Lighten.
	Difference	Subtracts the selected layer's color from the color of the underlying layers; however, no changes occur to black color and blending with white inverts the colors. The resulting image has a negative look to it.

Table 3-1 Blend Modes *(continued)*

Sample	Blend Name	Effect
	Dissolve	Creates a speckled effect by randomly replacing the colors of some pixels on the selected layer with those of the underlying layers. The layer must have an opacity setting of less than 100%.
	Exclusion	Similar to the Difference blend mode, by subtracting the selected layer's color from the color of the underlying layers, but does so with a softer color difference and less contrast. No changes occur to black color and blending with white inverts the colors.
	Hard Light	Adds highlights and shadows by combining the Multiply and Screen blend modes, depending on the color channel. It multiplies pixels greater than 50% gray and screens pixels less than 50% gray. Painting with pure black or white results in pure black or white.
	Hard Mix	Similar to Vivid Light mode, but also reduces the color channels to only include white, black, red, green, blue, yellow, cyan, and magenta. The result is a posterized effect.
	Hue	Blends the color of the top layer to the brightness and color intensity of the lower layers.
	Lighten	Creates a lightening effect by displaying pixels in the selected layer that are lighter than the underlying pixels. Any pixels darker than the underlying layers disappear. Lighten is the opposite of Darken.

Table 3-1 Blend Modes *(continued)*

Sample	Blend Name	Effect
	Linear Burn	Creates a darkening effect by looking at the color information in the layers and darkening the lower layers by decreasing the brightness. Blending with white produces no change.
	Linear Dodge	Creates a lightening effect by looking at the color information in the layers and lightening the underlying layers by increasing the brightness. Blending with black produces no change.
	Linear Light	Changes the lighting effect by decreasing the brightness if the top layer pixels are more than 50% gray or by increasing the brightness if the top layer pixels are less than 50% gray.
	Luminosity	Without affecting the hue or saturations, applies the lightness of the selected layer to the underlying layers. Luminosity mode is the opposite of Color mode.
	Multiply	Creates a darkening effect by mixing the colors of the selected layer with the underlying layers. There are two exceptions: multiplying any color with white leaves the color unchanged, and multiplying any color with black results in black. Multiply is the opposite of Screen.
	Normal	The default option, displays pixels of the underlying layers, based on the opacity of pixels on the selected layer. If opacity is at 100%, Normal mode lets each pixel appear with no adjustments.

Table 3-1 Blend Modes *(continued)*

Sample	Blend Name	Effect
	Overlay	Creates a lighting effect by showing patterns and colors of the selected layer, but preserves the shadows and highlights of underlying layers. Similar to the Hard Light blend mode in that it combines the Multiply and Screen blend modes, depending on the color channel value.
	Pin Light	Creates a lighting effect by examining the top layer pixels. If the top layer pixels are greater than 50% gray, it replaces the darker pixels on the lower layer, but leaves the lighter pixels alone. If the top layer pixels are lighter than 50% gray, Pin Light mode replaces the lower layer pixels that are lighter than those on top. but leaves the darker pixels alone.
	Saturation	Without affecting the hue, combines the brightness and the color intensity of the selected layer and applies it to the underlying layers.
	Screen	Lightens the colors of underlying layers by multiplying the inverse of the selected and underlying layers, resulting in a lightened color of the selected layer. Screening with black leaves the color unchanged and screening with white produces white. The effect is similar to projecting multiple photographic slides on top of each other. Screen is the opposite of Multiply.
	Soft Light	A lighting mode, soft light adds highlights or shadows by combining the Burn and Dodge blend modes, depending on the colors in the selected layer. It actually darkens pixels more than 50% gray and lightens pixels less than 50% gray. Painting with pure black or white produces a distinctly darker or lighter area, but does not result in pure black or white.
	Vivid Light	Also a lighting type of blend mode, it burns or dodges the colors by increasing or decreasing the contrast, depending on the pixel color. If the pixels are greater than 50% gray, the contrast increases making the image darker, and if the pixels are less than 50% gray, the contrast decreases, making the image lighter.

Let's take a look at another example. Looking at the beautiful forest seen in Figure 3-21, I added a layer of a colorful sunset and set the blend mode to Hue. The image on the left is the original photograph, and the image on the right is the one after applying the sunset fill layer with the Color blend mode.

Photo Size When Blending

When you are blending images, you should use photos of the same size or scale, making sure that one of them has an element that would look somewhat natural if placed in the second photo.

Figure 3-21
Blending image colors.

Photographer: Jonathan Hawkins

4

Organizing Your

Photographs

PICTURE YOURSELF PACKING your possessions, getting ready for the moving van. You carefully wrap each of your dishes in bubble wrap and newspaper, taking extra time to make sure each treasure is protected. Next, you carefully organize and mark each box so the movers know what room it goes in. After spending so much time looking after your property, you would be devastated if the antique vase Aunt Mary gave you were chipped or cracked or even worse…lost.

Well, what about your digital photographs? If you're like most digital camera users, you have hundreds, perhaps thousands, of priceless memories stored on your computer. You could spend an enormous amount of time looking for that one photograph…you know, the one where your brother has the really funny grin on his face. Even more to consider is that one bad lightning storm could crash your hard drive and permanently erase your entire photographical history.

Opening the Organizer

I N THE FIRST THREE CHAPTERS, you worked in the Editor workspace where you discovered the basics of working with Photoshop Elements. But an equally and even sometimes more important feature in Photoshop Elements is the Organizer workspace. Through the Organizer you can:

▶ Download and import images from a camera, media card, scanner, CD, DVD, or hard drive.

▶ Create catalogs and collections to organize images.

▶ Add tags to easily identify and locate images.

▶ Create slide shows and other creative ways to view multiple images.

▶ Back up images and catalogs to CD's and DVD's.

One way to access the Organizer is through the Photoshop Elements Welcome screen, which appears when you launch the program. Click the View and Organize Photos button along the top of the screen. Photoshop Elements closes the Welcome screen and launches the Organizer workspace.

You can also open the Organizer directly from the Editor window. In the Shortcuts bar you see in Figure 4-1, click the Organize button, which tells Photoshop Elements to load the Organizer window. If you open the Organizer from the Editor window, both the Editor and Organizer workspaces are loaded and appear in the Windows taskbar.

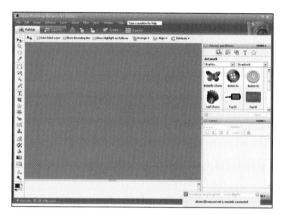

Figure 4-1
Launching the Organizer.

Start Up Options

Remember, if you spend a lot of time in the Organizer, you can tell Photoshop Elements to automatically start in the Organizer. Click the Start up in arrow and choose Organizer.

Reviewing the Organizer Workspace

CROSS THE TOP of the Organizer workspace, you see the traditional Windows menu from which you make many choices when managing your images. Under the menu, you see the Shortcut toolbar, which is the same toolbar as in the Editor workspace. On the left side, you see the large Organizer viewing area, called the *Photo Browser*, where Photoshop Elements stores thumbnail-sized links to your images. But there are a number of other helpful items in the Organizer workspace. In Figure 4-2, take a look at the following items:

▶ **Timeline:** The Timeline is the bar that runs along the top of the Photo Browser, and is divided into months and years, based on the file dates of the images currently in the Photo Browser.

View by Month

Pause your mouse over a bar in the Timeline to see the month the images were taken.

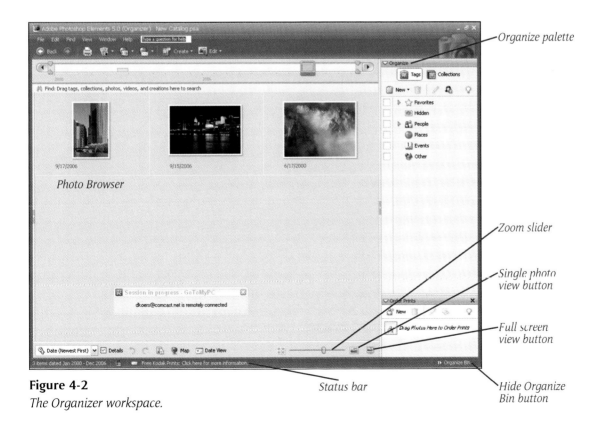

Figure 4-2
The Organizer workspace.

Status bar

▶ **Organize Palette**: In the Organize palette bin, you see the Organize palette. From the Organize palette, you can add tags to your images and create and manage your collections. You'll discover tags and collections later in this chapter.

▶ **Order Prints Palette**: Drag images from the Organizer viewing area here to order prints you want sent to you or someone else. See Chapter 8 for information on ordering prints online.

Hide Organize Bin

Click the Organize bin button to hide the bin, which stores your Organize palette and the Order Prints palette.

▶ **Zoom Slider**: Drag the slider bar right to increase the thumbnail image size or to the left to decrease the thumbnail image size.

▶ **Single Photo View**: Use this button to enlarge the view of a selected image.

▶ **Full Screen**: Use this button to hide the Photoshop Elements window and display the image in a full screen mode.

▶ **Control Bar**: Running along the bottom of the Photo Browser window are a series of tools, which help you sort, view, and manipulate your images. We'll work with these tools throughout this chapter.

▶ **Status Bar**: Appearing at the very bottom of the Organizer workspace, you see several informational items, including the number of images in the Photo Browser, the number of selected images, or the date range. The information changes as you perform various filters or searches. Additionally, there is a mailbox with prompts for special offers from Adobe, such as updates, promotions, or downloadable content such as creation templates.

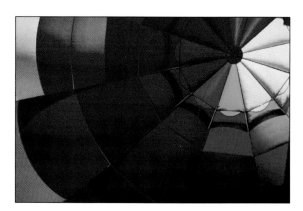

Adding Images to the Organizer

The catalog contains thumbnail-sized links to the original images, whether the images are stored on your hard drive or on a CD or DVD.

You can additionally scan images on a scanner and import them into your Photoshop Elements Photo Browser, or you can even get them from your digital camera or cell phone.

Once the images are in the Photo Browser, you can delete them, sort them, rotate them, and perform many organizational tasks on a single or multiple images.

Before you can organize your photos, you need to bring them into the Photoshop Elements catalog. By default, Photoshop Elements places images into a single catalog. A little later in this chapter, you'll discover how you can group the images into collections or even create additional catalogs where you can sort your images into additional categories, such as Business, or Web Site, or Personal. Until you create an additional catalog, Photoshop Elements places the images into a catalog called My Catalog.psa.

Automatically Include in Catalog

When you open a file in the Editor workspace, the Open dialog box contains a box to check so Photoshop Elements can automatically include the image in the catalog.

If you want to delete a photo from the Photo Browser, click the image you want to delete and press the Delete key. A Confirm Deletion from Catalog box appears. The image will only be deleted from the catalog unless you choose the option to delete the image from the hard drive as well.

Default Location

By default, Photoshop Elements stores catalogs on your hard drive in \Documents and Settings\All Users\Application Data\ Adobe\Catalog.

Dragging Photos from a Folder

One option for getting your images into the Photo Browser is to manually place them there. While not the fastest method, it gives you the flexibility of picking and choosing which images end up in the Photo Browser.

Open the folder containing the images you want in the Photo Browser. You may need to resize the window so you can see your image, but also see the Photoshop Elements window. Click and drag the image file from the folder onto the Photo Browser. A confirmation dialog box seen in Figure 4-3 appears. Optionally, click Don't Show Again if you don't need to see the confirmation box on future transfers. Click the OK button.

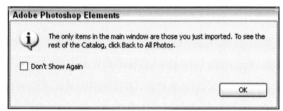

Figure 4-3
Drag-and-drop confirmation.

Each time you bring new images into Photoshop Elements, the images are loaded into a New Photos catalog window. Having them separated from other images makes it easier to tag and categorize your images before you group them up with other images.

Retrieving Images from Your Computer

One of the most common methods of bringing images into the Photo Browser is through the Get Photos menu. From photos retrieved from your

computer hard drive, the actual photos are left in their original folder location, and Photoshop Elements creates a link to it. When performing any type of editing or printing action, Photoshop Elements uses the link to open the original photograph.

The following steps show you how to retrieve images from your hard drive:

1. Choose File > Get Photos > From Files and Folders. The Get Photos from Files and Folders dialog box seen in Figure 4-4 appears.

Optional Methods

Two optional methods to get photos are to click the Get Photos drop-down button on the Shortcuts bar or to press Ctrl+Shift+G.

Figure 4-4
Retrieving images from your computer.

2. Use the Look in drop-down list to navigate to the folder containing the images you want to retrieve into your catalog.

3. Select the desired images. Photoshop Elements provides several methods for selecting images:

▶ **To select a single image, click on the image you want.**

▶ **To select all images in the current folder, click inside the box where the file names appear and press Ctrl+A.**

▶ **To select a sequential list of images, click on the first file you want; then Shift-click on the last file.**

Optional Selection Method

Optionally, to select a sequential group of images, click and draw an imaginary boundary box around the images.

▶ **To select a nonsequential list of images, click on the first image you want; then Ctrl-click on each additional image.**

5. If you want Photoshop Elements to automatically correct red eye in any images, make sure the Automatically Fix Red Eyes option is selected. Chapter 5 also shows you how you can manually correct image red eye.

My Preference

I personally prefer to fix my red-eye images manually. The Automatically Fix Red Eyes option is only a so so feature. While it doesn't usually make any incorrect fixes, it misses a great deal of red eye.

5. If you want Photoshop Elements to automatically create stacks for the images, make sure the Automatically Suggest Photo Stacks option is selected. (See "Stacking Photos" later in this chapter.)

6. Click the Get Photos button. Photoshop Elements retrieves the images into the Photo Browser. If you opted for automatic red-eye repair, a dialog box appears indicating how many and which images it repaired (see Figure 4-5).

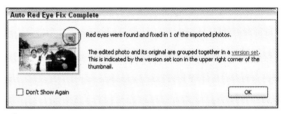

Figure 4-5
Automatically repairing red eyes.

If any of the photos already have tags attached to them, the Import Attached Tags dialog box seen in Figure 4-6 appears. (See "Tagging and Organizing" later in this chapter.) Select any tags you want to use and click OK. After Photoshop Elements retrieves the images, they appear in their own New Photos catalog window.

Figure 4-6
Importing tags from images.

Watched Folders

Photoshop Elements can monitor your file folders for the addition of new images. Watched folders alert Photoshop Elements Organizer when a new photo is added to the folder and then automatically add the photo to the Organizer or prompts you first. By default, the My Pictures folder is watched, but if you want to add additional folders to the list, choose File > Watch Folders, click Add, and then browse to the folder. Click OK after you select the folder.

Keep Original Photo Offline option   Disk reference name

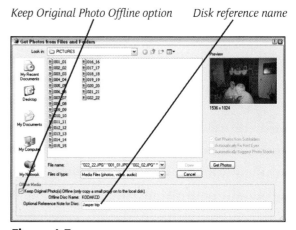

Figure 4-7
Save from CD to hard drive or save low-resolution proxy files.

Opening Images on a CD or DVD

Retrieving images from a CD or DVD isn't much different than those that are on your hard disk, except that you can choose to copy the actual files on the removable disk to your hard drive, or you can bring in low-resolution photocopies, called *proxy files*. Copying the images to your hard drive is the default option unless you choose Keep Original Photos Offline from the Offline Media section you see in Figure 4-7. If you choose to save only the proxy files, you can optionally assign a descriptive reference name to the original CD or DVD.

Later, if you want to edit the original image, Photoshop Elements prompts you to insert the CD or DVD. It supplies the reference name so you can locate the correct disk. Figure 4-8 shows the dialog box you see when Photoshop Elements needs the original disk.

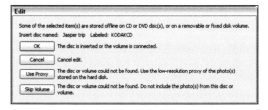

Figure 4-8
Insert the requested CD to edit the original image.

As with retrieving images from your hard drive, they appear in their own New Photos catalog window.

Label Your Disk

To make the disk easy to locate, write the reference name on the CD. Use a label or a felt tip pen.

Proxy Icon

A proxy image for an offline photo has the CD icon in its thumbnail image.

Searching for Files

Often, you know exactly which folders contain your images and, as you just discovered, you can import them through the File > Get Files> From Files and Folders options. But occasionally, images get misplaced, and you could spend an enormous amount of time looking for files that aren't in the usual locations. Instead of getting frustrated looking for them, let the Photoshop Elements Organizer do all the work with its Search feature. You can let it search your entire hard drive or even network drives to locate image and video files. The following steps show you how:

1. Choose File > Get Photos > By Searching. The Get Photos by Searching for Folders dialog box seen in Figure 4-9 appears.

Optional Method

Optionally, choose Get Photos by Searching from the Get Photos button on the Shortcut bar.

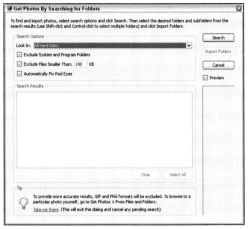

Figure 4-9
Set options when searching for image files.

2. If you want to search in a location other than your local hard drives, click the Look In drop-down list and select another location. If the location you want, such as a removable drive or a network drive, isn't listed, click the Browse button and select the location from there.

3. If you want Photoshop Elements to look in your system and program folders, remove the check mark from the option. You should know, however, that typically these folders don't contain images.

4. If you want Photoshop Elements to limit its search to only those images larger than a certain size (which typically represents higher resolution images), specify the size in the KB box. If you don't want to limit the image size, remove the check mark from the Exclude Files Smaller Than box.

5. If you don't want Photoshop Elements to automatically look for and fix any images with red eye, remove the check from the Automatically Fix Red Eyes option.

6. Click the Search button. The search returns a list of all folders containing photos and video clips (see Figure 4-10).

7. Click a specific folder to select it or press Ctrl and click another folder name to select multiple folders.

8. Click the Import Folders button, which imports the images into the Photo Browser.

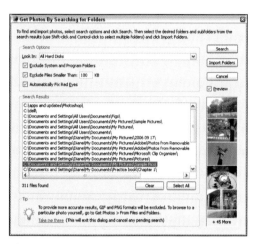

Figure 4-10
A found list of folders containing images.

Downloading Images from Your Camera or Card Reader

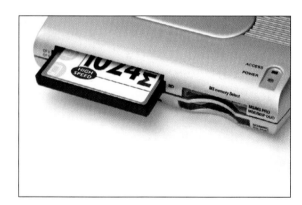

You can download images from your camera or memory card reader, either by moving and pasting them through Microsoft Windows into the folder of your choice, or by using software that came with the camera, or you can choose an even easier method of using the Adobe Download Manager.

Use the following steps:

1. Connect your camera or card reader to your computer and make sure it is switched on. If you don't know how to connect your camera or card reader, refer to the documentation that came with it.

2. The Adobe Download Manager window seen in Figure 4-11 should automatically open, but if not, click the Adobe Photo Downloader icon in the Windows system tray or choose File > Get Photos > From Camera or Card Reader.

Figure 4-11
The Adobe Download Manager dialog box.

3. The device's name should appear in the Source area, but if not, click the drop-down list and select your camera or card reader. If you don't see your device listed, try choosing the <Refresh List> option.

Modify Default Options

To modify the default options that appear in the Adobe Download Manager, click Edit > Preferences > Camera or Card Reader.

4. Select any desired options from the Import Setting area. Options include:

   ▶ **Location: This option determines in which folder the Adobe Photo Downloader should store the imported files. Click the Browse button to change the default location, which is typically under the My Documents\My Pictures folder.**

   ▶ **Create Subfolders: This option allows you to set a folder naming convention for the downloaded images.**

   ▶ **Rename Files: By default, your camera assigns a name to the images. For example, a Sony camera uses a file naming convention of DISC*xxxx*.jpg, where the *xxxx* represents the image number. If you want to use Photoshop Elements to rename the files while importing them, click the Rename Files drop-down list and select a different naming convention.**

   ▶ **Delete Options: This option tells Photoshop Elements whether to leave the photos on your camera or memory card or to delete the files after they are copied to the hard drive. You can also choose to verify that the files were really copied and match the files on the camera before deleting them from the camera. Any photos you do not download with the Download Manager are not deleted, no matter which option you select here.**

5. Click Get Photos. Photoshop Elements copies the images to your hard drive and displays a confirmation dialog box in preparation for importing the image into the catalog.

Automatic Download

If you click the Automatic Download Imports button, the next time the selected device is connected to your computer, Adobe Download Manager automatically downloads your photos using the default settings specified here.

6. Click OK. If you opted to delete the files after copying and importing, you see a couple of confirmation message boxes. Click Yes if you want to delete the images; then click OK to confirm the images are deleted.

Scanning Images

Similar to a copy machine, a scanner duplicates material, but instead of printing the item on a piece of a paper, the digital image gets placed on the computer screen. The two main types of scanners are a flatbed scanner and a sheetfed scanner. The differences are that with a flatbed scanner you raise a lid to reveal a glass plate where you lay the item you want to scan, while a sheetfed scanner may look similar to a fax machine in that it has a slot where a sheet of paper can be fed into the scanner. While the scanner itself is a piece of hardware, scanners usually have software that allows the hardware to communicate with the computer. You can use the software that came with your scanner to open your photos, negatives, and slide images, or you can let Photoshop Elements read directly from the scanner.

Let's take a look at letting Photoshop Elements retrieve the scanned image:

1. Make sure the power to the scanner is connected and the scanner is turned on.

2. Choose File > Get Photos > From Scanner or press Ctrl+U. The Get Photos from Scanner dialog box appears.

Get Photos Icon

Optionally, click the Get Photos icon on the Shortcuts bar and select From Scanner.

3. If not already displayed, select your scanner from the Scanner drop-down list.

Install Scanner Software

Before you try to scan and open your photos into Photoshop Elements, make sure that you've installed all the software that came with your scanner.

4. Optionally, click the Browse button and select a different file location for saving scanned images.

5. Choose a file format from the Save As menu. Choices are JPEG, which is the default format, TIF, or PNG.

6. If you choose JPEG, drag the Quality slider to the setting you want, but remember that higher quality also results in larger file sizes (see Figure 4-12).

7. If you don't want Photoshop Elements to automatically fix red eyes, remove the check mark from the Automatically Fix Red Eyes option.

Figure 4-12
Getting scanned images.

8. Click OK. Photoshop Elements launches either the Windows scanning interface or a scanning interface for your specific scanner.

9. Set the scan type, size, and resolution according to your scanner manufacturer's instructions and start the scan. After the photo is scanned, the image thumbnail appears in a New Photos window ready for you to assign a tag or category.

Retrieving Images from Your Cell Phone

Many of today's cell phones have cameras built into them, but it's traditionally been very difficult to get the photos from the camera onto your computer's hard  drive. If you have a Nokia brand cell phone, you're really in luck. Follow the manufacturer's instructions to physically connect the cell phone to your computer, and the Adobe Photo Downloader automatically appears. If the Photo Downloader doesn't automatically begin, you can start it by choosing

File > Get Photos > From Mobile Phone. The first time you attempt to get photos from your cell phone, you will see the Specify Mobile Phone Folder dialog box seen in Figure 4-13.

Get Photos Option

Optionally, choose the Get Photos button on the Shortcuts bar and choose From Mobile Phone. The shortcut key is Ctrl+Shift+M.

Figure 4-13
Specify a cell phone image folder.

The default folder location is \My Documents\My Pictures, but it's a really good idea to separate the cell phone images into their own folder. Click the Browse button and then click the Make New Folder button to create a new folder. Click OK twice to accept the changes.

Change Folder Location

To later change the folder location, choose Edit > Preferences > Mobile Phone.

But what if you don't have a Nokia cell phone that interacts with the Adobe Photo Downloader? You will probably have to contact your cell phone provider for instructions, but if you have a Bluetooth enabled cell phone, you can also purchase a Bluetooth to USB adapter that will allow you to copy or move media files from your cell phone to a computer folder you specify (which should be the same folder you designate when the Specify Mobile Phone Folder dialog box appears). The instructions for Bluetooth to USB adapters vary by brand, so once again, refer to the manufacturer's instructions.

After you copy the images from your cell phone to your cell phone images folder, you can use the Photoshop Elements File > Get Photos > From Mobile Phone option.

Stacking Photos

Sometimes when you take photos, you may take a number of the same image, perhaps by using your camera's Burst mode where each image shows a slightly different movement or pose. Stacking the photos lets you easily access all the visually similar images from a single thumbnail location instead of scattered across rows of thumbnails, thereby saving space and time by keeping the related images together.

Often, when importing images into the Photo Browser, if Photoshop Elements sees images that are visually similar and taken in close time intervals, it can automatically suggest image groups and place them into a stack. Figure 4-14 shows a stacked thumbnail icon. By default, Photoshop Elements places the newest photo on top of the stack.

Stack icon   *Expand button*

8/30/2006 8:31 PM

Figure 4-14
Stack similar images together.

Here are a few ways to manage Photoshop Elements stacks:

▶ **If you want to create your own stacks, select the images you want to stack; then choose Edit > Stack > Stack Selected Photos. Optionally, right-click the selected images and choose Stack > Stack Selected Photos.**

Stack Commands

You can optionally access all stack commands by right-clicking the images or stack.

▶ **If you want to expand a stack to view the underlying images, click the right-pointing (expand) arrow. Each image appears in its own thumbnail; however, all images in the selected stack are highlighted together. The expansion arrow turns into a left-pointing (collapse) arrow.**

Expand Stack

Photoshop Elements edits, e-mails, and prints only the top-most item in a collapsed stack. To apply an action to all or individual stacked photos, expand the stack and select the photos you want to edit.

▶ **If you want to restack the images, click the collapse arrow.**

▶ **If you want to find only the images stacked together, choose Find > All Stacks.**

▶ **If you want to remove a photo from a stack, expand the stack, click the photo you want to remove, and choose Edit > Stack > Remove Selected Photos from Stack. When you remove a photo from the stack, it's not removed from the catalog or the computer hard drive.**

▶ **If you want to make a photo the top image in the stack, expand the stack and select the image you want as the top thumbnail. Choose Edit > Stack > Set as Top Photo.**

▶ **If you want to delete all the photos in a stack, select a collapsed stack and press the Delete key. In the Confirm Deletion from Catalog dialog box, select the Delete All Photos in Stack option and if you want to permanently delete the images from your computer, select the Also Delete Selected Item(s) from the Hard Disk.**

▶ If you want to delete all but the top photo in a stack, from a collapsed stack, choose Edit > Stack > Flatten Stack. You will see the confirmation box shown in Figure 4-15 . Optionally, choose the Also Delete Photos from the Hard Disk option if you want the image files removed from your computer as well.

▶ If you want to combine multiple stacks, select the stacks you want to combine and choose Edit > Stack > Stack Selected Photos. A confirmation dialog box appears warning you that the stacks will be combined. Click OK. The newest photo will appear at the top of the new stack.

Figure 4-15
Deleting images from a stack.

Viewing Photos in the Photo Browser

NOW THAT YOU'VE SEEN the power the Photo Browser has to gather together images imported from your computer, CD, camera, scanner, or phone, it's probably looking pretty full and maybe a bit intimidating. All those little thumbnails may be difficult to view, especially if you're viewing them with "older" eyes. Let's take a look at some of the options for looking at your photographs and other media files.

View Details

Click the Details option in the Control bar to turn on and off the display under the photo. By default, you can see the image date and any assigned tags. If you want to see the file name as part of the detail information, choose Edit > Preferences and click Show File Names in Details from the General category.

Sorting Files in the Photo Browser

When you import images from your camera or media card, the images usually contain additional information (metadata), which includes the date the photograph was taken. When you scan an image, the scanned date is the image date, and if the image originated from another source, such as the Internet, and was then saved to your hard drive, the date you first saved the file to your disk becomes the image date.

So why is this information necessary? Because, by default, Photoshop Elements displays the images by their date, showing images with the newest dates first. If multiple images have the same date, then Photoshop Elements displays them in the order they were taken, with the oldest of those images first. But that's not the only way Photoshop Elements can display images in the Photo Browser. Choose View > Arrangement and select a different sort option. Other sort options include:

▶ **Date (Oldest First):** This option displays the images in chronological order.

▶ **Import Batch:** This option groups the images together by the batches in which they were imported and shows how the photos were imported, such as by scanner or from the hard drive (see Figure 4-16).

Choose Sort Option

Optionally, select a sort option from the Photo Browser Arrangement drop-down list.

Arrangement drop-down arrow

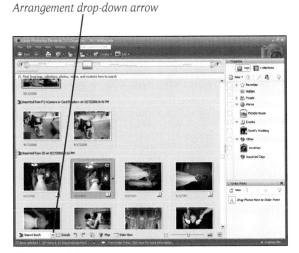

Figure 4-16
Images sorted by import batch.

▶ **Folder Location:** This option displays the images grouped together by the folder where the images are stored on your hard drive. A folder tree also appears on the left side where you can click any folder to jump to the images it contains.

From the Folder location view, you can also manage your folders and files. Right-click a folder and choose to rename the folder, delete the folder, or even create a new folder.

Resizing Thumbnails

Earlier I mentioned those "older" eyes that sometimes make things more difficult to see clearly. Rather than get nose prints on the computer screen to see the images better, you can change the size of the thumbnails. Located along the bottom of the Organizer workspace, you see the Zoom slider. Drag the Zoom slider handle to the right to make the thumbnails larger like those you see in Figure 4-18 or to the left to make them smaller. Drag the slider all the way to the right to view only one thumbnail at a time.

View Single Photo

Optionally, to view a single photo, click the Single Photo button located to the right of the Zoom slider.

Folder tree

Figure 4-17
Images sorted by folder.

Small thumbnail button

Figure 4-18
Zooming in on thumbnail images.

To display the smallest thumbnails possible, providing the most thumbnails on the screen, drag the slider all the way to the left or click the small thumbnail button located to the left of the Zoom slider. The number of thumbnails you see depends on your screen resolution and monitor size.

Viewing Photos in a Slide Show

Another perspective is to view the images at full screen without seeing all the Photoshop Elements toolbars, palettes, and other screen items. You can peruse through the images at a leisurely pace, which, by default, also includes background music.

The slide show previews all the images visible in the current catalog. If you want to view only certain slides in the slide show, select those images first. You can also choose the images you want by their tag. See "Tagging and Organizing" later in this chapter.

Start the slide show by choosing View > View Photos in Full Screen. The Full Screen View Options dialog box seen in Figure 4-19 appears.

Figure 4-19
Launching a slide show.

Start Slide Show

You can optionally start the slide show by pressing the F11 key or by clicking the Full Screen View button located to the right of the Zoom slider.

Table 4-1 describes the many options available in the Full Screen View dialog box.

Table 4-1	The Full Screen View Options dialog box
Option	**Function**
Background Music	Choose any desired options, including whether you want to play background music while the screen show plays and if so, what music file you want to hear. You can choose from the supplied list of music or browse to any music file stored on your computer.
Play Audio Captions	Plays voice-recorded captions previously applied to images. See "Working with Captions" later in this chapter.
Page Duration	Sets the time interval each image should remain on the screen before the next one appears. The default duration is 4 seconds and the maximum time is 3600 seconds, which is 1 hour.
Include Captions	Displays previously applied text captions along the bottom of the screen. See "Working with Captions" later in this chapter.

Option	Function
Allow Photos to Resize	Resizes photos to fit the screen. If your image is small, resizing it may make it appear grainy or distorted at a larger size.
Allow Videos to Resize	Resizes video to fit the screen. If your video resolution is small, resizing it may make it appear grainy or distorted at a larger size.
Show Filmstrip	Check this box to display thumbnail size images along the right edge of your window. Showing the filmstrip allows you to jump quickly to a specific image.
Fade Between Photos	Uncheck this if the next image should just appear on your screen, or leave it checked if you want the previous image to fade out before the new one appears.
Start Paying Automatically	Check this box to launch the screen show as soon as you click the OK button. Without the option checked, you must first press the spacebar to launch the show.

Option	Function
Repeat Slide Show	Check this option if you want the screen show to play repeatedly until you manually stop it from running.
Show This Dialog Before Viewing Photos in Full Screen	Uncheck this option if you don't want to see this dialog box before your screen shows begin.

Click the OK button, which closes the Full Screen View Options dialog box. The first image remains on your screen and a control bar appears across the top, as you see in Figure 4-20. Press the keyboard spacebar to begin the slide show, which displays according to the options you selected. After a few seconds, the control bar disappears, but you can display it again by simply moving your mouse. While in the slide show, you can use the control bar for the following actions:

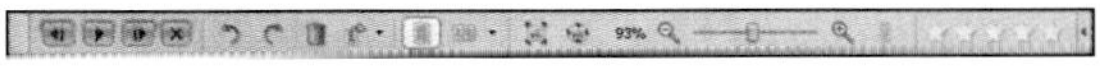

Figure 4-20
Slide show control toolbar.

▶ **Previous Photo:** Displays the previous image shown in the slide show. You can also press the left arrow key.

▶ **Play:** Starts the slide show and changes to a Pause button while the slide show is running. You can also press the spacebar to play and pause the show.

▶ **Next Photo**: Jumps ahead and displays the next image shown in the slide show. You can also press the right arrow key.

▶ **Exit**: Quits the screen show. You can also press the Escape key to exit the show.

▶ **Rotate 90° Left**: Rotates the current image. The image remains rotated when you return to the Photo Browser.

▶ **Rotate 90° Right**: Rotates the current image. The image remains rotated when you return to the Photo Browser.

▶ **Delete**: Deletes the image from both the slide show and the Organizer, but doesn't delete it from the hard drive unless you specify so.

▶ **Action Menu**: Pauses the slide show and lists a series of commands, as seen in Figure 4-21, including showing the filmstrip and the Full Screen View Options dialog box.

Figure 4-21
Control bar action items.

▶ **Full Screen View**: The default screen show view; it shows the image using the full resources of the screen.

▶ **Side-by-Side View**: Displays the current image and the next image side by side. Click the arrow next to the Side-by-Side view button and optionally choose Above and Below.

▶ **Fit in Window**: Zooms the image so it fits in the current window.

▶ **Actual Pixels**: Displays images at their actual sizes.

▶ **Zoom Out**: Zoom out on an area of the image.

▶ **Zoom Slider**: Controls the slide zoom. Drag it to the left to zoom out and to the right to zoom in.

▶ **Zoom In**: Zooms in on an area of the image.

▶ **Sync Panning and Zooming**: Used when you have slides displayed side by side or above and below. When activated, and you zoom in on one image, the other image zooms in also.

▶ **Specify a Favorites Rating**: Applies a Favorites tag based on a 1 to 5 scale rating. See "Tagging and Organizing" later in this chapter.

▶ **Show Only Navigation Controls**: Collapses the control bar so it only shows the first four tools—the navigation tools. Click the arrow while the toolbar is collapsed to expand it to show all tools.

Viewing the Photos in a Date/Calendar View

Another method of viewing your images is by their dates, which Photoshop Elements calls the *Date view*. Date view is not the same as sorting the images by newest or oldest date. In Date view, the images appear in a monthly, daily, or yearly calendar.

Access the Date view by clicking the Date View button located at the bottom of the Photo Browser window. Optionally press Ctrl+Alt+D to display the Date view. The images appear in a default monthly calendar, such as the one shown in Figure 4-22. As you pause your mouse over any day with an image, a tool tip appears advising how many images were taken on that date.

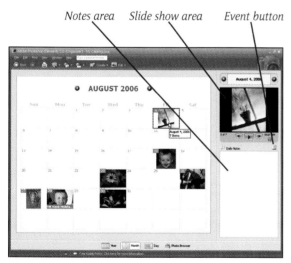

Figure 4-22
Images in a monthly calendar.

Click any calendar day with an image on it. Toward the top right of the screen you see controls to launch a miniature slide show of the images for the selected day. At the bottom right, you see a

white area where you can click and type notes about the selected day. Dates that have notes attached display a small yellow icon on the date. Click the Event button to create a reminder event, such as a birthday or anniversary or a reason you took pictures that day. Optionally, you can repeat the event every year (see Figure 4-23).

Figure 4-23
Creating an event.

> **Add Event**
>
> Optionally, right-click any day to add an event.

Double-click any image to switch to Day view where you see a large screen view of the top image, along with all the other images for that day that appear as a filmstrip along the side, similar to what you see in Figure 4-24. Click the controls along the bottom of the screen to launch a repetitive miniature slide show of the day's images.

Along the bottom of any of the calendar windows, you also see buttons to jump to the other views (yearly, monthly, and daily). Figure 4-25 shows the yearly calendar where you can see highlighted calendar squares representing the days that have images attached to them.

Figure 4-24
Daily view.

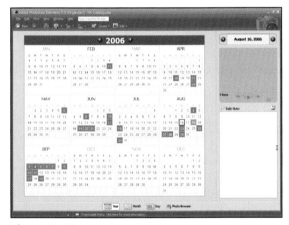

Figure 4-25
Yearly view.

Click the Photo Browser button at the bottom of the window to return to the Photo Browser window.

Specifying Media Types

Since the Photo Browser includes a variety of media types, you may want to review only certain types. Fortunately it's very easy to filter the thumbnails so they only display selected media types. Use the following steps:

1. Choose View > Media Types or press Ctrl+M. The Items Shown dialog box seen in Figure 4-26 appears.

Figure 4-26

2. *Displaying only selected media types.*

   Remove check marks from the media types you don't want to display and add check marks to the media types you do want to display. Removing the check marks only hides them from the Photo Browser catalog. It doesn't remove them from the catalog or the computer hard drive.

3. Click the OK button. Photoshop Elements displays only the selected media type thumbnails.

Watching Video Clips

The Photo Browser displays video clip thumbnails with a small icon of a filmstrip. Double-click the video thumbnail to display a video window, such as the one you see in Figure 4-27. Along the bottom edge of the window, you see a set of controls similar to your VCR or DVD players that you can use to play, pause, stop, or rewind the video.

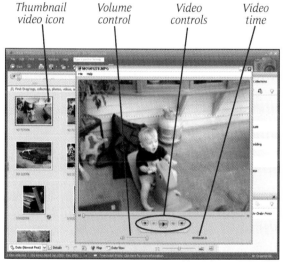

Thumbnail video icon   Volume control   Video controls   Video time

Figure 4-27
Viewing video clips in the Photo Browser.

Controls include Rewind, Stop, Play, Pause, and Fast Forward. Along the bottom of the window, you can control the volume with the volume slider.

Working with Captions

You can add a descriptive title to your image in the form of a caption, which appears along the bottom of the image. When you print your image or view it in a slide show, you have the option of displaying the image caption. While captions are generally text based, they can also be an audio file that you record with a microphone or any recorded MP3, WAV, and WMA file.

Photoshop Elements provides a number of different methods to add a caption. One method is to double-click the image thumbnail so the image appears in Single Photo View and then type in the Click Here to Add Caption area, which is beneath the photograph. Another common method to add a text caption is to choose Edit > Add Caption, which displays an Add Caption dialog box where you can type your description.

If you want to add an audio caption, from the Single Photo View, click the Record Audio Caption button, which displays the Select Audio File dialog box. Click File > Browse and locate the audio file you want to use. Choose File > Close and when prompted to save the audio caption, choose Yes.

Figure 4-28
Adding an audio caption.

Looking at File Metadata

Every time you take a picture with your digital camera, the camera records additional information called *metadata*. Metadata includes the date and time you took the picture, as well as the camera make and model, shutter speed, aperture, and all sorts of other little pieces of information. When you add an image to the Photoshop Elements Organizer, the metadata information also comes along. As you work with the image in Photoshop Elements (for example, adding captions, tags, or editing changes), Photoshop Elements adds the changes to the file's metadata.

In addition, Photoshop Elements automatically scans opened images for Digimarc watermarks, which are digital watermarks designed to prevent copyright violations. If a watermark is detected, Photoshop Elements displays a copyright symbol in the image window's title bar and includes the information in the Copyright Status, Copyright Notice, and Owner URL sections of the File Info dialog box.

Resize Properties Box

Resize the Properties box by dragging any edge of the box.

You view all the data assigned to an image by viewing the image properties. Select the image and choose Window > Properties. A small Properties box appears. In Figure 4-29, you see the four versions of the Properties box. The first image shows the General Properties, such as captions, file name, size, date, and location. The second image shows any tags and collections assigned to an image, and the third image shows import information. The tall image shows some of the detailed metadata, including camera information.

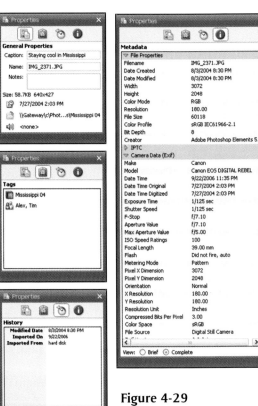

Figure 4-29
Viewing image properties.

Tagging and Organizing

ALL THROUGH THIS CHAPTER and through much of the book so far, you've seen tags mentioned. Tags are keywords for people (such as Tommy), events (such as Bob's Wedding), or places (such as Our Trip West). You assign one or more tags to your images so you can easily locate and organize them. Photoshop Elements provides an unlimited number of categories, subcategories, and tags.

Hidden Category

You can also assign the Hidden category to images to prevent them from being displayed in the catalog until you want them to appear.

Creating Tags

The easiest way to work with tags is from the Tags palette, which is located on the right side of the Organizer window in the Organize palette. By default, the Photoshop Elements Organizer creates categories of tags, including People, Places, and Events, as well as tags to hide images or mark them as a favorite. You can create an unlimited number of new tags by adding them under any category. The following steps show you how to create new tags:

1. From the Tags palette, click the New button.

2. Choose New Tag. The Create Tag dialog box appears.

3. Click the Category drop-down menu and select a category for the new tag.

4. Type a name in the Name text box.

5. Optionally, type a description or other information in the Note box.

6. Click OK. The tag appears in the Tags palette under the category you selected. By default, new tags have a question mark on them; however, as soon as you attach a tag to a photograph, that photograph becomes the tag icon.

Rename Tag

If you need to change the name or tag category, right-click the tag and choose Edit *tag name* tag. If you want to delete a tag, right-click the tag and choose Delete *tag name* tag. Deleting a tag only deletes the tag, but not the image, from the Organizer.

Adding Tags to Images

After you create your tags, you can associate a photograph and a tag together. Remember that images can have more than one tag associated with them. For example, suppose that you create and attach tags called *Niagara Falls* to the images you took from your last vacation. Now you might have another tag for your individual friends or family members, such as Mom or Uncle Joe. The picture of Mom standing close to Niagara Falls could have both the Niagara Falls tag and the Mom tag.

You can assign tags one at a time to individual photographs, or you can select a group of images and assign them all the same tag (such as all the Niagara Falls trip images). The Organizer provides several different methods to attach tags to photographs:

In the Photo Browser, select the photo or photos to which you want to attach the tag. (To select more than one photo, Ctrl-click the photos.)

To attach one photo to one tag, do one of the following:

> ▶ **Right-click the mouse over any selected photo. From the Shortcut menu, choose Attach Tag to Selected Items>*tag category* > *tag name*.**

> ▶ **Drag the tag from the Tags palette onto the selected photos. In Figure 4-30, I'm attaching the images to the tag named Scott's Wedding.**

After you apply a tag, an icon appears either in the thumbnail image or directly below it (depending on the thumbnail size). Each category of tag has its own icon. Pause your mouse over any thumbnail tag icon to see the tag name.

Cursor dragging the tag icon

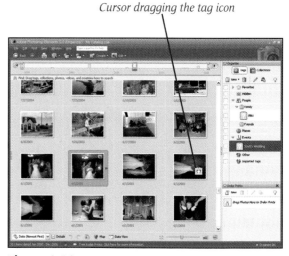

Figure 4-30
Drag the desired tag to the selected images.

Remove Tag

To remove a tag from an image, right-click on the thumbnail tag icon and choose Remove tag.

If you apply a tag to a collapsed stack, the tag is applied to all items in the stack. When you search on the tag, the top photo, the one with the tag icon, appears in the search results. If you want to apply a tag to only certain photos in a stack, expand the stack and then apply the tag to those photos.

After you have your images tagged, you can easily filter out the Photo Browser window to show only specific tagged images. From the Tags palette, click the gray box next to the tag name. A pair of binoculars (indicating Search) appears and only the images with that specific tag appear. You can choose multiple tags, such as you see in Figure 4-31, which shows only the images from Mackinaw Island and Washington DC.

Search tag icon

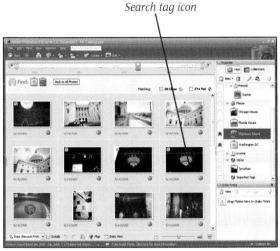

Figure 4-31
Filter the thumbnail display by using tags.

The bar across the top of the Photo Browser indicates how many images did and did not meet your filter. In this example, 30 images matched and 274 images did not match. Click Back to All Photos to display the entire catalog or click the Tag palette gray box to remove the Search.

Finding Faces for Tagging

A really cool feature of the Organizer is that it can isolate images with faces for you so you can quickly tag those images. It's fast and pretty accurate, too! In a search of over 1,000 images, it was able to locate almost 300 images that had a human face in about five minutes. Oh yeah...it found one dog nose, too! One of my photographs was of a Washington DC memorial called Fallen Heroes of Operation Enduring Freedom, and the memorial had pictures on display of military men and women who lost their lives. The Organizer face tagging function caught every single face from that one photograph. Here's how to use the Face Tagging function:

1. Select the images you want to search. If you want to search all images in your catalog, press Ctrl+A or choose Edit > Select All.

2. Choose Find > Find Faces for Tagging. Photoshop Elements searches through the selected images and returns a thumbnail for every face it finds. If your photograph has three different people in it, you'll get three thumbnails—one for each person in that photograph. Figure 4-32 shows an example of the face tagging results window.

Figure 4-32
Identifying faces for tagging.

Face Tagging

Face tagging only works on photographs. If your selection includes other media, such as videos or Photoshop Elements creations, you get a dialog box noting that those items will be skipped from the face tagging.

3. Select the images you want to assign to a specific People tag, such as Mom or Adam, and either drag the selected images on top of the tag or drag the tag on top of a selected image. Photoshop Elements immediately assigns the tag to the face and removes the image from the results window so you can assign the rest of the faces to their tags.

4. When you're finished with tagging the faces, click the Done button.

Working in Map View

A FEATURE NEW TO Photoshop Elements Version 5 is the Yahoo! Map. With an Internet connection, you can use the map to view images by specific geographic regions, or you can share the map and the associated images on your Web site or save the map to a CD.

Click the Map button at the bottom of the Organizer window. The Map window appears on the left side of your screen (see Figure 4-33).

First Use of Map

The first time you use the map feature, a dialog box appears. Click OK.

At the bottom of the Map window, you see several viewing controls. Use the Zoom In or Zoom Out buttons to click on the map to zoom in or out. Use the Hand tool to click on the map and drag it in any direction. There's also a Move tool, which you'll use if you need to move map pins.

While you can drag photos from the Photo Browser to the map, a more accurate method is to let the map find the location. Select one or more pictures you want to appear on the map. Choose Edit > Place on Map, which displays the Photo Location on Map dialog box. Type the city, state, or country where you want the image associated. For example, type Cincinnati, OH, or Chicago or Egypt. A Look Up Addresses dialog box like the one you see in Figure 4-34 appears. Select the location that most closely matches your destination; then click OK.

Zoom In   Zoom Out   Hand   Move

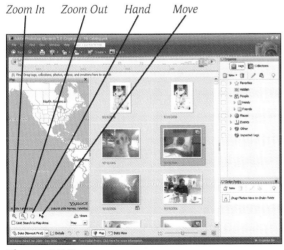

Figure 4-33
Displaying the Yahoo! Map.

Figure 4-34
Select the appropriate location.

Photoshop Elements zooms into the designated location and places a red pin. Click the pin to see mini representations of the images associated with the location.

> **Multiple Pins**
>
> Locations that have multiple pins in close proximity show a three-pin cluster.

Figure 4-35 illustrates a map with several pins. Here are some of the functions of the Map View:

Figure 4-35
View photos by their geographical location.

▶ Select **Limit Search to Map Area** to limit the Photo Browser view to only the photos related to the visible map pins.

▶ You can quickly navigate to a particular map location by right-clicking on a photo or a tag that has a location assigned to it and choosing **Show on Map.**

▶ To remove an image from a map area, select the image you want to remove and choose **Edit > Remove from Map** or optionally right-click the image and choose **Remove from Map.**

▶ To remove a map pin from the map, right-click the pin you want to remove and choose **Remove from Map.** A confirmation box will follow.

▶ To move a map pin, zoom in to the area so you can clearly see the pin; then select the **Move** tool. Drag the pin to a new location. Optionally, right-click the pin and choose **Place on Map.** When the **Photo Location on Map** dialog box appears, type the new location.

▶ In the Map, click the drop-down list to display the standard map or the map from a satellite view. Choose **Hybrid** to view the map as a combination of both the standard map and the satellite view map.

▶ Choose **Share** to publish the map to your Web site or to a CD. A prompt from Yahoo! Maps appears, and you must first agree to their license agreement.

> **Close Map**
>
> Click the Map button to close the Map View.

Creating Collections

NOTHER WAY PHOTOSHOP Elements sorts and organizes your photographs is by using collections. You can use a collection when putting together slide shows or creations such as scrapbook pages or calendars. You'll learn about creations in Chapter 10.

Collections work a lot like tags, but are more for grouping photos you want to work with, rather than for identifying photos for searches. Also, collections differ in that pictures in a collection are numbered and sequenced. When you use the collection in a slide show or a creation, Photoshop Elements uses the picture sequence. As an example, you might create a collection called "Holidays at Home" or "Family Vacations." Think of collections as a digital photo album or a container for holding similar groups of photos.

One other important difference between tags and collections is that images in a collection can be arranged into a custom order. When you select images using tags, they are displayed according to

date, import batch, or folder, depending on what option you choose from the arrangement menu. You can display collection images in any order you want.

Using the Collections Palette

You create and work with collections in the Collections palette, which is stored in the Organizer bin. Click the Collections button at the top to see your current collections. No collections are provided as a default since collections tend to be very specific, such as Christmas 2005 or Camping Trips.

To create a new collection, click the New button in the Collections palette and choose New Collection. The Create Collection dialog box you see in Figure 4-36 appears. Enter a name for the collection and optionally enter a descriptive note to describe it; then click the OK button. The collection appears in the Collections palette with a question mark in the icon. As soon as you add images to the collection, the question mark will turn into one of your images.

Figure 4-36
Create a new collection.

Adding images to a collection is identical to adding tags. You select the images you want in the collection and either drag the selected images to the collection icon or drag the collection icon to the selected images. The same photograph can be a part of several different collections. Photoshop Elements places an icon under the thumbnail, indicating the image is part of a collection.

Add to Collection

Optionally, right-click an image and choose Add to Collection and select the desired collection.

Each image in the collection displays a number in the upper-left corner of the thumbnail, indicating its sequence. You can drag and drop the photos within a collection to arrange them into any order you want.

Creating a Collection Group

When you have several similar collections, you might want to semi-group them together. For example, you may have a number of collections, all relative to vacations, with each vacation in its own collection. Creating a collection group called *Vacations* keeps all the individual vacation photographs together.

In the Collections palette, click the New button and choose New Collection Group. The create Collection Group dialog box, shown in Figure 4-37, appears. Click OK.

Figure 4-37
Create a new collection group.

One Collection at a Time

Different than tags, you can only display the contents of one collection at a time. Limit the display to a specific collection by clicking the gray box next to the collection name. A pair of binoculars (indicating Search) appears and only the images with that specific collection appear.

Editing a Collection Properties

After you create a collection, you may decide that you'd rather have a different name or prefer it be part of a collection group, so Photoshop Elements provides an easy method to modify it. The following steps show you how to change a collection's properties:

1. Select the collection you want to modify.

2. From the top of the Collections palette, click the Edit button. The Edit Collection dialog box appears.

3. Make any desired changes, such as selecting a group to place the collection, changing the collection name, or adding or editing the collection note.

4. If you want to change the photo that appears in the collection icon, click the Edit Icon button and by using the next or previous arrows, locate the image you want for the icon; then click OK.

5. Click OK to close the Edit Collection dialog box.

Take a look at Figure 4-38. You see two collection groups: Family Vacations and Holidays. Each collection group has several collections (for example, the Family Vacations collection group has collections for each individual vacation).

Figure 4-38
Viewing the Collections palette.

Merging Collections

The Merge Collections command lets you merge multiple collections into a single collection. For example, if you create a Vacation 2005 collection, and then later inadvertently create an Our Trip to California collection for the same photos, you can merge both collections into one. When you merge collections, Photoshop Elements places all photos into one collection and removes the other collection.

First, select the collections you want to merge; then right-click any of the selected collections and choose Merge Collections. A Merge Collections dialog box appears with a listing of the selected collections. Select which collection you want to receive the photos. Click the OK button.

Delete Collection

If you want to delete a collection or collection group, select the collection or collection group and from the Collections palette, and then click the Delete button. Deleting a collection or collection group does not delete photos from the catalog or hard drive. It removes only the collection, the group and any collections in the group.

Finding Photos in the Organizer

ONE OF THE GREAT benefits of organizing your photographs in the Photo Browser is the enormous power of the search options provided. There are so many ways to look for specific images that Photoshop Elements includes an entire menu devoted just to searching. Through this menu, you can search for images based on dates, names, caption, type, history, and even by similarities such as image color.

Understanding the Timeline

The Timeline, which is located directly above the Photo Browser, represents visually the chronological dates of your images. The Timeline spans a number of years and displays a bar for each month that has pictures dated in that month. The taller the bar, the more photos fall into that time period. Look at Figure 4-39. As you pause your mouse over a bar, the timeline displays the month it represents.

Resize Timeline

If the timeline is too wide to show every year for which you have photos in your catalog, use the arrows on either end of the timeline to scroll through it.

Left end marker   Find bar   Slider   Right end marker

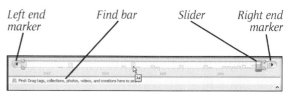

Figure 4-39
The Organizer's Timeline.

In the Timeline you see a square slider, which you can drag back and forth to jump quickly to a specific month of images in the Photo Browser. The Photo Browser still shows all your images, but scrolls to the specified month.

If you want to restrict the Photo Browser to a smaller range of photos, you can do so by dragging the left and right end markers to enclose the time frame you want. The status bar changes to show how many items fall in that date range and how many items are not shown. You can also restrict the date range by choosing Find > Set Date Range. Enter both a start date and end date and then click OK.

You can return the Timeline to normal so it displays all images by dragging the left and right end markers back to the end or by choosing Find > Clear Date Range.

Timeline Changes

If you are sorting the Photo Browser by folder view or import batch view, the Timeline bars change to represent folders or import batches.

Finding with the Find Menu

The Organizer Find menu is filled with ways you can locate specific images. When the requested images are located, the Photo Browser displays them exclusively and at the top shows how many images best matched your request and how many images did not match your request.

View Other Images

If you want to see the images that do not match your request, remove the check mark from Best and check the Not box.

The following list shows you some of the choices in the Find menu and how to use them:

▶ **By Caption or Note**: Displays the Find by Caption or Note dialog box where you enter any part of the caption or note you're looking for. You can specify to match only the beginning of the text or to match any part of the text.

▶ **By Filename**: Displays the Find by Filename dialog box where you can enter any part of the file name you want. You can also type a file extension (JPEG, BMP, and so on) in the Find by Filename dialog box to find files of a certain file type.

▶ **By History**: Displays a submenu from which you can select (see Figure 4-40). Each option prompts you for more specific options.

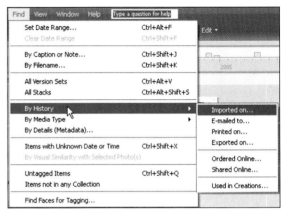

Figure 4-40
Find by History options.

▶ **By Media Type:** Displays a submenu where you can select to see only Photos, Video, Audio, Creations, Items with Audio Caption, PDF files, or Photo Creations.

▶ **By Details:** Displays the Find by Details (Metadata) dialog box seen in Figure 4-41. Click the first criteria drop-down list and choose from 24 different choices, including Camera Make, Camera Model, Pixel size, F-Stop, and Exposure options. After selecting the data type you want to search on, you choose if the images should contain or not contain settings you specify in the third box.

Add Additional Criteria

Click the + (plus sign) to add additional filter criteria.

Figure 4-41
Find by Metadata details.

▶ **All Stacks:** Displays only stacked images. The images are still stacked and not expanded.

▶ **Untagged Items:** Displays only the images with no tags assigned to them.

▶ **Items Not in Any Collection:** Displays only the images not used in any collection, regardless of whether the image is tagged or not.

▶ **All Version Sets:** Displays only the images with original and edited images in version sets. (See "Understanding Version Sets" later in this chapter).

▶ **Unknown Date or Time:** Displays only the images with no date or time associated with the image.

Uncovering Hidden and Tagged Images

Earlier in this chapter, you found that by assigning tags to images you could click the box next to a tag and the Photo Browser would display only items with those tags. You also discovered you could assign the Hidden tag to images that you generally didn't want to view or sort through. The Photo Browser then hides them from the window. Hidden tags work the same way as other tags, in that if you

click the box next to the Hidden tag category, only the hidden images appear. If you want to find hidden photos of a specific tag subject, click the square next to the Hidden tag and then click the tag for the category you want.

Using the Find Bar

Above the Photo Browser images is a thin horizontal bar called the *Find bar*. You can use the Find bar as another method of finding images by their tags. When you drag a tag on top of the Find bar, the bar expands to accommodate the tag and searches for the images that match the tag.

If you want a more comprehensive search, you can drag additional tags onto the Find bar. Multiple tags on the Find bar, by default, result in an *and* condition, meaning the search result images must match both criteria. Take a look at Figure 4-42. With the tag *Drew* search, the Photo Browser shows a result of 18 images. With the tag *Chris* search, the Photo Browser shows a result of 21 images. With both tags on the Find bar, the Photo Browser finds only five images that have both Drew and Chris in them.

Figure 4-42
Using tags on the Find bar.

Also notice the other two options seen in Figure 4-42. When you search using tags, Photoshop Elements ranks the results of the search in groups of Best, Close, or Not. *Best* represents the images that match all the criteria, which, in the previous example, meant Drew *and* Chris. *Close* represents images that match one or more of the criteria, in the example Drew *or* Chris. *Not*, of course, represent those images that *don't* show Drew and Chris. Check the option (or combination of options) you want to see. *Close* matching image thumbnails have a blue circle with a white check mark and *Not* matching image thumbnails have a not symbol.

Click Back to All Photos to clear the Find bar and display all images in the catalog.

Drag Collection

Optionally, drag a collection to the Find bar; however, only one collection at a time can be searched.

Searching for Matches by Visual Similarity

A very unique search function is the ability to look for images with similar images, color, or general overall appearance. You use the Find bar to locate images by visual similarity.

Drag one or more (up to four) images you want to search for onto the Find bar. (You may get a warning that the visual similarity index must be rebuilt. If you get this message, choose OK.) Your images are displayed, with the photos that are most similar in visual appearance displaying at the top of the Photo Browser window. The images are displayed by a decreasing order of similarity and each image displays a percentage of similarity rating (see Figure 4-43).

Percentage rating

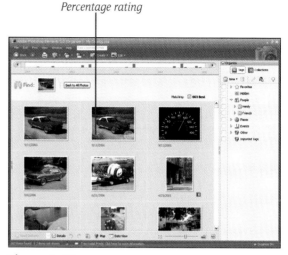

Figure 4-43
Matching visual similarities.

Excluding Photos from a Search

Before finding an image, you can tell Photoshop Elements to exclude images containing specific tags. For example, say you want to find all images in the date range of April through July, but you don't want the ones with your brother Bob in them. From the Tags palette, right-click the tag of the photos you want to exclude from a search and choose Exclude Photos with *tag name* from Search Results. The exclude (universal Not) symbol appears in the gray box next to the tag. You then proceed with the Find command of your choice.

Disable Exclude

To disable the exclude command, click the Exclude icon next to the tag.

Managing Catalogs

BY DEFAULT, Photoshop Elements places images into a single catalog, which is really a database that could contain thousands of photographs. You might, however, want to separate your images into additional catalogs. For example, you might want to place all your personal photographs into one catalog and those you take for your company into another one. Another example of using multiple catalogs is if you have one for your personal images and your kids want to manage one with their own images.

Catalog Information

Remember that a catalog doesn't contain the actual images, but links to the images and a collection of information about each image.

Photoshop Elements allows for as many catalogs as you want, but only one catalog can be open at a time, and you cannot move photos or tags from one catalog to another. You can create a new blank catalog, or you can create a copy of your current catalog. Use the following steps to create a new catalog:

Single Catalog Search

Photoshop Elements doesn't allow a search across multiple catalogs.

1. From the Organizer window, choose File > Catalog. The Catalog dialog box seen in Figure 4-44 appears.

2. Click the New button.

Figure 4-44
Creating a new catalog.

3. Type a name for the new catalog in the File Name text box.

Use Caution Naming Catalogs

Don't use the name "My Catalog," or you'll overwrite your original catalog.

4. Click the Save button. A new blank catalog appears on your screen, ready for you to bring in images.

Last Used Catalog

The next time you open the Organizer workspace, the last used catalog automatically opens.

Switch Between Catalogs

To switch back and forth between catalogs, choose File > Catalog; then click the Open button. You'll see the Open Catalog dialog box where you can select the catalog you want to work with.

Backing Up

Y OU'RE GOING TO FIND yourself spending many hours organizing your images. After putting all that time and effort into the project, you don't want to risk losing all your work or even worse, all your photographs. Do the right thing and do it right away. MAKE A BACKUP!

Hard drives get full and they have a tendency at the most inopportune moment to quit working. Most of the time when hard drives fail, the files are nonrecoverable and even when they are recoverable, you're usually looking at thousands of dollars to have them recovered. If you don't do one other thing in this book, please do this one. MAKE A BACKUP!

Photoshop Elements has a Backup Catalog command that copies not only your catalog with all its tags and collections, but also your photographs in their full resolution on to a CD, DVD, or external hard drive or a network hard drive. Additionally, since the Organizer not only holds photographs but creations, audio files, and video files, they get backed up, too. Here's how you can make a backup to protect your precious photographs:

1. From the Organizer, choose File > Backup Catalog. The Backup Options dialog box seen in Figure 4-45 appears.

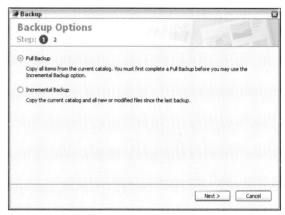

Figure 4-45
Make a backup!

You can make two different types of backups:

▶ **Full Backup: This option copies the entire catalog and all its items (photos, videos, and so forth). This option is required the first time you make a backup.**

▶ **Incremental Backup: This option copies the catalog but only copies the items that have been added or edited since the last backup.**

2. Select a backup type; then click Next. Step 2 of the backup window appears (see Figure 4-46). Notice the number at the bottom of the dialog box. That's the total file size needed for the backup.

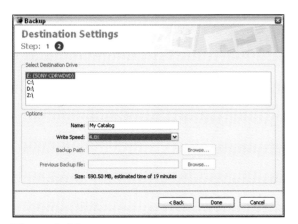

Figure 4-46
Selecting more backup options.

3. From the Destination Drive list, select the CD, DVD, or hard drive to which you want to burn the items.

4. If you're backing up to an external, internal, or network hard drive, click the Backup Path Browse button and choose a specific folder location.

Map Network Drive

If you are making a backup to a network drive, your computer must have a drive letter mapped to the network drive. Contact your network administrator to map a network drive.

5. If you're making an incremental backup, select which backup you want to use as the basis for determining which files have changed.

6. Choose Done. The backup process begins. Be patient, as backing up to a CD or DVD can take a fair amount of time. Figure 4-47 illustrates a dialog box like the one you see when backing up to a CD or DVD. The dialog box you see when backing up to a hard drive is very similar.

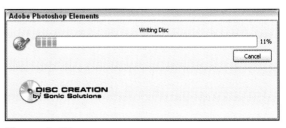

Figure 4-47
Backing up progress indicator.

7. After burning a CD or DVD, Photoshop Elements prompts you to verify that the disk was correctly created.

Verify Disk

I strongly recommend you take the time to let the disk verify.

8. Click OK at the reminder message.

9. Remove the CD or DVD and put a label on it or write on it with a felt tip pen.

Restoring a Backup

HOPEFULLY YOU'LL NEVER have a disaster where you need to restore a backup, but if you do, you'll find the restoration process quite simple. Choose File > Restore Catalog, which displays the Restore dialog box you see in Figure 4-48. Choose a location for the backup file and determine if you want to restore the files to their original locations or to an alternative location. Click the Restore button, and Photoshop Elements begins the restoration process. If you elected to restore the files to their original location, you may see a warning message. Read the message carefully and decide if you want to continue.

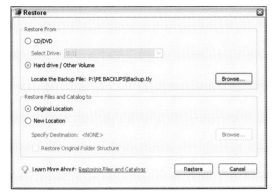

Figure 4-48
Restoring from a backup.

Understanding Version Sets

SIMILAR TO STACKS, version sets contain multiple images, but where stacks contain a group of similar but individual images, version stacks contain only a single original image and any edited copies. Version sets allow you to monitor and control the progress of changes you make and if you don't like the changes, you can easily revert back to the original image. With version sets, you are doing a Save As command and saving a new copy of the image with the same name and the word edited after it.

When you edit the photo by choosing Edit > Auto Smart Fix, the Organizer automatically puts the photo and its edited copy together in a version set. When you edit the photo in Full Edit or Quick Fix and choose File > Save As, you can choose the option to save it in a version set.

Photoshop Elements automatically creates version sets when you edit your image by choosing Edit > Auto Smart Fix (see Chapter 6), but if you make edits to the image in the Full Edit or Quick Fix workspace, you need to tell Photoshop Elements if you want to maintain a version set for the image. Make your image edit; then choose File > Save As, which displays the Save As dialog box seen in Figure 4-49. Select the Save in Version Set with Original option to put the photo and its edited copy together in a version set. After you click Save, a notification message appears explaining version sets. Click OK or choose Don't Show Again.

Each time you want to save another copy of the image in the version set, you must choose the Save As command. If you choose the Save command, Photoshop Elements simply updates the latest version with the changes.

Figure 4-49
Creating a version set.

In the Organizer, version sets appear as stacks with the right-pointing arrow to expand the set, but they also have an icon with a paintbrush across the stack icon, which indicates this is a version set, not a standard stack.

Maintaining History

If you edit your image in another program beside Photoshop Elements, the history link becomes broken and version sets cannot be maintained.

Do Not Delete Original

It's not a good idea to delete an original photo unless it has been compressed or has lost information.

Here are several notes about working with version sets in the Organizer:

▶ **If you want to apply a tag to a version set, Photoshop Elements applies tags to all items in a selected version set.**

▶ **If you want to remove images from the version set, expand the set, select the photos you want to remove, right-click the image, and choose Version Set > Remove Item(s) from Version Set. The image isn't removed from the catalog—it's only separated from the version set.**

▶ **If you want to break apart a version set so all images appear as individual photos, right-click the collapsed version set image and choose Version Set > Convert Version Set to Individual Items.**

▶ **If you want to delete all the images in a version set except the most recently edited version, right-click the collapsed version set image and choose Version Set > Flatten Version Set.**

▶ **If you want to delete all the images in a version set except the original image, right-click the collapsed version set image and choose Version Set > Revert to Original.**

Photographer: Tresee Koers

5

Understanding Color *Management*

Photographer:
Tresee Koers

PICTURE YOURSELF STANDING on a veranda looking out over the gentle ocean waves. It's a gorgeous day with clear skies. The green trees are gently stirring with the breeze and the warm azure water is beckoning you. Now picture the same scene where the skies look green, the trees look brown, and the water appears gray. It's not the same feeling at all, is it? Skies are supposed to be blue, not green. When images aren't the color you expect them, the feeling behind the image changes dramatically. Sometimes, our photographs don't come out in the same color we viewed with our eyes.

The visual world, the world as we see it, is a world populated by colored objects. So much of our perception of physical things involves our identifying objects by their appearance, and since colors are essential to an object's appearance, any account of visual perception must contain some account of colors. Because visual perception is one of the most important species of perception, of our acquisition of knowledge of the physical world, and of our environment, a theory of color is doubly important.

This chapter provides an in-depth look at the color theories that are useful when working with Photoshop Elements. You'll learn more about the most frequently-used color models and the differences between the way color is viewed in the real world and how it is captured by a film or digital camera, displayed on your monitor, and output by your printer.

Describing Color

OUR LIVES ARE FULL OF COLOR and generally we accept color as part of our lives in a casual and nonchalant manner. But color affects us very deeply, on a physical level, an emotional and psychological level, and a spiritual level. Our individual identities are largely expressed by our own personal understandings or feelings toward color. We learn to manipulate it and master it even while most of us have no true understanding of what color is.

Our nervous system requires input and stimulation. With respect to visual input, we become bored in the absence of a variety of colors and shapes. Consequently, color addresses one of our basic neurological needs for stimulation.

If we question how we relate to color in our lives, we see that our personal color preferences affect our fashion, our art, and our interior and exterior environments. Color is cool. Color is hot. Color can encourage or adversely affect our health and well being. Color portrays feelings in that color can be erotic and sensual, calming and passive, or expressive and vital. Colors represent emotions, as well as conveying subliminal messages. Take a look at the following color representations:

▶ **Red: A symbol of liveliness and power, considered a warm color because of its relationship with fire and heat. It represents danger, anger, blast, fire, heat, liveliness, love, blood, and revolution.**

▶ **Yellow: It shows brightness and represents the sun. It is a color of life and light. It represents wealth, happiness, freshness, brightness, fulfillment, richness, and spirituality.**

▶ **Blue: In a first look, it shows silence and coolness. It is related to sky and water. In our perception of this color, we feel the distance. It represents faith, truth, seriousness, silence, and stability.**

▶ **Orange: A symbol of knowledge. It also represents happiness, freshness, and knowledge. It is also used for showing patriotism. Orange also is known to make us hungry.**

▶ **Green**: It is nature's color, and nature gives us freshness. A green color makes us feel relaxed. It represents liveliness, freshness, wealth, and clarity. You'll often see green in hospitals.

▶ **Purple**: Being a mixture of red and blue, it somehow represents qualities of both colors. It is associated with spirituality, mystery, aristocracy, and passion. It may also symbolize mourning, death, and nausea.

▶ **Black**: The absence of all colors, which indicates darkness. Darkness gives rise to ill-omened things, such as murder, theft, and robbery. The color black is used to represent inauspicious events.

▶ **White**: It is light consisting of all colors It represents purity, clean nature, truthfulness, brightness, etc.

Colors of the sun and fire such as red, yellow, and orange express warmth and appear on the right side of the color wheel, while colors of snow and ice, such as blue, violet, and green emit the feeling of being cold or cool and appear on the left side of the color wheel. Take a look at this photograph of a church in winter. The blue hue surrounding the snow outdoors feels cold and lonely, but the red roof welcomes you into the warmth of the church.

In reality, color is a scientific phenomenon, measurable and definable with rules and boundaries. Throughout this chapter, we'll take a look at some of those measurable rules and boundaries. But the way we experience color is personal. No color is seen the same way by any two people, and color has different meanings to people in different cultures.

Why Is Color Important?

Color is a science, although considered a "soft science," but it plays a pivotal role in all our visual experiences. Earlier I mentioned about wearing white for coolness in the summer and black in the winter for warmth. I also mentioned some of the emotions put into play with color. Here is more research study information about colors:

▶ **Studies show that color can improve readership by 40 percent, learning from 55 to 78 percent, and comprehension by 73 percent.**

▶ **Color influences brand identity in a variety of ways. Remember the green ketchup?**

▶ **Color increases participation. Studies of telephone directory ads show that ads in color are read up to 42% more often than the same ads in black and white.**

▶ **Color affects your appetite. If you're hungry, seeing blue may help ward off snacking, while seeing orange can make you even hungrier. Why? Because blue food is a rare occurrence in nature. There are no leafy blue vegetables, no blue meats, and aside from blueberries and a few blue-purple potatoes from remote spots on the globe, blue just doesn't exist in any significant quantity as a natural food color. Consequently, we don't have an automatic appetite response to blue. Furthermore, our primal nature avoids foods that are poisonous. A million years ago, when our earliest ancestors were foraging for food, blue, purple, and black were "color warning signs" of potentially lethal food.**

▶ **Tests indicate that a black-and-white image may sustain interest for less than two-thirds a second, whereas a colored image may hold a person's attention for two seconds or more. (A product has one-twentieth of a second to halt the customer's attention on a shelf or display.)**

▶ **People cannot process every object within view at one time. Therefore, color can be used as a tool to emphasize or de-emphasize areas. For example, a large insurance company used color to highlight key information on its invoices. As a result, they began receiving customer payments an average of 14 days earlier.**

▶ **In another recent study of business professionals, from 76% to 92% of the participants believed the following statements: Color presents an image of impressive quality. Color can assist in attracting new customers. Customers remember presentations and documents better when color is used. Color makes them appear more successful. Color gives them a competitive edge. The use of color makes their business appear larger to clients.**

As you see, color influences many aspects of our lives, whether or not we realize it when it happens.

What Makes Up Color?

WHAT MAKES COLOR WORK? Technically, you don't have to understand how color works to use it to make photograph corrections or add striking effects. It's entirely possible to use trial-and-error experimentation to arrive at the results you want. It's just a good idea to understand the basic concepts behind color.

Daylight, or white light, is made up of numerous waves or impulses, each having different dimensions or wavelengths. When separated, any single wavelength will produce a specific color impression to the human eye. What we actually see as color is known as its color effect. We see color because of light. However, it's not the light waves that are colored. When light rays strike an object, the object absorbs certain waves and reflects others, and this is what determines the color effect.

For example, what we actually see when we observe a blue ball is that the ball appears blue because it reflects only blue light and absorbs all other light. The ball does not have color in itself. The light generates the color. What we see as color is the reflection of a specific wavelength of light rays off an object.

That's because human perception of color originates in our brains from the variation of the wavelengths of light that reach our eyes. We see color because the retina of the eye contains rod cells and three types of cone cells, which respond to a different wavelength of light. Different wavelengths reflect different light that we see and perceive as color. We typically see an object as a color, such as a blue sky, green grass, or a pink ribbon. But, in a sense, color is an optical illusion.

Color Characteristics

The human eye perceives color in terms of three characteristics—hue, saturation, and brightness (HSB), while computer monitors display colors by generating varying amounts of red, green, and blue (RGB) light. But color is really what we see as a result of the three factors interacting: light, the object, and the observer.

When light rays hit an object, the object absorbs some light and reflects some light. All the colors we see reside in a continuous color spectrum; however, we can't directly sense each of those individual colors. Instead, each of the three kinds of cone cells in our eyes "see" a different set of frequencies, which happens to correspond to what we call red, green, and blue (RGB). Our brains process this RGB information and translate it into a distinct color that we perceive.

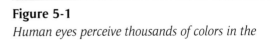

Figure 5-1
Human eyes perceive thousands of colors in the spectrum.

White results when light waves are reflected from a surface. Everyone knows that to keep cooler in the summer you wear white or very light colors, which also keep the sun rays reflected, not absorbed. Just the opposite however, is true when wearing darker colors or black in winter because the color black absorbs the light waves, converting them into heat.

The Color Wheel

TO HELP UNDERSTAND COLOR concepts, we use a color wheel. A color wheel is the color spectrum bent into a circle and is used to describe the relationship between colors. Traditional color wheels use three primary colors: red, yellow, and blue (the first or starting colors used to mix the wheel). Primary colors are hues that are mixed to create all other colors. Between them are shown the secondary colors: orange, green, and purple (colors made by mixing the primary colors). The colors between the primary and secondary colors are called *tertiary colors.* They are named for their parent colors, listing the primary color first, as in yellow green.

There are many different types of color wheels, the simplest being a red, yellow, and blue one. Primary colors are basic and cannot be mixed from other elements.

The red, yellow, and blue color wheel is useful as a conceptual model for color since the relationships are easy to see. This system is easy to understand and has been used for years to teach color relationships. It does, however, fail to accurately depict color relationships and does not show the relationship between the additive and subtractive color theories. It also does not work well to mix all of the colors of the spectrum. Figure 5-2 illustrates a simple red, yellow, and blue color wheel.

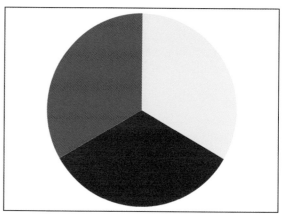

Figure 5-2
Primary colors.

To get a secondary color of green, orange, or purple, you mix together two primary colors. Notice that each secondary color on the color wheel is bounded by two primaries. These are the components that you need to mix to get a secondary color. For example, you mix primary red and primary yellow to get secondary orange, while you mix primary blue and primary yellow to get secondary green, and finally you can mix primary red and primary blue to get purple (or violet). See Figure 5-3.

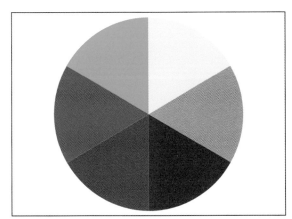

Figure 5-3
Primary and secondary colors.

When viewing the color wheel, look at the colors directly across from each other. These are called complementary colors or color opposites. Violet and yellow are complementary; blue and orange are complementary; and red and green are complementary. These colors contrast with each other in the most extreme way possible.

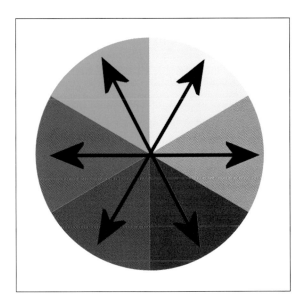

Next, we look at the tertiary, or intermediate, colors, which occur by mixing a secondary color with a primary color. In Figure 5-4, you see there are six intermediate colors: red-orange, red-violet, blue-violet, blue-green, yellow-green, and yellow-orange.

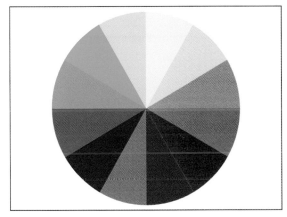

Figure 5-4
A simple color wheel showing primary, secondary, and intermediate colors.

If you continue blending the colors along with different hue, saturation, and lightness settings, you end up with millions of different color variations. We'll take a look at hue, saturation, and lightness later in this chapter.

Color Models

A COLOR MODEL is a system for specifying the components of color, and there are a number of different generic and some specific color models. Artificial color systems, which include computer scanners, monitors, printers, and other peripherals, attempt to reproduce, or model, the colors that we see, using various sets of components of color. If the model is a good one, all the colors we are capable of detecting are defined by the parameters of the model. The colors within the definition of each model are termed its color space. Nearly all color spaces use three different models, such as colors like red, green, and blue or qualities such as hue, saturation, and brightness.

The international standard for specifying color was defined in 1931 by the Commission Internationale L'Eclairage (CIE); it is a scientific color model that can be used to define all the colors that humans can see. However, computer color systems are based on one of three or four other color models, which are more practical because they are derived from the actual hardware systems used to reproduce those colors.

None of these systems can generate all the colors in the full range of human perception, but they are the models with which we must work. In Photoshop Elements, you use the RGB and HSL color models to select and manipulate color.

The RGB Color Model

RGB stands for red, green, and blue, the colors used by most monitors and video output devices. If you're old enough, you might remember when you had to adjust your TV color because the people's faces were too red or too green. You were working with RGB settings. All colors on the screen, whether on your television or computer screen, are a combination of red, blue, and green.

Computer monitors produce color by aiming three electronic guns at sets of red, green, and blue phosphors (compounds that give off photons when struck by beams of electrons), coated on the screen of your display. LCD and LED monitors use sets of red, green, and blue pixels to represent each picture element of an image that are switched on or off, as required. If none of the colors are displayed, we see a black pixel. If all three glow in equal proportions, we see a neutral color—gray or white, depending on the intensity. We call this color model the *RGB model*.

The RGB color model is called an *additive model*, so-called because the colors are added together. As you discovered when working with the color wheel, a huge selection of colors can be produced by varying the combinations of light. In addition to pure red, green, and blue, we can also produce cyan (green and blue together), magenta (red and blue), yellow (red and green), and all the colors in between.

No display device available today produces pure red, green, or blue light. Only lasers, which output at one single frequency of light, generate absolutely pure colors, and they aren't used for display devices. We see images through the glow of phosphors, LEDs, or LCD pixels, and the ability of these to generate absolutely pure colors is limited. Color representations on a display differ from brand to brand and even from one display to another within the same brand.

Moreover, the characteristics of a given display can change as the monitor ages and the color-producing elements wear out. Some phosphors, particularly blue ones, change in intensity as they age, at a different rate than other phosphors. So, identical signals rarely produce identical images on displays, regardless of how closely the devices are matched in type, age, and other factors.

In practice, most displays show far fewer colors than the total of which they are theoretically capable. Actually, the number of different colors a display can show at one time is limited to the number of individual pixels or the screen resolution you set on your monitor. For example, at 1024×768 resolution, there are only 786,432 different pixels. Even if each one were a different color, you'd view, at most, only around three-quarters of a million colors at once.

Adjusting the amount of red, green, and blue in your image makes color corrections by changing the overall color cast. Reducing blue adds yellow, reducing green adds magenta, and reducing red adds cyan to the image. A value of 0% indicates the original value. If you want to add more of a color, you should use a positive number, but if you want to remove some of a color, use a negative number.

You can either increase its opposite color on the color wheel or reduce the amount of adjacent colors on the color wheel. For example, to color correct an image containing too much yellow, either increase the amount of blue or decrease the amount of red and green. In Chapter 6, we'll take a look at adjusting the colors in our photographs.

The HSL Color Model

Another color model, HSL, illustrates hue, saturation, and lightness. HSL uses RGB values but allows you, the user, to modify the RGB values even further.

Color has three properties:

▶ **Hue: Hue is the color reflected from an object and represents the shade or tint of an RGB color.**

▶ **Saturation: Saturation represents the vividness of the color, which is actually from the amount of light in the color. Values range from 0 (entirely gray) to 255 (fully saturated) so the higher saturation produces more vivid color, whereas a lower saturation produces more gray.**

▶ **Lightness: Lightness represents the quantity or intensity of light in the color. Lightness ranges from 0, which is no light, or black, to 255, which is total lightness, or white, so the higher the lightness value, the whiter the image becomes. At a low value, the image becomes darker or black.**

Of the most common color models, the one based on the hue, saturation, and lightness (HLS) is the most natural for human eyes to perceive color because it deals with a continuous range of colors that may vary in brightness or richness. You use this type of model when you adjust colors with the Hue/Saturation dialog box seen in Figure 5-5.

Figure 5-5
Adjusting the HSL values.

Capturing Color Images

I N CHAPTER 4, you discovered how, by using a digital camera or scanner, you could get your images into the Photoshop Elements Organizer. But how do those images get into the camera or scanner in the first place? Color scanners have been around the longest, for around 50 years, in fact. The first ones we saw many years ago cost more than a million dollars when you included the computer equipment needed to drive them, and they were intended only for professional graphics applications at service bureaus and large publications. Today, color scanners, like the one shown in Figure 5-6, cost less than $100.

Figure 5-6

Today's scanners are cost effective and easy to use.

Color scanners are nothing more than a system for capturing the proper amount of each of the primary colors of light in a given image. So these scanners use three different light sources—one each of red, green, and blue—to scan a color image.

To do so, some older scanners actually made three passes over the image—once for each color. More recent scanners use multiple light sources, or "rotate" their illumination, using red/green/blue light in succession to capture an image in a single pass.

The amount of light reflected by the artwork for each color varies according to the color of the pigments in the original. Cyan pigment, for example, absorbs red light and reflects blue and green. So when a cyan area is illuminated by the red fluorescent light in a scanner, relatively little light is reflected. Most of the light produced by the blue and green fluorescents is reflected. Your scanner software records that area of the original as cyan. A similar process captures the other colors in your subject during the scan. Even if you don't use a scanner yourself, you may work with scanned images that are captured by your photofinisher when converting your color slides or prints to digital form for distribution online or as a PhotoCD.

Digital cameras cut out the middle step by creating color images directly. Where scanners use a linear array that grabs an image one line at a time, digital cameras use a two-dimensional array that grabs a complete bitmap in one instant. Today, digital cameras with 3.3 to 8 megapixels (or more) of resolution can capture images that are virtually indistinguishable from those grabbed on film when reproduced or enlarged.

Color Modes

OW IS A COLOR MODE DIFFERENT from a color model? Color mode determines *how* the selected model combines the components of a color, based on the number of color channels in the color model. An image mode determines the number of colors that can be displayed in an image and can also affect the file size of the image. Color modes include grayscale (1 channel), RGB (3 channels), and CMYK (4 channels), among others. Photoshop Elements supports bitmap, grayscale, indexed, and RGB color modes, each of which is exhibited in Figure 5-7. The following list describes each mode:

▶ **RGB Mode:** Digital cameras use RGB mode, and it's also the default mode for Photoshop Elements. In RGB mode, the red, green, and blue components are each assigned an intensity value from 0 to 255 for every pixel. For example, a lime green color might have a red value of 59, a green value of 208, and a blue value of 0. When the values of all three components are equal, such as 25, 25, 25, the result is a shade of neutral gray. When the value of each red, blue, and green is 255, the result is pure white; conversely, when red, green, and blue each have a value of 0, the result is pure black.

▶ **Grayscale Mode:** Grayscale mode uses a single-channel image that includes only 256 colors of black, white, and shades of gray. Depending on the bit depth, grayscale images can reproduce various shades of gray. Every pixel of a grayscale image has a brightness value ranging from 0 (black) to 255 (white).

Figure 5-7
Color modes from left to right: RGB, grayscale, indexed, bitmap.

▶ **Indexed Mode:** Indexed color mode is specifically developed for images that appear on Web pages and uses a maximum of 256 colors. By limiting the palette of colors, indexed color can reduce file size. When converting from RGB to indexed color, Photoshop Elements builds a color lookup table (CLUT), which stores and indexes the colors in an image. If a color in the original images does not appear in the table, the program chooses the closest one or simulates the color using available colors. Figure 5-8 illustrates the color table for the image you saw in Figure 5-7.

Figure 5-8
An Indexed mode color table.

▶ **Bitmap:** Bitmap mode uses only two colors—black and white. Typically, images don't start in bitmap mode so you usually convert to bitmap after any editing. However, before you can convert an image to bitmap mode, you must first convert it to grayscale mode. Converting it first to grayscale removes the hue and saturation information from the pixels and leaves just the brightness values, thereby reducing file size.

Edit in Grayscale First

If you're planning on extensive editing, you should work in Grayscale mode and then convert to Bitmap when you are finished.

To change an image mode, choose Image > Mode and then select the desired color mode. Neither Bitmap or Index mode supports layers, so if the original image has layers, Photoshop Elements discards the hidden layers and flattens all the layers.

Which Mode for Editing

If you're planning on extensive editing, you should work in RGB mode and then convert to indexed color when you are finished.

Color Correction

COLOR IS A POWERFUL TOOL that can grab the eye, lead our attention to specific areas of an image, and through some unknown process, generate feelings that run the emotional color range from passion to anger. Conversely, *bad* color can ruin an image. It's a fact of life that a well-composed image that might look sensational in black and white can be utterly ruined simply by presenting it in color with inappropriate hues or saturation.

Sometimes, a horrid-looking image may have nothing more wrong with it than the balance of colors used to represent the image. Other times, the balance may be okay, but you'd like to make the colors look horrid in order to produce a desired special effect in your image.

The most interesting thing about color is that the concepts of "good" and "bad" can vary by the image, the photographer's intent, and the purpose of the finished photograph. The weird colors of a cross-processed image are very bad if they show up in your vacation pictures, but wonderfully evocative in a fashion shoot. A photo that has a vivid red cast may look terrible as a straight portrait, but interesting when part of a glamour shot taken by the glowing embers of a fireplace. A picture of a human with even the tiniest bit of a blue tinge looks ghastly, but might add the desired degree of chill to a snowy winter scene.

Color balance is the relationship between the three colors used to produce your image, most often red, green, and blue. You need to worry only about three different factors:

▶ **Amount of red, green, and blue:** If you have too much red, the image will appear too red. If you have too much green, it will look too green. Extra blue will make an image look as if it just came out of the deep freeze. Other color casts are produced by too much of two of the primary colors when compared to the remaining hue. That is, too much red and green produce a yellowish cast; red and blue tilt things toward magenta; and blue and green create a cyan bias. Figure 5-9 shows the same image with red and green color casts.

▶ **Saturation:** That is, how much of the hue is composed of the pure color itself, and how much is diluted by a neutral color, such as white or black. Figure 5-10 shows an image with low, normal, and high saturation.

▶ **Brightness/contrast:** Brightness and contrast refer to the relative lightness/darkness of each color channel and the number of different tones available. If, say, there are only 12 different red tones in an image, ranging from very light to very dark, with only a few tones in between, then the red portion of the image can be said to have a high contrast. The brightness is determined by whether the available tones are clustered at the denser or lighter areas of the image. Many professionals use something called histograms to represent these relationships, but you don't need to bother with those for now. You'll learn more about histograms later in this chapter. Figure 5-11 shows an image with the contrast and brightness set low, normally, and high.

Figure 5-9

Too much of one color can corrupt the entire image.

Figure 5-10

An image with different saturation levels: low (left), normal (center), high (right).

Figure 5-11

Change an image's contrast and brightness

Understanding Resolution

O NE OF THE MOST MISUNDERSTOOD topics in the digital realm is the field of resolution. A writer once said that trying to understand resolution is easier than spit-roasting jellyfish—but only marginally. Unfortunately, that's true. A quick way to describe resolution is that it is the fineness of detail you can see in an image.

Digital images are made up of pixels, and pixels (short for *picture elements*) are the small sections of color and light that make up a digital image like pieces of a mosaic. A digital image is really a grid of those pixels and when the pixels are viewed together, the image is formed. When there are enough pixels and they are small enough so as not to be individually discernible, the digital image can achieve photo quality.

A digital image, as it is stored on a hard drive or a flash card, is simply an informational record of the image pixels and has no physical size. But when an image is displayed on a monitor or printed, it takes on physical form. At that point the image has spatial dimensions—width and height. The physical dimensions are the number of pixels a digital image is made of, and it is expressed in pixel dimensions, such as 1600×1200.

The resolution of a digital image is defined as the number of pixels per inch it contains. So when considering resolution, you need to determine what you intend to do with the image. Are you going to use it on a Web page? Are you going to print it? If so, at what size? Fine detail is rendered by having an ample amount of pixels. Too few pixels and the picture appears jagged or pixilated.

It is measured in pixels per inch (PPI). The more pixels per inch, the greater the resolution. Generally, the higher the resolution of your image, the better the printed image quality will be.

Let's take a look at the two principal types of resolution measurements and how they are used.

PPI

PPI, which stands for *pixels per inch*, is a measurement of how many pixels can fit into a square inch of your image. If they are large pixels, obviously you won't get as many into an inch as you would if they were smaller. Think of it as how many peas you can fit into a sandwich bag versus how many apples you can fit into that same sandwich bag.

PPI actually has a dual purpose. One place that uses PPI is your screen display, which is called *monitor resolution*. You set monitor resolution by adjusting Display Properties from your Windows desktop. Settings you select for the monitor resolution affect all programs that you run on your computer, including Web pages. The options you choose are based upon the graphics card installed in your computer, your overall monitor size, and how good your eyes are. When you are setting the pixel resolution in the Display Properties dialog box, remember that as you increase the number of pixels, you can display more information on your screen, but the information, including text and icons, gets smaller in size. Figure 5-12 shows the Display Properties dialog box where you set monitor resolution.

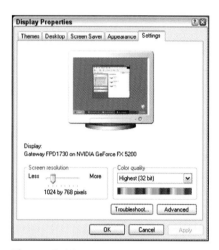

Figure 5-12
Monitor display settings.

An image's pixel dimensions correlate to the image size. A combination of the image size and pixels determines how large you can print your image. Obviously, you can physically make your image any size you want, but that doesn't mean it will print well. Images that are printed too large for their pixel size lose their quality. You'll learn later in this chapter how you can change your image size or resolution.

Different Measurements

Even though the term is PPI—pixels per inch—Photoshop Elements allows you to measure your image in either inches or centimeters.

Change Display Properties

To display the Display Properties dialog box, right-click a blank area of your desktop and choose Properties. Optionally, you can choose Display Properties from the Windows Control Panel.

Unlike conventional photographs where we refer to a 4×6-inch or 8×10-inch print, the overall size of a digital image is measured by its pixels. The image's final destination, whether to a good printer or to the screen, also factors into the image size. Check the actual dimensions, as well as the resolution of your image, to know how it will print.

For example, if you have an image that is 1200×1500 pixels and the resolution is set at 300 PPI, the image will print a 4×5 inch size, but if the image resolution is set at 200 PPI, the image will print approximately 6×7 inches.

The use of PPI discussed in this chapter refers to how PPI is used in image resolution, and how it relates to the photo dimensions. People often get confused about how many inches a digital image is. To understand digital image size, you simply have to understand that pixels are more tightly packed for printing than for display on a computer screen.

Required pixel dimensions can be calculated by multiplying the print size by the resolution, so an 8×10-inch print at 300 DPI requires an image size in pixels of 2400×3000. Or let's look at it from another perspective and divide the size by resolution. If we know the image size in pixels and we know the resolution, what size print can we get?

If we know our image is 2400×3000 and the resolution is 300, we'll take 2400 and divide it by 300, then we'll take 3000 and divide it by 300, which gives us a print size of 8×10 inches. Got it?

Figure 5-13 shows an image at an 8×10 inch size at a 200 PPI resolution. This image is 1600×2000 pixels.

Image size information

Figure 5-13
Image size.

Photographer: Jonathan Hawkins

DPI

DPI represents *dots per inch* and refers to your *printer resolution.* Printer resolution is independent of and unrelated to image resolution. DPI is the measure of how many dots of ink or toner a printer can place within an inch (or centimeter) on paper. The maximum value is determined by your printer and cannot be changed through Photoshop Elements, although most printers provide settings where you can select low, medium, or high settings from within the printer's DPI range. DPI affects the quality of your printed image, but does *not* affect the size of your printed image.

Most printers print the same number of dots horizontally and vertically, so basically a 600 DPI printer prints 600 tiny little dots across one inch of space and 600 dots vertically, creating a one-inch square. The lower the DPI, the less fine the detail it will print and the fewer shades of gray it will simulate.

Better printers have a higher DPI resolution. For photographs, you will probably want to print between 250 and 1000 DPI. Anything less than 250 DPI can produce spotty, pixelated images, and DPI over 1000 provides little extra benefit. In addition, the paper you use can have some bearing on the final outcome. You'll learn more about paper types in Chapter 8. With good printer resolution, you get better tones, especially in areas that have uniform color and density, such as a sky. Good printer resolution also provides a smoother transition from one color to another. In general, the more dots, the better and sharper the image will be.

Resizing and Resampling

ADJUSTING AN IMAGE RESOLUTION'S PPI, or its size in inches, has no effect on the actual pixels. This is called *resizing* or *scaling,* and it involves specifying the printing resolution, if and when, the image is printed. The image remains the same grid of pixels with the same pixel dimensions and pixel data.

However, if you change the image's size in pixels, changing the actual pixel dimensions, this is called *resampling.* Resampling changes the actual image file, which results in a different number of pixels and alters some pixel color and tonal data to maintain the same appearance over the altered amount of pixels.

The bottom line is that there are two different ways to make the same digital image print at different sizes. You can resize it, which changes the print resolution to yield the desired physical dimensions without changing the existing pixel dimensions, or you can resample it, which changes the existing pixel dimensions to yield the desired physical dimensions at a given output resolution.

Resampling changes the amount of pixels the image consists of, whereas resizing changes how many pixels are being printed per inch. Resampling affects the nature of the digital image itself; resizing affects only the printing of the image.

Table 5-1 illustrates an example of what happens to an image when you modify your image size.

More pixels per inch creates smaller printed pixels and a smaller printed image, while fewer pixels per inch creates larger printed pixels and a larger printed image. As you can see, as the output resolution gets smaller, the print size gets larger. It sounds strange and in a way it is, but that's how the image sizing process works.

Resizing

As stated earlier, when you resize an image, you're changing the image's physical dimensions. Photoshop Elements provides a dialog box where you can change your image size.

Choose Image > Resize > Image Size or press Alt+Ctrl+I. You'll see a Resize dialog box like the one in Figure 5-14. The Document Size area is where you resize your image.

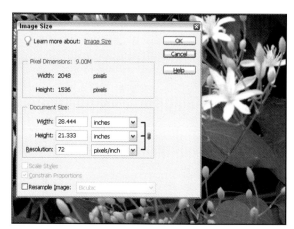

Figure 5-14
Image Size dialog box.

Table 5-1 Modifying Image Size

Goal	Dimensions in PPI	Print Size	Resolution	Resize Type PPI	Result
Original Image	900×600	6×4	150	N/A	N/A
Increase size only to 200%	1800×1200	12×8	150	Resize	Increases print size, but decreases quality
Increase resolution only to 300 PPI	900×600	3×2	300	Resample	Decreases print size, but improves quality
Increase size to 200% and resolution to 300 PPI	1800×1200	6×4	300	Resize	Keeps print size the same, but improves quality *best option*
Decrease resolution only to 100 PPI	900×600	9×6	100	Resample	Enlarges print size and decreases quality
Decrease size only to 50%	450×300	3×2	300	Resize	Reduces print size and maintains quality

Reset the Image

Before clicking the OK button, if you want to return to the original image settings, hold down Alt and click Reset.

When you make a change, you should make sure the Constrain Proportions is checked. As you make changes to the image width, Photoshop Elements also changes the height, maintaining image proportions. If you change the aspect ratio, it can distort your image by making it larger or smaller in one dimension than the other. If you need specific heights and widths, try using the Crop tool after you resize the image.

In Figure 5-15, at its original dimensions, the image is 2048 pixels×1536 pixels, with a print size of 28.444×21.333 inches at a 72 PPI resolution. If we resize the print size to 10 inches, the width automatically changes to 7.5 inches and the resolution adjusts to 204.8 PPI.

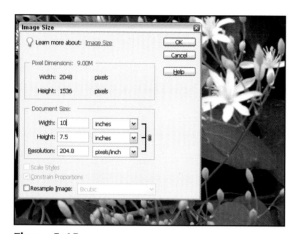

Figure 5-15
Changing image size.

Resize Once

For best results, only resize your image once. If you resize it and aren't happy with it, use the Undo Resize command and try it again.

Resampling

When you downsample, you decrease the number of pixels in your image and information is deleted from the image. When you upsample, you increase the number of pixels in your image. New pixels are added based on color values of existing pixels, and the image loses some detail and sharpness.

When you resample an image to a larger size, Photoshop Elements must do some interpolation. Interpolation is the process of upsizing a photograph by adding pixels that were not there originally. Since every pixel must have a color, this process usually involves assigning a color to the newly created pixels based upon the colors of the pre-existing pixels surrounding the new ones. The result is a larger image in terms of resolution, but one that now has less clarity because you simply cannot produce something from nothing.

Photoshop Elements has several resampling type methods to calculate the interpolation. All of them are based upon mathematical calculations:

▶ **Nearest Neighbor:** When creating new pixels, this option looks at nearby pixels and then by calculating a weighted average color value, uses that result to create the new pixels. However, this method can create jagged edges, which become apparent when distorting or scaling an image or performing multiple manipulations on a selection.

▶ **Bilinear:** The Bilinear method determines new pixels by using the two pixels nearest each existing pixel.

▶ **Bicubic:** Bicubic is similar to the Nearest Neighbor calculation in that it does use a weighted average, but the Bicubic method uses a larger area of pixel samples to calculate the new pixel values. The Bicubic method generally takes a little more time, but it usually produces a more accurate sample and is often the best method to use.

▶ **Bicubic Smoother:** Use this option when you're enlarging images.

▶ **Bicubic Sharper:** Use this when you reduce the image size. This method maintains the detail in a resampled image. It may, however, oversharpen some areas of an image. In this case, try using Bicubic.

Like the resizing options, you make your resampling choices through the Image Size dialog box. Make sure the Resample Image check box is selected and you have selected a resampling type (see Figure 5-16).

After you resample an image, you should run the Unsharp Mask filter. See Chapter 6 for more information on the Unsharp Mask filter.

Reset the Image

Before clicking the OK button, if you want to return to the original image settings, hold down Alt and click Reset.

Resample Only Once

For best results, only resample your image once. If you resample it and aren't happy with it, use the Undo Resize command and try it again.

Resample check box   *Resample type selection*

Figure 5-16
Resampling options.

6

Manipulating
Photographs

PICTURE YOURSELF SITTING at your computer desk, all ready to download the pictures you took from your family reunion. It's your goal to put together a memorial scrapbook that you can send to others. Now you've downloaded the images, you take a peek...and you gasp! Some of them are too dark and some are too light! And the picture of Uncle Fred looks like he's got devil red eyes! Everyone is counting on you—this just won't work. What are you going to do? First, you need to take a deep breath, and then you're going to let Photoshop Elements go to work for you.

Using Photoshop Elements isn't going to make you a better photographer. That only comes with knowledge, time, talent, and lots of practice. In most cases, however, Photoshop Elements can help you make your photographs look like they should.

Previously, photographic technicians and specialists, called retouchers, worked directly on film negatives and other media with brush and color. It was a time-consuming and expensive process, but an important area of photography. Most published photographs and other media images were retouched in some manner. Today, virtually all the images you see in advertising and magazines have been retouched and manipulated digitally.

There is a difference between photo correction and photo enhancement. If you need to make the image look like it should, say for example, to remove digital noise or adjust the color, that's a correction. If you want to actually modify the contents of the photograph, that is called photo enhancement.

Photoshop Elements provides you with the tools you need to retouch images in resourceful and creative ways. You can remove or disguise blemishes, touch up dust spots, repair scratches, and perform many tasks that were once available only through the realm of the film retoucher. Each of these tools offers basic settings, but you should know that these aren't the only tools to work with your images. Photoshop Elements includes many in-depth tools allowing you to get to the very heart of your images and make the most minute changes you can imagine. However, most people find the automatic tools work quite to their satisfaction.

In this chapter, you'll discover methods to correct those types of image defects, as well as correct perspective, remove red eye, and rectify lighting and distortion problems. We'll take an in-depth look at the many different retouch brushes and filters you can use to modify your image details. Many photos need multiple corrections, so you should look at each image as a project.

If you can identify the parts of your photo that need improvement, Photoshop Elements can provide ways to make these improvements, from automatically balancing your color or contrast to the ability to make very specific, detailed adjustments, such as working with channel mixers, thresholds, and histogram modifications.

Just keep in mind that as you try to improve the color balance, brightness/contrast, and other attributes of photographs, none of the methods can add detail or color that isn't there. All techniques work well with photographs that have, say, all the colors somewhere, but with too much of one hue or another. The extra color can be removed, leaving a well-balanced picture behind. Or you can beef up the other colors, so they are in balance once again. Photoshop Elements can do that by changing some pixels that are relatively close to the color you want to increase to that exact color.

But remember that removing one color, or changing some colors to another color, doesn't add any color to your image; either way, you're taking color out. So, if you have a photograph that is hopelessly and overpoweringly green, you're out of luck. When you remove all the green, there may be no color left behind. Or you can add magenta until your subject's face turns purple, and all you'll end up with is a darker photo. You must start with a reasonable image; color correction is better suited for fine-tuning than a major overhaul.

Playing It Safe

I N THIS CHAPTER, YOU'LL DISCOVER lots of ways you can correct and edit your images. Hopefully, after you apply some of these techniques, you'll have images you're quite happy with. But if not, let's take a look at some of the things you can do after you totally goof up the image:

▶ **The most important step is to never work on an original image until you are absolutely sure you are happy with it. Before you begin retouching a photograph, always make a copy (File > Duplicate) and work on the copy.**

▶ **Use the Undo function. From the Edit menu, choose Undo (or press Ctrl+Z). Each time you choose Edit > Undo, Photoshop Elements backtracks your actions one step. You can undo up to the last 50 actions you took.**

Undo Settings

You can change the number of Undo actions by choosing Edit > Preferences > General. Enter a number in the History States box and click OK.

▶ **Use the Undo History palette. Choose Window > Undo History, which displays the History palette. Like you discovered in Chapter 1, for quick and easy access, you can place the History palette into the Palette Bin. The Undo History palette lists all your actions (up to the limit you specify in your preferences). Your actions are listed with the most recent action on top. You can click any action to revert back to the selected step.**

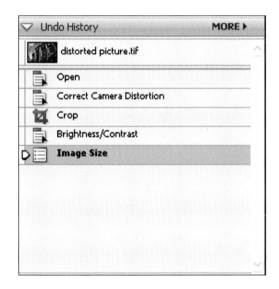

Exploring Photoshop Elements Automatic Fixes

THE EASIEST WAY TO FIX a disrupted photograph is through one of the Quick Fix options. As part of the Editor workspace, Quick Fix provides you with the basic tools needed for image editing. Quick Fix provides six automatic lighting, contrast, and color correction tools that take the guesswork away from image editing, although you can still manage each control yourself.

The automatic fixes are extremely easy to use, and you don't have to be a photographic expert full of knowledge about color, lighting, and contrast. The Quick Fix options are usually the place to start, and if you aren't happy with the results, you can click a simple button and start over and repair the photograph manually.

Photoshop Elements provides several ways to access Quick Fix:

▶ **From the Welcome window, select the Quickly Fix Photos option.**

▶ **From the Editor workspace, click the Quick Fix tab.**

▶ **From the Organizer workspace, click the Edit button on the Shortcuts bar and choose Go to QuickFix.**

From the Quick Fix window, as shown in Figure 6-1, you see an abbreviated toolbar on the left and a Palette Bin on the right with four different palettes: General Fixes, Lighting, Color, and Sharpen. We'll take a look at each palette and its tools individually.

Figure 6-1
The Quick Fix window.

You can work on any photograph in the Quick Fix window, and you can have multiple photos open and displayed in the Photo Bin, but unlike the Full Edit window, Quick Fix only displays one image at a time—the image currently being edited.

Rotate Image

Click either the Rotate Left or Rotate Right buttons to rotate your image.

By default, the Preview window shows the image as it looks after you apply any automatic fix controls; however, directly above the Photo Bin you can see a View Control. The View Control controls what you see in the Preview window. One particularly helpful choice is the Before and After option, which allows you to see both images side by side so you can compare what changes Photoshop Elements makes during the automatic fixes.

Generally, you use only one of the Auto controls on a photo. If that control doesn't achieve what you want, click the Reset button and try another one. However, that's not a set rule. Some images just need a little more fixing than others.

Quick Fix Changes

After an image leaves the Quick Fix window, either because you chose another image or you switched over to Full edit, the image retains the Quick Fix changes, and you can no longer reset it to the default. For that reason, it's really a good idea to work on a copy of your image instead of the original.

General Fixes

Two options exist in the General Fixes area: Auto Smart Fix and the Red Eye Fix.

Auto Smart Fix

Auto Smart Fix is an all-in-one command that adjusts lighting, improves detail, and adjusts the color balance. If you click the Auto button, Photoshop Elements examines the image and repairs what it sees as needing to be fixed. If you

see that the Auto Smart Fix command "overfixes" your photo, you can manage it yourself. Drag the slider bar until your image is the way you want it. It works just like the Auto command, but you control how much change Photoshop Elements applies.

In Figure 6-2, you see a photograph that was way too dark as you see in the Before picture, but the Auto Smart Fix command dramatically improved the image in the After picture.

Figure 6-2
Images before and after using Auto Smart Fix.

Auto Smart Fix

From the Organizer workspace, you can select one or more images and choose Edit > Auto Smart Fix (or press Ctrl+Alt+M). Photoshop Elements automatically applies the Auto Smart Fix and saves the adjusted image as *image name* edited.

Auto Red Eye Fix

In Chapter 2, you discovered what causes the glare that sometimes appears in human or animal eyes and how you can use the Red Eye tool to quickly remove red eye. In Chapter 4, you also learned that the Organizer workspace tries to automatically fix red eye when you bring images into the Photo Browser. Photoshop Elements also has another method, although quite honestly, it's the least effective of the three methods, and you have no control over where or how much it changes. (Using the Red Eye tool is the best method.)

However, if you have an image with red eye, give the Auto Red Eye button a shot. It just might work! If it doesn't, the Quick Fix window also has the Red Eye tool on the toolbar.

Before and After Images

If you have set your Quick Fix View to display both the Before and After pictures, you can only use the toolbar tools on the After image.

Lighting Fixes

One of the most common problems in photography is a picture that's too dark. But thankfully, it's also one of the easiest things to fix. Photoshop Elements looks for things that it thinks should be white, things that should be gray, and things that should be black and then adjusts them. Photoshop Elements calls the light areas highlights, the gray areas midtones, and dark areas shadows. You have a number of tools at your disposal that work on each of these areas independently.

Auto Levels

Levels is a lighting control that adjusts overall contrast and brightness. The Auto Levels command works by individually mapping the lightest and darkest pixels in each color channel to black and white and works best on images that have high contrast details to begin with and just need a little minor adjusting. The drawback to the Auto Levels command is that it may produce a slight color cast to your image. If you try the Auto Levels command and don't like the result, click the Reset button and try using the manual Levels command. In Figure 6-3, you can see an image of a dog that was seriously washed out, but the Auto Levels command brought life back into the image.

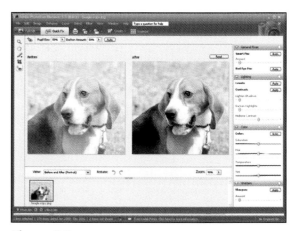

Figure 6-3
Images before and after using Auto Levels.

Manual Levels Command

The obvious solution isn't always the best solution, so sometimes you have to do the work manually. Another way to adjust image brightness and contrast is with the Levels command. Additionally, many professionals like to use the Levels command to correct the white balance in their images. However, before you manually adjust the levels, you need to understand a histogram such as the one you see in Figure 6-4.

Figure 6-4
You use a histogram to adjust levels.

Recalling Histograms

You've already discovered several Photoshop Elements tools to adjust color, contrast, and brightness, but one way to view the image tonal values is the histogram, which provides a useful graphical representation of the red, green, blue, grayscale, color value (hue and saturation), and luminosity (lightness) values in your image. Casual users may not want to use the histogram, but for image-editing professionals, the histogram is a powerful tool for understanding and correcting images.

A histogram consists of a series of up to 256 different vertical lines in a graph, arranged horizontally with the black tones represented on the left side of the graph, the white tones at the right side, and the middle tones located (you guessed it) in the middle of the graph. The taller each of the lines is, the more tones that are present at that brightness level. A typical histogram has one or more peaks, and the black-and-white tones often don't extend to the theoretical limits possible for the image (0 for pure black at the left side and 255 for pure white at the right side).

As a general example, if you are working with an overexposed photo, you might see most of the tones concentrated at the right side of the histogram, where an underexposed photograph might have most tones concentrated on the left side. With such an image, you could analyze the image weaknesses using the histogram and then use the other Photoshop Elements adjustment tools to correct the problem.

Photoshop Elements includes a Histogram palette, which represents how many pixels are at each value in the selected channel. You display the Histogram palette while in Full Edit mode by choosing Window > Histogram. (You can't display the Histogram in Quick Fix mode.) Like other palettes, you can keep it in the Palette Bin, or you can let it float over your image.

Recalling Histograms *(continued)*

When viewing a histogram, the vertical axis represents the number of pixels from zero to the highest number and the horizontal axis represents the 0 to 255 value for each channel.

▶ **If a line spikes, there are lots of pixels in that value range.**

▶ **If a line is relatively flat and close to the horizontal axis, there aren't many pixels in that value range.**

▶ **If the graph is spread out, the image is probably pretty balanced and can be easily corrected if needed.**

▶ **If the lines are compressed into a narrow area, the image probably doesn't contain enough detail to be easily corrected.**

▶ **If the grayscale is mostly on the left, the image is probably too dark, and if the grayscale is mostly on the right, the image is probably too light.**

▶ **If the grayscale lines aren't spread out much, you might want to increase the contrast.**

The numeric display beneath the histogram probably looks like a lot of mumbo jumbo at first glance, but as you become experienced using the Histogram palette, you'll find this information is increasingly valuable. As you move your mouse over the histogram, it displays statistical information regarding the various channels and the image pixels:

▶ **Mean: This represents the average intensity value of all the pixels in the image. If the number is very low, that will confirm that the image is rather dark; a high number means that the image is, on average, very bright.**

▶ **Std Dev: This value represents how widely intensity values vary.**

▶ **Median: The median is the middle number in the range of intensity values; half the individual values are higher than the median, while half are lower.**

▶ **Pixels: This value represents the total number of pixels used to calculate the histogram.**

▶ **Levels: This value displays the intensity level of the area underneath the pointer.**

▶ **Count: This value shows the total number of pixels at the intensity level underneath the pointer.**

▶ **Percentile: This value displays the percentage of pixels at and below the level underneath the pointer. This value is expressed as a percentage of all the pixels in the image, from 0% at the far left to 100% at the far right.**

▶ **Cache Level: This value displays the setting for the image cache but only if the Use Cache for Histograms option is selected in the Preferences dialog box. When this Preferences option is deselected, Photoshop Elements more accurately displays the histogram, although just a slight bit slower than if the Use Cache for Histograms option is selected.**

You can't actually change levels from the Histogram palette, but you can view the results of the changes as you make them by using the other Photoshop Elements commands.

Okay, now that you've got a fair handle on a histogram, let's take a look at manually adjusting the image levels. Choose Enhance > Adjusting Lighting > Levels. You see the Levels dialog box in Figure 6-5. While this is technically not a histogram, notice the similarity, but while you cannot make any adjustments in the histogram itself, you can make adjustments from the Levels dialog box.

Levels Shortcut Key

Optionally, press Ctrl+L to display the Levels dialog box.

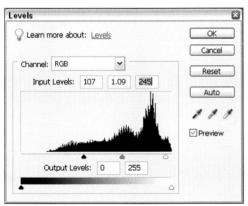

Figure 6-5
Adjust color channels together or independently.

You can adjust the RGB channels together or independently by selecting an option in the Channel drop-down list. Notice the two sliders, Input and Output, and notice that both have a black diamond on the lcft and a clear diamond on the right. The Input level slider also has a gray diamond, which is for the Gamma, or gray levels. Adjusting the gamma changes the brightness values of middle gray tones.

The Input level bar indicates the image's brightness values, and you can increase the contrast by dragging the black triangle to the right to darken the dark values or the white triangle to the left to lighten the lighter values. To change the value of medium gray, drag the gray gamma triangle left or right; the range of the gamma value is 0.10 to 9.99, with 1 being in the middle.

Just the opposite is the Output level, which you use to decrease the contrast. To lighten the darkest pixels, drag the black triangle to the right. To darken the lightest pixels, drag the white triangle to the left.

Auto Contrast

In photography, contrast designates the relative difference between light and dark areas of a print or negative. But, you say, isn't that what the Levels command did? Yes, but the Levels command sometimes changes the color tint as well. In Photoshop Elements, the Contrast commands adjust the overall contrast of an image without affecting its color. Auto Contrast works by converting the lightest and darkest image pixels into white and black, making highlights lighter and shadows darker.

Click the Auto button next to Contrast to apply Auto Contrast. If the Auto Contrast doesn't do what you want, try using the slider controls to adjust the individual settings:

▶ **Lighten Shadows: Lightens the darkest areas of your photo without affecting the highlights. Pure black areas are not affected.**

▶ **Darken Highlights: Darkens the lightest areas of your photo without affecting the shadows. Pure white areas are not affected.**

▶ **Midtone Control:** Adjusts the contrast within the pixels that are about halfway between pure white and pure black without affecting the extreme highlights and shadows.

These adjustment tools are great for making modifications in images that need fixing in one area or the other, or different amounts of compensation in each area. For the purpose of an exaggerated example, I've taken a selected area of the figure (the third man) you see on the left in Figure 6-6 and added brightened shadows and darkened highlights, creating the version seen on the right.

Color Correction Fixes

The first way we'll color correct an image is by using the color balance controls. This section lays down some principles you can use to create wild color effects, even if you decide to perform normal color corrections by one of the other methods.

Color Quick Fixes

The Auto Color command works by adjusting the contrast and color through the image shadows, midtones, and highlights. It neutralizes the midtones and clips the white and black pixels using a default set of values. Like the other Quick Fix controls, you can adjust the individual components:

▶ **Saturation:** Makes colors more vivid or more muted. That is, how much of the hue is composed of the pure color itself, and how much is diluted by a neutral color, such as white or black.

▶ **Hue:** Shifts all colors in an image. This control is best used in small amounts or with selected objects whose color you want to change.

▶ **Temperature:** Use this control to make your image colors warmer or cooler.

▶ **Tint:** Use this control after you adjust the temperature, to fine-tune the image by adding more green or magenta.

Figure 6-6

Adjust contrast for a selected area of an image or the entire image.

Figure 6-7 shows a before and after image of Bryce Canyon. After manually adjusting the Saturation and Temperature, the After picture looks more like the real Bryce Canyon.

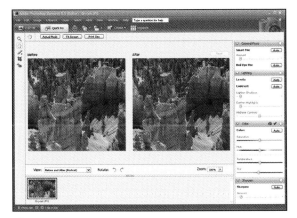

Figure 6-7
If you haven't seen Bryce Canon for yourself, it's worth a trip!

If adjusting the image in the Quick Fix window isn't quite enough, from the Photoshop Elements menu, you can further manually adjust several different color settings. For example, you can select Enhance > Adjust Color > Adjust Hue/Saturation, which displays the Hue/Saturation dialog box seen in Figure 6-8.

From the dialog box, you can manually adjust the Hue, Saturation, and Lightness using the slide controls, but you can also click the Edit drop-down list and select the specific color range you want to modify.

Hue/Saturation Shortcut Keys

Optionally, pressing Ctrl+U also displays the Hue/Saturation dialog box.

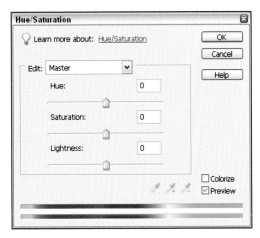

Figure 6-8
Adjust the image Hue, Saturation, and Lightness.

Manually Adjusting Curves

Just as the Levels command allowed you to make tonal corrections in a controlled way, the Adjust Color Curves command provides even more precise color adjustment. The Adjust Color Curves command allows you to further tweak the image colors by adjusting highlights, midtones, and shadows in each color channel.

Using Curves to obtain color balance is comparable to using the Levels tool—in that it is best for global color shifts because it compresses/stretches the tonal values across the image.

Choose Enhance > Adjust Color > Adjust Color Curves. You will see the Curves dialog box shown in Figure 6-9. On the basic level, Adjust Color Curves uses image thumbnails to make adjustments. These include Increase Midtones, Lighten Shadows, Backlight, Increase Contrast, Darken Highlights, and Solarize. Clicking on any of these buttons will make visual changes to the image you are working on.

Expand the Curves Dialog Box

If you don't see the six preview images, click the Preview button to expand the dialog box.

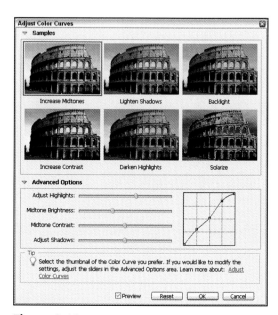

Figure 6-10
Advanced curve options.

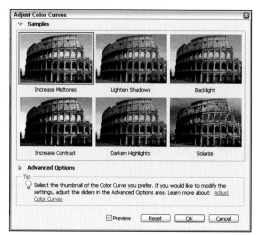

Figure 6-9
Modify the image curves.

However, you can obtain even more control by clicking the Advanced Options triangle to expand the dialog box for even more choices. You see the actual curve tool, where, by using sliders you can further adjust highlights, midtone brightness and contrast, and shadows (see Figure 6-10). The curve line in the Advanced Options uses 256 levels in the image with white in the lower left and black in the upper right. Apply the adjustment to your image by clicking the OK button, or cancel the adjustment by clicking the Reset button.

Adjusting Color Variations

Photoshop Elements provides several ways to remove a color cast on an image, but the best way is through the Color Variations feature. The Color Variations dialog box allows you to change a specific range of image colors, such as the darkest or lightest parts. You determine whether to increase or decrease any of the RGB values. You can also modify image lightness and darkness. Follow these steps to use the Color Variations function:

1. Choose Enhance > Adjust Color > Color Variations. You see the Color Variation dialog box shown in Figure 6-11. The Color Variation dialog box provides a before and after image to preview your selections.

Modify Selected Areas

If you only want to adjust a portion of your image, select the portion before performing step 1.

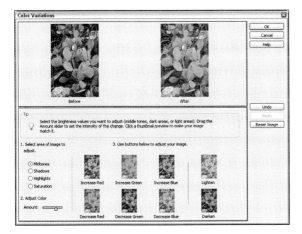

Figure 6-11
The After image shows the image after increasing the green value.

2. Select the image area you want to modify. Choose from Midtones, Shadows, Highlights, or Saturation.

3. The eight option windows show you the effect if you choose a specific option. You can intensify or decrease the amount of change by adjusting the Amount slider.

4. Select the adjustment you want, such as Increasing the Reds or Decreasing the Greens. The After image changes to reflect your choice.

5. Click OK to accept the changes.

Sharpen

High acutance, or sharpness, is a fundamental element of photography. Photography awards are won and lost because of sharpness. A problem arises with digital photography or scanning that can make edges appear blurred because of detail being lost during the digitization process.

Can you ever recover the lost detail? Not really, but through sharpening, you can make it appear as though you have. By increasing differences between neighboring pixels, Photoshop Elements enhances image edges, thereby making the edge appear sharper, whether they really are or not.

You can use sharpening commands to enhance detail in photos, but remember that none of the sharpening commands can add detail that was not saved in the original image. For example, sharpening cannot correct a severely blurred image.

Apply Sharpening Last

You should not apply sharpening effects until you are finished with other corrections, including color and tone. Sharpening should be the last effect you apply. This general rule applies to all sharpening tools.

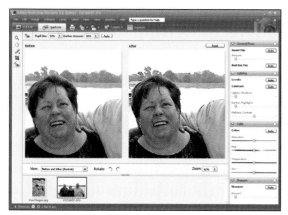

Figure 6-12
Ouch! Oversharpening hurts the image.

AutoSharpen

In the Quick Fix window, the last adjustment tool is the AutoSharpen. You can click the AutoSharpen button to apply the Photoshop Elements default sharpening amounts, or you can drag the slider bar to choose a definitive amount of sharpening. Don't oversharpen though. Take a look at what happens to an image when you oversharpen as seen in Figure 6-12.

Unsharp Mask

As mentioned, Photoshop Elements includes a number of different tools you can use to sharpen your images, including Sharpen, Unsharp Mask, and Adjust Sharpness. Each has a specific use; however, most professionals prefer the Unsharp Mask tool over the others.

Unsharp Mask works more on the mid- to high-contrast edges of an image, but you have much more control over the process. Despite what its name indicates, Unsharp Mask actually sharpens your image. The principle behind it involves exaggerating the light-dark contrast between the two sides of an edge.

The process actually mimics a traditional film compositing technique by taking two or more copies of the image, manipulating them, and then merging them back together. One copy is translated into a negative image, while the others are slightly blurred. The images are then combined together; the light areas of the blurred images cancel out the dark areas of the negative, but the blurring around the edges has nothing to cancel it out, which results in lighter and darker lines on either side of the edges. That, in turn, adds the appearance of sharpness.

You access the Photoshop Elements Unsharp Mask feature by clicking the Enhance menu and selecting Unsharp Mask. There are three settings for the Unsharp Mask feature: Amount, Radius, and Threshold. Let's take a look at what each of these settings do:

▶ **Amount: The Amount setting refers to how much sharpening you are applying. In other words, it controls the contrast change along the edges in your photo, making dark colors darker and light colors lighter. The Strength range is from 1 to 500, but as a general rule, 100 to 150 percent is the most useful range for this variable. Start with a small amount and see if you like the effect; if not, increase it gradually. But be careful about increasing it too much; you can end up with a noisy photo with harsh edges and too much contrast.**

▶ **Radius**: The Radius setting determines the number of pixels to adjust around each edge. The practical effect of this is to specify how large a region is darkened or lightened. As this number increases, so does the apparent sharpness of the image. Setting too high a number, though, can result in harsh edges with lighter pixels around all the edges, especially if you also increase the Strength setting. The range is from .01 to 100, but the default setting is only 2.

Lower values sharpen only the edge pixels, while higher values sharpen a wider band of pixels. The effect is much less noticeable in print than on-screen because a small radius (for example, 1 pixel) represents a smaller area in a high-resolution printed image. Therefore, use lower values for on-screen images and higher values for high resolution printed images.

The main thing to keep in mind is the original resolution of your image. Low-resolution images can't benefit from much more than one to three pixels worth of edge sharpening, while higher resolution images can accommodate values of 10 or more. You'll know right away if you have set your values too high because you will see thick, poster-like edges that aren't realistic, accompanied by a high degree of contrast.

▶ **Threshold**: The Threshold setting determines how much contrast must exist between the pixels before the filter will be applied to an area. Low contrast equals a blurry, soft image, whereas high contrast tends to mean a sharp, hard image. A very low setting value means that edges with relatively small contrast differences will be accentuated. High setting values mean that the difference must be very great before any additional sharpening is applied.

The Threshold setting has a range of 0 to 255. Normally, you'll need to change the Threshold only when the default value produces an image with excessive noise or some other undesirable effect. Try setting the Radius and Strength settings first; then experiment with Threshold to see if you like the results any better.

Also, remember that all three of these values work together. If you use a high Threshold value because your picture was taken in low light and suffers from some digital noise, you may want to increase the amount to 150 percent to beef up the sharpening effect. Figure 6-13 illustrates an image before and after applying the Unsharp Mask function.

Figure 6-13
Unsharp Mask shows more detail in the flower leaf and petals along with making the ice crystals crisper.

Adjust Sharpness

The Adjust Sharpen tool gives you more control to add sharpness to your images. Adjust Sharpen helps to fix such issues as motion blur caused by the camera or subject being photographed, as well as to sharpen detail in the image. It features a dedicated workspace that enables you to adjust the amount of the sharpness in percentages with a slide bar, as well as the radius. Optionally, you can remove any blurs such as Gaussian blur, lens blur, and motion blur. Choose the Adjust Sharpness tool by clicking Enhance > Adjust Sharpness. The dialog box you see in Figure 6-14 appears.

Figure 6-14
Using Adjust Sharpness brought out the detail in the cat's whiskers and fur.

Replace Color

ANOTHER COLOR COMMAND PROVIDED with Photoshop Elements is the Replace Color command. Using this tool, you can easily replace designated colors in your image with other colors. You can optionally adjust the hue, saturation, and lightness. In Figure 6-15, you see two images side by side, one with purple flowers and one with yellow. By using the Replace Color command, the first image changed into the second. Let's take a look:

Figure 6-15
Easily replace colors within an image.

1. Choose Enhance > Adjust Color > Replace Color. The Replace Color dialog box opens. The dialog box has two major sections: Selection and Replacement. The Selection area is where you specify what color you want to change; in the Replacement section, you specify what color you want to change to.

2. From under the preview pane, choose Selection or Image. I usually start with Image so I can see the overall image, but often switch back and forth between Image and Selection, which displays the image as a black-and-white masked version.

3. Click the first Eyedropper tool icon. You need this tool to select your original color.

4. Drag the Fuzziness slider to control the degree to which related colors are included in the selection. Think of the Fuzziness slider as a Tolerance indication.

5. Click the Results color box and choose a new color. Optionally, you can select a color by dragging the Hue, Saturation, and Lightness sliders or even by manually entering color values in the boxes next to the sliders.

6. Click in the image on a color you want to change. Photoshop Elements immediately changes colors within the tolerance range you specified into the new color choice. Depending on the shade variances in your image, you may need to select a different sample for other portions of the image.

More Adjustment Options

Optionally, adjust the Hue, Saturation, and Lightness sliders to modify your color replacement tones further.

7. Click the second Eyedropper tool icon. This icon adds more colors to your original selection.

Subtract Colors

Choose the third Eyedropper tool icon to subtract colors from your original selection.

8. Click another area in your image.

9. Keep repeating steps 6 through 8 until your image takes on the color changes you want (see Figure 6-16).

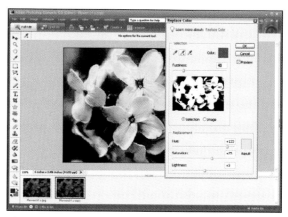

Figure 6-16
Replacing one color with another.

The Color Replace tool is a great tool you can use to brighten a person's smile by whitening their teeth. Take a look at Figure 6-17. By using the Magic Wand tool, I selected the teeth (first image) and then used the Color Replace to replace the original teeth color (second image) with a lighter color (third image).

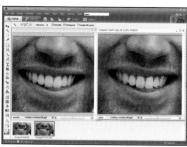
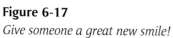
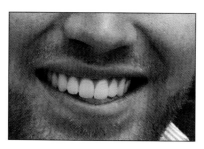
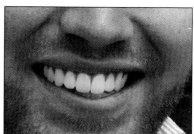

Figure 6-17
Give someone a great new smile!

Removing Blemishes and Wrinkles

HOW ABOUT A FREE FACE-LIFT? No one over the age of 21 wants to look older than he or she is; in fact, most of us want to look younger than we are! Photoshop Elements contains several powerful brushes you can use to quickly remove aging features, such as blemishes and wrinkles, as well as plain old image dust and scratches, all of which distract from your photograph. You first discovered a couple of them in Chapter 2 where you saw the Spot Healing brush remove a blemish from a tomato and the Healing brush remove a date stamp from an image. But these tools and several others can do even more.

Take a look at the beautiful girl in Figure 6-18. It's an unusual pose, with the girl looking up to the camera lens. However, the physical position she's in made wrinkles appear in her forehead. We can use a couple of different tools to soften and remove the wrinkles.

First, we need the Spot Healing brush, so we need to make sure we are in Full Edit mode since the Spot Healing brush is not available in the Quick Fix window. From the toolbar, we'll choose the Healing brush or the Spot Healing brush, whichever is displayed on top. Next, we select the necessary options from the Options bar, starting with choosing the Spot Healing brush itself if it's not already selected.

Now we need to select a brush type. The brush type you select can definitely affect your results. Feathered or soft edges brushes blend pixels differently than those with harder edges. For this example, we need a soft edge brush so we click the brush type drop-down list and select the Soft Round 21 point brush. We need a larger brush for the larger wrinkles, but we'll switch to a smaller brush when we do the fine lines. Just remember to choose a brush slightly larger than the area you want to fix. In order to create a smoother blend, we'll also choose the Create Texture option.

Now you can brush away the wrinkles, either by clicking different areas of the wrinkle or by clicking and dragging across small areas at a time. If you choose to drag across the wrinkles, be sure to choose only small sections at a time.

Finally, we'll smooth out the skin tones by using the Dodge tool set at a 39-point dry brush in a Highlights range. Our finished result shows in Figure 6-19.

Figure 6-18　　　　　　　　　　**Figure 6-19**

Getting a digital makeover.　　　*Beautiful skin!*

Photograph by Hossley Partington

Repairing Cracks

MANY OF US HAVE BOXES FULL of old photos that we will put into beautiful albums "someday." Unfortunately, since the images are not generally protected, they are inclined to get dust, scratches, tears, or creases. When you scan those images digitally, they pick up the same blemishes as are on the original. Fortunately, Photoshop Elements includes several tools to remove some of these marks from the digital image. You could take them to a professional for restoration, but you can do a pretty good job of it yourself. Save the money and buy yourself that new gadget you've been wanting instead.

By using just a few Photoshop Elements tools, you can seamlessly restore the image. Take a look at the image you see in Figure 6-20. This is a scanned image, and you can see multiple cracks in the photograph along with a tape mark along the top. While nothing short of a miracle could restore this image completely, you can generate quite a few improvements and repairs.

The three main tools used to repair cracks are the Spot Healing brush, the Clone Stamp, and the Blur tool. Starting with the main crack going through the middle of the image, we'll start with the Spot Healing brush. Choose the Proximity Match type and choose a brush size. Use a soft brush that is larger than the crack size.

Figure 6-20
A scanned image in need of lots of repairs.

Zoom in on the crack so you can clearly see it; then click and drag in small segments over the crack. Use your mouse as though it were a paintbrush in your hand with small easy strokes. Photoshop Elements uses the surrounding area to intelligently determine the missing image parts. Sometimes, you may be unhappy with a change, but choose Edit > Undo and try again. Try altering your angle slightly for a different result.

The Spot Healing brush is not the right tool to repair large damaged areas such as the tape spot. When the area is large, Photoshop Elements doesn't have enough information, or it has only "wrong" information, from the surrounding areas to figure out what's missing.

Instead, we'll use the Clone Stamp to duplicate image information from another part of the image. When using the Clone Stamp, besides selecting a brush size, you need to determine where you want to copy image data from and where you want to put it. In our example, since the tape area is over some bare tree limbs, we'll use another portion of the tree as our "what" to fill it over the tape (the "where").

Select the Clone Stamp tool from the toolbar. Now you need to set your tool options. The first option is the brush shape that the tool uses. Choose a soft-edged circular brush because with hard edge brushes, the cloned edges turn out hard as well. By using a soft edge brush, you get a gradual transition between the original image and the repairs you make. Also, choose a brush size according to where you are working. Generally the bigger the better, but don't use a brush so big that you over-write data that you want to keep. For this example, we'll use a size 45 brush.

One of the most important settings when working with the Clone Stamp is the opacity setting. Using the default setting of 100% tends, like a hard edge brush, to leave hard edges. For a softer transition when cloning, set your opacity at somewhere between 60 and 70%. You may have to go over your area several times, but you'll definitely get a smoother edge and a less noticeable clone.

Now you're ready to clone the area. Select the source by positioning the mouse over the area you want to copy, which, in our example, is the upper-left corner. Hold down the Alt key and click the area. The destination area is relative to the source area, and you determine that by the next place you click. Click and drag over the tape area. Voilà! The tape is replaced with tree limbs.

Once you finish your repairs, you'll probably notice that some of the repairs are still noticeable. That's where the Blur tool comes in. If an area of your image looks a little bit suspect, and the Clone tool has left some edges or other marks, gently blur the mark until it merges into the background. Use the same settings as you do with the Clone tool in that you use a soft-edged brush and a lower opacity. Depending on the area, you might even drop the opacity to 20 or 30%.

Take a look at the image now in Figure 6-21. There are still plenty of finishing touches needed, such as contrast adjustments and dust removal, but you can clearly see the three tools we used did a good job of removing the scratches.

Figure 6-21
The image after some improvements.

Reducing Noise

I'M ONE OF THOSE PEOPLE who doesn't like a lot of noise. When I'm driving, I rarely listen to the radio or play CD's as I prefer the silence of my thoughts and the ability to absorb the beauty around me. Similarly, I don't like the distraction of having the television going when I'm trying to read or write. In photographic images, the same idea applies. Keep the noise and distraction away. Digital noise appears as tiny speckles that appear on the image and distract from the subject matter. Noise typically gives an image a grainy appearance.

Most digital images contain some noise, some more than others, which usually results from taking photos with the camera set at extreme high-speed levels, but with longer than normal exposure. Many high-end digital cameras offer noise reduction features, but you can remove most unwanted noise with Photoshop Elements. A noise reduction tool should remove objectionable noise but still retain a natural low level of noise.

Image Compression

Some image compression techniques can cause digital image noise.

While Chapter 7 is all about using filters, Photoshop Elements includes four different filters that can help reduce image noise. These filters typically blend pixels from surrounding areas to remove noise; however, because they are blending pixels, too strong a filter can blur your image so it's important to find the right combination of noise removal. You can apply a noise filter by choosing Filter > Noise and selecting one or more of these options:

Add Noise

Photoshop Elements also includes an Add Noise filter that applies random pixels to an image. You might add noise to an image to give a more realistic look to heavily retouched areas or to create a textured layer. An Add Noise dialog box allows you to determine the amount and type of noise.

▶ **Despeckle: This filter looks at the edges, which is where major color changes occur, and it blurs everything except those edges. This type of blurring removes noise while preserving detail.**

▶ **Dust & Scratches: This filter reduces noise by changing dissimilar pixels.**

▶ **Median**: This filter reduces noise by blending the brightness of pixels. It searches for pixels of similar brightness and replaces the center pixel with the median brightness value of the searched pixels. You may find this filter helpful when working with a scanned image.

▶ **Reduce Noise**: This filter reduces the noise, typically created from photographing with insufficient light.

In Figure 6-22, the image on top depicts a magnified original image with noise around the dome of a building. The lower image shows the same detail after using the Despeckle filter. For the sake of emphasis, I used the Despeckle filter twice so you could see where it has cleaned up the noise in the blue sky but blurred the edge of the building dome.

Figure 6-22
Removing digital noise.

Adjusting Skin Tone

SOMETIMES, YOUR PHOTOGRAPHS CAN give human subjects an odd skin color. They may be too green, too red, or some odd combination. The Photoshop Elements Adjust Color for Skin Tone command can often repair the skin tones by adjusting the overall color in a photo to bring out more natural skin tones.

From either the Standard Edit or the Quick Fix mode, choose Enhance > Adjust Color > Adjust Color for Skin Tone. The Adjust Color for Skin Tone dialog box appears as shown in Figure 6-23.

Make a Selection First

The Adjust Color for Skin Tone feature also slightly adjusts the overall color in your image. If you've already tweaked the rest of the image and are happy with the colors, protect the rest of the image by selecting the skin areas before you display the Adjust Color for Skin Tone dialog box.

Click the mouse pointer on any area of skin in the image. Photoshop Elements immediately determines the skin tones and adjusts them. You can also further adjust the skin color by using the Tan or Blush sliders. You can manually adjust the brown and red colors separately to achieve the final color you want. The Tan slider increases or decreases the level of brown in skin tones and the Blush increases or decreases the level of red in the skin. Optionally, slide the Temperature control towards the right to make the overall skin color warmer or to the left to make the overall skin color a little cooler.

Figure 6-23
Remove the unsightly skin tint.

Take a look at the mother and baby in Figure 6-24. The image was taken on a camera phone, which often doesn't give the best results anyway, but in the image on the left, both the mother and baby have a pale almost green cast to them while their skin color looks much more natural in the adjusted image on the right.

Figure 6-24
Image before and after adjusting for skin tone.

Generating Black, White, and Grayscale

W E'VE SPENT A LOT OF TIME working with improving color in our images, and Photoshop Elements has lots of tools designed to help you fine-tune your image color to perfection. There may be times, however, when you don't want any color at all. And while you can use the black-and-white mode on your camera to take the picture, what about all those images you already have that are in color? Photoshop Elements can easily convert color images to black and white. The conversion process changes the photograph from a three-color channeled image (RGB) into a single channel containing only the image detail. Remember that black-and-white isn't only black and white, but includes many shades of gray in between; however, a black-and-white picture has no saturation.

When it comes to converting color images to black and white images, you have several choices. The method you select depends on the look you want for your image and the original image itself. Some photographs lend themselves better to one way over another. Let's take a look at four different methods, and then we'll view the image you see in Figure 6-25 after using each of the methods.

Figure 6-25
Image that is taken in color.

Photograph by Griffing Partington

The first method is with the Photoshop Elements grayscale conversion feature. The Grayscale function is under the Image menu and offers no options—it simply converts the photo by replacing each pixel in the image with a gray that matches its lightness value.

Choose Image > Mode > Grayscale. A confirmation dialog box appears, confirming that you want to discard the color information. Click Yes to continue. In Figure 6-26, the walls are darker and the shadows are deeper than the other black-and-white images. You may want to adjust the image lighting with the Levels and the Contrast commands.

Create a Layer

As with most image modifications, it's best to create a layer first and make any adjustments to that layer.

Figure 6-26
Image in Grayscale mode.

Figure 6-27
Image with color removed.

The second method, like the first, provides no options. Choose Enhance > Adjust Color > Remove Color (Shift+Ctrl+U). As with many other Photoshop Elements commands, if you only want to remove color from a portion of your image, select the area you want to modify before choosing the Remove Color command. Notice that Figure 6-27, which has a feeling of flatness and drabness, could use some serious contrast adjustments.

Modify Contrast

Occasionally, you may find your image flat after using the Remove Color command. You may need to use one of the lighting fixes to repair this problem.

You just discovered that using the Remove Color command removes all the color with no questions asked. If you want a little more control over the conversion, you can use the third method. Choose Enhance > Convert to Black and White. (Alt+Ctrl+B). The Convert to Black and White workspace dialog box shown in Figure 6-28 appears, and you have access to all the tools necessary to create a perfect black-and-white photograph.

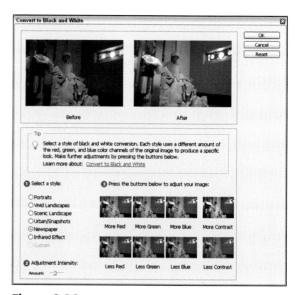

Figure 6-28
Select a conversion style.

Photoshop Elements displays a number of prede-fined image styles, and you can select a style that most suits your image. In Figure 6-29, for example, the Newspaper effect left the white rose and the walls a little lighter than the rest of the image. You can also create a customized option by changing the Adjustment Intensity slider and then selecting an option from the More or Less (red, green, blue, or contrast) options. Using a More or Less (color) option doesn't add any color to your black and white image; it simply doesn't remove as much of the selected color from the original color.

Reset Button

Clicking multiple options combines the effects. Click the Reset button to start over.

Figure 6-29
Image converted to black and white.

The last option is one that many retouchers like to use and one you've already discovered in Chapter 5 and earlier in this chapter. This method of black and white involves removing color by adjusting the image hue and the saturation. Remember that a black-and-white picture has no saturation. Choose Enhance > Adjust Color > Adjust Hue/Saturation (Ctrl+U). In the Hue/Saturation dialog box, drag both the Hue and the Saturation sliders all the way to the left. Optionally, adjust the lightness and click OK. See Figure 6-30 for the results.

Figure 6-30
Image with adjusted hue and saturation.

Black-and-white photos are a personal preference, and everyone is different, so you need to experi-ment with the different methods. As you can see, there's usually no right or wrong method when converting images to black and white. It depends on your taste and the image itself.

Creating a Sepia Tone

H OW ABOUT A LITTLE "SEPIA 101" before we use it? When photographs were first taken, they were all black and white, but people wanted a little color in their images. So the photographers began a slightly different process when developing their images. They started replacing the silver in the black-and-white photographic print with silver sulphide, which is brown. Adding the brown tint gave the images a warmer tone and made the photographs more visually appealing.

Today's digital cameras have a setting that allows the initial rendering of an image with a sepia effect. Don't use that. Create the effect using Photoshop Elements instead, because you have much more control over the final image when you let the camera capture the image to the maximum of its ability.

The following steps walk you though using adjustment layers to create a sepia tone image:

1. Choose Layer > New Adjustment Layer > Hue/Saturation. Click OK, and you see the Hue/Saturation dialog box.

2. Remove the color by dragging the Hue and Saturation sliders all the way left and then clicking OK. A new layer appears on the layer palette, and the image appears in a flat black and white.

3. Add another adjustment layer to adjust the black-and-white levels. Choose Layer > New Adjustment Layer > Levels and click OK. The Levels histogram seen in Figure 6-31 appears.

Figure 6-31
Working with a Levels layer.

4. From this, you can see that the resulting image has a lot of highs and midtones and most of them are to the left, but very few lows. We need to compress the color levels, so in this example, we need to slide the right slider triangle, which represents the highlights, to the left until it hits the midtones area.

5. Slide the middle slider until you achieve the look you want and then lighten the image just a little more. We'll need that lightness for when we put a little color back into the image.

6. Create a third layer by choosing Layers > New Fill Layer > Solid Color. Click OK.

7. Now you need to select a color for the sepia tone, as mentioned earlier, a shade of medium brown. Click OK when finished.

Sepia Color Settings

A good sepia tone color is Red 91, Green 56, and Blue 17.

8. With the Color Fill layer selected in the Layers palette, click the Blend mode drop-down list and choose Soft Light.

9. Decrease the opacity to 70%, and you will see a final result like the image shown in Figure 6-32.

Colorize to Sepia

A quick optional way to achieve sepia-like tones is to choose Enhance > Adjust Color > Adjust Hue/Saturation and check the Colorize option from the Hue/Saturation dialog box.

Figure 6-32
Adding sepia toning aged this picture at least 75 years.

Fixing Photo Errors

EVEN THE BEST OF PHOTOGRAPHERS don't create perfect photos every time. That's why you see professional photographers take many different pictures from lots of different angles so they can pick the best of the best. Taking multiple pictures got much easier with digital cameras because there's no film to waste. But sometimes you get that "almost perfect" opportunity, and you discover later that something's not quite right. Your angle was wrong, or you had the wrong lens. Let Photoshop Elements try and help you rid an image of camera distortion.

Perspective

Photograph by Griffing Partington

When you take pictures of tall objects, the results may have a perspective illusion; that is, the objects seem to be leaning or angled. This happens when the camera is at an angle to the subject. The best remedy is to take the picture with a longer lens or a perspective control lens, but that's not always an available option. Sometimes, you just need to tilt the camera upwards to capture your subject.

Unfortunately, that can give you a result similar to what you see in Figure 6-33. In this image, you see a church that captured the photographer's interest. Besides all the unwanted extraneous elements in the photo, the subject building appears to lean back, due to a bad perspective when shooting the photograph. Photoshop Elements can help correct perspective problems with the Transform option.

Figure 6-33
Lean back and adjust the image perspective.

Photograph by Hossley Partington

Follow these steps to modify an image perspective:

1. If your image is only on a background layer, you must first convert it to a regular layer. Right-click the background layer and choose Layer from Background. Click OK to accept the default layer name.

2. Choose Image > Transform > Perspective. A bounding box appears around the image perimeter.

3. Drag each corner handle as needed to straighten the image subject. In Figure 6-34, in order to change the viewing angle so the building doesn't appear to be leaning back, we need to make the image smaller at the bottom, which brings the top forward.

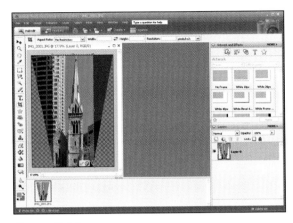

Figure 6-35
Crop the image to remove transparencies.

Figure 6-36 illustrates the image after applying the transformation and cropping.

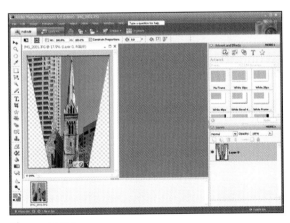

Figure 6-34
Drag a corner handle from the bounding box.

4. Click the Apply check mark or double-click the image to accept the change.

5. Next, we need to crop the image, or it will print in this unusual shape. Choose the Crop tool from the toolbar.

6. Crop until all the transparent areas are gone (see Figure 6-35).

Figure 6-36
A straighter, taller angle.

Correcting Distortion

Often, pictures can suffer from lens distortion issues, including barrel distortion, where the subject lines bow outward making the subject appear spherical, or from pincushion distortion, where the subject lines bow inward and look pinched at their center. Another form of camera distortion is when the image has darkened edges, which are usually caused by lens faults or improper lens shading. Although distortion is frequently found in cameras with inexpensive lenses, such as disposables, you'll sometimes find it in digital camera images, too. Digital camera lenses must be wider than their film counterparts to capture the same area. As a result, pictures taken with digital cameras can suffer from lens distortion. Typically, you'll find wide-angle lenses can cause barrel distortion and telephoto or zoom lenses can cause pincushion distortion.

One other type of lens distortion is called *fisheye*. Fisheyed images look like they have been pasted onto a sphere or blown up like a balloon. Lines that should be straight are curved and edges look compressed. Unwanted fisheye distortion is rare.

In general, distortion is most noticeable when you have a very straight edge near the side of the image frame. Take a look at the image in Figure 6-37, which shows quite a bit of barrel distortion. The brick pillars are curved, and the building almost looks full, like it could pop at any moment. Additionally, the perspective is off on this image.

Fortunately, Photoshop Elements includes correction tools to manage image distortion. For the lens corrections to work properly, the axis of the camera lens must coincide with the center of the image; therefore, you should apply any lens distortion corrections before you crop your image.

Distortion

Figure 6-37

An image in bad need of distortion repair.

Photograph by Griffing Partington

1. If your image is only on a background layer, you must first convert it to a regular layer. Right-click the background layer and choose Layer from Background. Click OK to accept the default layer name.

2. Select Filter > Correct Camera Distortion. The Correct Camera Distortion dialog box seen in Figure 6-38 appears. Notice the image has gridlines covering it to assist you in correcting the flaws.

Figure 6-38

Correct camera distortion through this dialog box.

Begin making changes as needed:

▶ **Remove Distortion**: Use this control to correct barrel or pincushion distortion. Notice the icons on the left (barrel) and right (pincushion) side of the slider. In our example, we need to drag the slider to the right to correct the barreling problem.

▶ **Vignette**: Vignette is what causes loss in clarity towards the corners and sides of an image. In our example, the clouds are too dark in the upper-left corner so we need to drag the slider to the right to lighten the edges and corners.

What Is Midpoint?

Midpoint determines the width of the area affected by the Amount slider. If you want to affect more of the image, drag the slider to the left, but if you want to restrict the change to the edges of the image, drag the slider to the right.

▶ **Perspective Control**: The perspective controls allow you to fix perspective issues caused by tilting the camera up or down, even easier than using the Transform command in the previous section. Drag the sliders until your image attains the perspective you want. There's also an angle setting that rotates the image, if needed, after correcting perspective. Change the angle by dragging the angle dial until the image is rotated as needed.

▶ **Edge Extension**: After changing the image, you may have some transparency areas. After closing the Correct Camera Distortion dialog box, you can crop the image, which can make the image much smaller, or you can, while still in the Correct Camera Distortion dialog box, use the Scale option. The Scale option crops the image for you *and* adjusts the image size to the original pixel dimensions.

3. Click the OK button when you are finished making changes. Figure 6-39 illustrates the image both before and after making changes.

Figure 6-39
What a difference!

Batch Renaming

A GREAT TIME-SAVING FEATURE included with Photoshop Elements is a batch processing function, which the fine folks at Adobe call *Process Multiple Files*. You can rename files, convert images to another file type, change file sizes, and even apply quick fixes to a group of files (although I typically don't recommend using this option).

Most digital cameras name their images by assigning a number to each image you take. Unfortunately, that's not very intuitive to the photographic contents. Suppose you have a large batch of vacation photos that your camera named DISC101, DISC102, DISC103, and so forth, but you'd rather they be named in a more descriptive manor such as Florida 2006–1, Florida 2006-2, Florida 2006–3, and so forth. Renaming these images one at a time can be very tedious, especially if you have lots of them.

Take a look at the list of files in Figure 6-40. This is a list of 74 images taken by the proud grandparents of a new baby. We can use the Photoshop Elements batch rename command to rename them all at once. The following steps walk you through using the batch rename command:

1. Choose File > Process Multiple Files. The Process Multiple Files dialog box appears.

2. Click the Browse button on the Source line and locate and select the folder containing the files you want to rename.

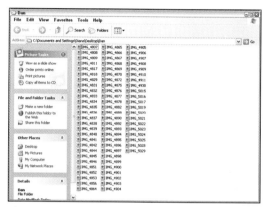

Figure 6-40
Rename any number of files at one time.

3. Click the Destination Browse button to locate and select the folder where you want to store the renamed files. It can be the same folder as the originals or a different folder.

4. In the File Naming area, check Rename Files.

5. In the first box under Rename Files, type the name you want to describe these images, such as Mary's Party, or New Baby, or 2006 Trip West. Optionally, click the drop-down list and choose from Photoshop Elements' suggestions. All the images you rename will begin with whatever you enter here.

6. In the second box, click the drop-down list and choose how you want the images sequenced. Choose a Serial Number sequence if you want the images to read like New Baby–001, New Baby –002, and so forth. Or choose a lettering sequence such as New Baby–A, New Baby–B, etc. (see Figure 6-41).

Choose a Unique Sequence

You must include at least one field that is unique for every file (for example, file name, serial number, or serial letter) to prevent files from overwriting each other.

Delete Original Images

The images with their original names are still in the folder. You need to manually delete these using the Windows Explorer, My Computer window or the Photoshop Elements Organizer workspace.

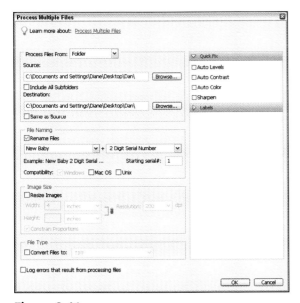

Figure 6-41
Choose a new name sequence for the images.

7. Click OK. Photoshop Elements begins the renaming process by temporarily opening each image in Photoshop Elements, renaming the file, and then closing the image.

A second option available from the Process Multiple Files dialog box is to resize your images if you want each file resized to a uniform size. Click the Resize Images option and then select the Constrain Proportions option so you don't distort your images. Enter a desired width or height and resolution.

The third function of the Process Multiple Files dialog box is the ability to convert a batch of images from one file format to another. Since most digital cameras automatically save your image in JPEG format which uses compression, you might want to change the photos from a JPEG format to a TIFF format or even a PSD (Photoshop) format to prevent you from accidentally resaving the images in JPEG again, which can cause quality loss. All you have to do is click the Convert Files to check box and select a new file type from the drop-down list. Like the renaming command, when you convert images to a new format, the batch process leaves the originals alone, and it creates duplicate images with the new format.

Dividing Scanned Photos

ONE FINAL FEATURE I THINK you should know about is Photoshop Elements' ability to divide up multiple images.

You learned in Chapter 4 that you could import images directly into Photoshop Elements through your scanner; however, when you have lots of images to scan, it can be very tedious to scan them one by one. Since most flatbed scanners allow you to place and scan multiple images at one time, you can let Photoshop Elements divide the images for you.

Scanning Tips

Here are a couple of tips to make the Divide Scanned Photos feature work better. The Divide Scanned Photos feature works by looking for clearly defined edges to differentiate between the photographs, so when scanning your images, don't place them too close together, and be sure to lay them as straight as possible. Sometimes, putting a sheet of colored paper over the back of the images helps Photoshop Elements distinguish their edges as well.

Open the image you want to separate and choose Image > Divide Scanned Photos. Photoshop Elements divides the images into separate files. See Figure 6-42.

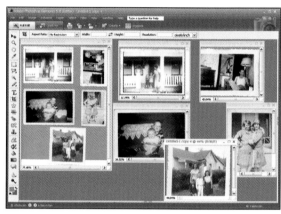

Figure 6-42
Save time by scanning multiple images and letting Photoshop Elements divide them for you.

Using *Filters*

Photograph:
Griffing Partington

PICTURE YOURSELF AS AN ACTOR or actress. Before you go on stage or in front of the camera, you spend time with a makeup artist. Changes are made—some subtle, others not. The makeup helps get your message across to the audience. But you're still the same person underneath—you just have this layer on top of you making you look different. Consider that look as a filter.

Filters are important correction and creativity tools. The function of a filter is to change the way the camera lens sees the subject. Some filters have a tint and can block certain colors, while others blur the image or even add distortion and special effects.

With digital image manipulation, you don't have to take your shots using those expensive and sometimes cumbersome filters. You can add the effect later using Photoshop Elements.

The filters we'll look at in this chapter have more to do with distorting your images into unique works of art. We'll take a brief look at the many deformation effects available with Photoshop Elements and see how they can easily give your images extra touches of character.

Effects and Filters

Photoshop Elements includes many different creative and sometimes mystical filter effects, designed to radically change the nature of your images. Some are subtle and barely detectable, while others make the image jump right out at you. As a photographer, you probably won't use these effects much, but in special situations you may find them helpful, if not downright amusing.

Effects work on selections or the individual layers of an image, so you can apply a different effect for each layer, or you can apply multiple effects to a single layer. Like most filters you've already encountered, most filters work only on raster images and only if the image is full color or in certain grayscale settings. Photoshop Elements includes over 100 different effects in 13 different categories:

- ▶ **Adjustment Effects**
- ▶ **Artistic Effects**
- ▶ **Blur Effects**
- ▶ **Brush Strokes Effects**
- ▶ **Distort Effects**
- ▶ **Noise Effects**
- ▶ **Pixelate Effects**
- ▶ **Render Effects**
- ▶ **Sketch Effects**
- ▶ **Stylize Effects**
- ▶ **Texture Effects**
- ▶ **Video Effects**
- ▶ **Other Effects**

We won't be able to look at each and every one of the effects, but we'll review each category and the type of effect the categories manage. Certain categories and effects we'll delve into more deeply than others. Several of the filters are applied without any dialog box or options while others require input from you; some require more information than others. Most filters do allow a good amount of customization, but the options vary depending on the individual filter.

Easy Undo

While you're experimenting with different filters, it's handy to have the Undo History palette displayed and easily accessible. Choose Window > Undo History.

Here are a few tips you might like when working with filters:

- ▶ **When using a filter on a selection, you can soften the edges of the filter effect by feathering the selection before you apply the filter.**
- ▶ **Apply filters to individual layers or to several layers in succession to build up an effect.**
- ▶ **Try applying a filter to a duplicate layer and adjusting the layer opacity.**
- ▶ **Try different blending modes to mix the filter effect.**
- ▶ **Apply filters to solid color or grayscale images to create textures you can use in other places.**

▶ Use a filter to hide blemishes and faults in an image.

▶ Apply the same filter to a series of images to make them look similar.

▶ Since some filters use the foreground and background colors in their process, select the colors you want to use before applying the filter.

Adjustment Filters

In Chapters 5 and 6, you learned quite a few ways to adjust brightness and color in your images. Photoshop Elements also includes several adjustment filters you can use to change brightness values, color, grayscale range, and pixel tonal levels. In the Adjustment category, you'll find six filters: Equalize, Gradient Map, Invert, Posterize, Threshold, and Photo Filter. Let's look at a couple of them.

▶ The **Equalize filter** redistributes the brightness values of the pixels in an image so that they more evenly represent the entire range of brightness levels.

▶ The **Threshold filter** converts grayscale or color images to high-contrast, black-and-white images.

▶ The **Photo Filter** command mimics the technique of putting a colored filter in front of the camera lens to adjust the color balance and color temperature of the light transmitted through the lens and expose the film.

▶ The **Invert filter** reverses your image colors making a black-and-white image into a negative image. See Figure 7-1 for an example.

Figure 7-1
The Invert filter as applied to a black-and-white image.

Artistic Filters

Artistic effects are one of my favorite categories and the largest category of all. Choose an Artistic filter if you want to simulate painting and drawing effects. There are 15 different artistic effects including:

▶ **Colored Pencil**: Imitates using colored pencils on a solid background along with a crosshatch appearance.

▶ **Cutout**: Makes the image look as though it is on rough cut-out pieces of colored paper.

▶ **Dry Brush**: Simulates using a dry brush technique by reducing its range of colors to areas of common color.

▶ **Film Grain**: Applies a grainy pattern to an image placing a more saturated pattern to lighter areas.

▶ **Fresco**: Uses short round dabs that look like they were hastily applied.

▶ **Neon Glow**: Takes the current foreground and background color from the color swatches and combines it with a selectable glow color.

▶ **Paint Daubs:** Makes the image appear hand painted.

▶ **Palette Knife:** Gives the effect of a thinly painted canvas.

▶ **Plastic Wrap:** Makes the image look as though it were shrink wrapped.

▶ **Poster Edges:** Locates the image edges and paints black on them.

▶ **Rough Pastels:** Looks like you've used colored pastel chalk. Also adds a textured background.

▶ **Smudge Stick:** Uses short diagonal strokes to smear darker areas in the image.

▶ **Sponge:** Creates a highly textured effect with contrasting colors.

▶ **Underpainting:** Adds a textured background.

▶ **Watercolor:** Simplifies the image details making it look painted with water and color.

Here are four Artistic filter samples for your review:

Dry brush

Plastic Wrap

Poster Edges

Sponge

Blur Filters

Most good photographic images demand clarity. Sharpening and Unsharp Mask help clarify your images as well as remove the noise with the noise filters. Sometimes, though, instead of clarifying your image you want to blur or soften all or part of the photograph. Blur filters, which actually add noise to your image, include Average, Blur, Blur More, Gaussian, Radial, and Motion blur.

Blur filters compare pixels to nearby pixels and average their value, which in turn, reduces the contrast between them. Most of the blur filters focus primarily on high-contrast areas, and all blur filters only work on grayscale and 16 million color images.

Blur and Blur More

You might use the Blur and Blur More filters to reduce graininess in your image. These filters remove noise by applying smooth transitions and decreasing the contrast in the image. As you might expect, the Blur More effect applies the Blur effect with more intensity.

You apply the Blur and Blur More filters by clicking the Filter menu, selecting Blur, and choosing Blur or Blur More. Neither filter provides you with any options; they simply apply a preset amount of blur to the image.

Figure 7-2 shows a portion of an image with no blur, Blur, and Blur More applied.

Controlling the Blur

Control the blur area by applying the filters to only selected areas of the image.

Figure 7-2
Decrease image contrast with the Blur and Blur More filters.

Photograph by Hossley Partington

Average Blur

The Average Blur filter is really helpful at removing dithering that often occurs when you increase the color depth of an image. By reducing the contrast between pixels, you get less waffling and a smoother more consistent appearance. Access the Average Blur filter by clicking the Filter menu, selecting Blur, and then choosing Average Blur.

Gaussian Blur

Another type of blur is Gaussian Blur, which originates from German mathematician and astronomer Karl Friedrich Gauss. Mr. Gauss had many mathematical theories, some of which are what Photoshop Elements applies when you use Gaussian Blur. Gaussian refers to the bell-shaped curve that Photoshop Elements generates when it applies a weighted average to the pixels. Gaussian Blur is very similar to the Average Blur, but Gaussian Blur is a little stronger and gives more realistic results. It works by controlling the amount of blurring applied to any given pixel or edge by an adjustable amount, making the blurring appear

dense in the center and soft and feathery around the edges. The Gaussian Blur filter adds low-frequency detail and can produce a hazy effect. From the Gaussian Blur dialog box, you set the blur radius to determine how far the filter searches for dissimilar pixels to blur.

Like other blurring effects, you can apply the blur to an entire image or just a selected portion of it. Most of the time, you won't want to apply the blur to the entire photograph but only to a portion of it, which changes the depth of field.

You'll have best results if you place the area you want to modify on its own layer and then add the Gaussian Blur to the layered image. Follow these steps:

1. Promote the background to a regular layer. (Right-click the layer and choose Layer from Background).

2. Select the area you want to blur. In the example used here, we'll select the large iceberg using the Magnetic Lasso tool, and to give a softer edge, set feathering to 2.

3. Copy the selected area to its own layer by choosing Edit > Copy and then choosing Edit > Paste.

4. Now you can apply the blur. Again, making sure you are on the background Layer 0, click the Filter menu, select Blur, and then select Gaussian Blur. You'll see a Gaussian Blur dialog box like the one in Figure 7-3.

5. Set the blur radius you want and click OK. Values range from 0 to 100 with 100 being totally blurred. Figure 7-4 shows the image before and after adding a 5 radius Gaussian Blur.

Figure 7-3

Set the amount of blur you want.

Figure 7-4

Photoshop Elements applied the blur only to the lower layer and not the iceberg on the upper layer.

Motion Blur

Today's cameras have built-in features that reduce the chance of getting motion blur during a shot; however there will be times when you want a motion blur to add to the visual impact an object has on the image. The filter's effect is comparable to taking a picture of a moving object with a fixed exposure time. Photoshop Elements includes a Motion Blur filter, which simulates the process. This filter works best when used inside a selection.

Motion effects are placed in a directional manner to achieve the illusion of motion. You can adjust not only the intensity of the blur but also the direction in which the blur effect is applied. The Motion Blur filter blurs in a particular direction (from −360° to +360°) and at a specific distance (from 1 to 999). You can set the blur angle and distance.

Take a look at the golf ball and club shown in Figure 7-5. It's a nice photograph with the ball precisely placed on the beautiful green grass, lacking even a hint of motion. How boring is that? Let's add a little action to it, giving the impression of movement.

We want to add the blur from the golf club and because we want to isolate the motion blur area, we have to make a selection first.

Figure 7-5

Put some action in your swing with the Motion Blur filter.

Again, using the Magnetic Lasso tool, in the Tool Options palette, set the Feather to 3, and enable Anti-alias. Select a rough selection around the area you want to blur, in our example, the golf club. Keeping the selection area rough prevents the blur from looking too stiff.

Now you can apply the blur filter. Choose Filter > Blur > Motion Blur, which displays the dialog box you see in Figure 7-6.

Figure 7-6
Use the dial control or enter an angle value to set the blur direction.

The blur angle is a circular value ranging from 0 to 359 degrees. The strength value runs from 1 to 100 with 100 being a total blur. For our example, we want the blur angle at −7, which sets the motion blur direction from the back of the golf club, and we will use a strength of 21. We do not want a full Motion Blur, as it would be too much for what we are trying to achieve. Click OK when you select your settings.

More Motion

To add additional motion, apply a second Motion Blur, but feather the selection size first.

Notice that the blur is applied only to our selected area. Figure 7-7 shows our golf club appearing as if it's at the end of a swing just about ready to meet the ball.

Figure 7-7
Fore!

Other Movement

Another way to add the illusion of movement is to apply the Wind filter.

Radial Blur

One other type of blur you can achieve with Photoshop Elements is a Radial Blur. Radial Blur simulates blurring like spinning a camera in circles or zooming in quickly with a slow shutter speed. The Radial Blur filter can also give your image a twirling look to it.

Like many of the blur filters, you probably won't use the Radial Blur often, but with the bottom photograph, it produces a stunning effect like the one you see in Figure 7-8, which makes the fire look alive.

Figure 7-8
Add a zoom effect with Radial Blur.

Photoshop Elements Radial Blur filter provides two different blur types: Zoom and Spin. Using the Zoom type blurs pixels away from the center of the image. The Spin type blurs pixels circularly around the image center. Figure 7-9 shows the same image with a Spin effect. Notice the circular motion.

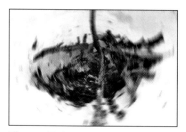

Figure 7-9
Sort of makes you dizzy, doesn't it?

The following steps walk you through applying the Radial Blur filter to your image:

1. Click the Filter menu, select Blur, and then select Radial Blur. You see a dialog box like the one in Figure 7-10.

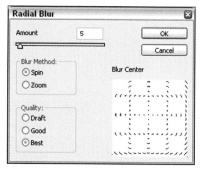

Figure 7-10
Zoom or spin your image.

2. Select a Blur type: Zoom or Spin.

3. Choose an Amount. Measured in percentages from 1 to 100, lower values lessen the effect, while higher values intensify the effect.

4. Select a blur quality. The quality runs from Draft for fast but grainy results to Good and Best for smoother results, which are indistinguishable except on a large selection.

5. Click OK after making your selection.

Experiment with the blur settings. You could even use blur to create some awesome backgrounds that you could use in other images.

Smart Blur

The last blur filter, Smart Blur, allows you to specify precise blur data. For example, you can specify how far the filter searches for dissimilar pixels to blur, a ceiling to determine how different the pixel values must be before being eliminated, and a blur quality. The filter also gives you the options of setting the blur to Normal for the entire selection, or for the edges of color transitions called Edge Only and Overlay Edge. When an image has significant contrast, the Edge Only option applies black-and-white edges and Overlay Edge applies only white edges.

Brush Strokes Filters

The eight brush filters are an artist's dream. You can use them to make your image look as if it were hand-painted or drawn. Choices include Accented Edges, Angled Strokes, Crosshatch, Dark Strokes, Ink Outlines, Spatter, Sprayed Strokes, and Sumi-e. The Sumi-e filter is interesting because the filter makes it look as though you used a brush with black ink on rice paper, giving soft blurry edges. Here are a few samples of the Brush Strokes filters:

Angled Strokes

Crosshatch

Ink Outlines

Sumi-E

Distort Filters

Just like their name implies, the Distortion Filters distort your image. Another large category of effects, this one contains 13 choices, many of which can completely turn your image into an unrecognizable but artistic form. Select from Diffuse Glow, Displace, Glass, Liquify, Ocean Ripple, Pinch, Polar Coordinates, Ripple, Shear, Spherize, Twirl, Wave, and ZigZag.

These are all great filters, but one filter in particular bears mentioning, and that's the Liquify filter. The Liquify filter doesn't just drop on an image. Instead, it allows you to interactively warp, twist, twirl, pinch, and pull parts of your image creating your own level of distortion. Like other filters, you can apply it to the entire image, on a separate layer, or to just a selected image area. When you choose the Liquify filter, you get the dialog box you see in Figure 7-11.

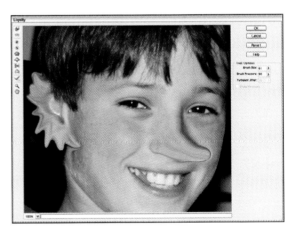
Figure 7-11
Have some creative fun with the Liquify filter.

On the left side of the Liquify dialog box is a toolbar with a number of helpful tools:

▶ **Warp:** Like a smudge brush, this tool pushes the pixels around creating a stretched effect.

▶ **Turbulence:** Use this tool to scramble pixels to create fire, clouds, water, waves, and many other effects.

▶ **Twirl Clockwise** or **Twirl Counterclockwise:** As you drag your mouse, these tools rotate pixels either clockwise or counterclockwise.

▶ **Pucker:** The Pucker tool pinches pixels toward the center of the brush area. It's just the opposite of the Bloat tool.

▶ **Bloat:** The Bloat tool moves pixels away from the center of the brush area. It's just the opposite of the Pucker tool.

▶ **Shift Pixels:** This tool moves pixels to the left if you drag straight up or moves pixels to the right if you drag downward.

▶ **Reflection:** By copying pixels, this tool drags a reversed image of your pixels at an angle to the brush motion. Use overlapping strokes to create an effect similar to a reflection in water.

▶ **Reconstruct:** This tool fully or partially reverses any changes you've made. Select the tool and drag the mouse over the area you want to reverse.

Start Over

Click the Revert button to start all over.

You also see a hand (pan) tool and a zoom tool. On the right side, you see options where you can set your brush size and pressure. When selecting a brush pressure, the higher the pressure, the faster the distortion effect is applied. Select the tool you want and drag away! Click OK when you are finished. See Figure 7-12.

Figure 7-12
My grandson said it was OK to have fun with his picture!

Here are some other distortion effects:

Ocean Ripple   *Pinch*

Shear   *Spherize*

Noise Filters

When retouching your photographs in Chapter 6, you discovered you use the noise filters to remove image noise by blending areas into the surrounding pixels. The five Noise filters are Add Noise, Despeckle, Dust & Scratches, Median, and Reduce Noise.

Pixelate Filters

The seven Pixelate filters modify your image by either sharply defining the edges or by clumping together similar color pixels. Options include Color Halftone, Crystallize, Facet, Fragment, Mezzotine, Mosaic, and Pointillize. Here are a few representations of the Pixelate filters:

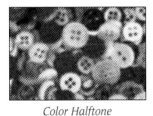
Color Halftone

Mezzotint

Pointillize

Crystalize

Render Filters

If you like special effects, you'll love the Render filters. The Render category includes seven special effects designed to give your selection or image a sense of depth and dimension. Filters include: 3D Transform, Clouds, Difference Clouds, Fibers, Lens Flare, Lighting Effects, and Texture Fill. Let's take a look at a couple of the rendering effects:

3D Transform

With the 3D Transform filter you can use a tool to draw a cube, sphere, or cylinder around any or all of your image and then move and rotate the object in three dimensions. You get the experience of manipulating a flat, two-dimensional image as if it were a solid, three-dimensional object. The 3D Transform filter provides a dialog box, seen in Figure 7-13, where you select the shape you want from options on the left side of the dialog box; then using the rotate tool, you can rotate the shape projection. It's not an easy filter to use, but it's fun.

Figure 7-13
Manipulate images as though they were three-dimensional.

Lens Flare

The Lens Flare filter simulates a bright light shining into a camera lens. In the Lens Flare dialog box seen in Figure 7-14, you can control the flare shape, which is the lens type and the flare brightness. You can change the location of the flare by dragging the crosshair in the preview window until the flare is in the desired location.

Figure 7-14
Create a reflective effect with a lens flare!

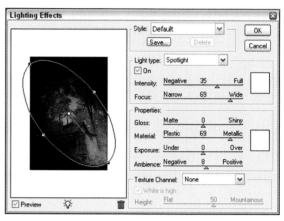

Figure 7-15
Be creative with lighting effects.

On the left side, you have a Preview area where you can see each light you choose. The light area is indicated by a white circular or elliptical shape line with four handle boxes and a center dot. From the Preview area, you can do any of the following:

▶ **Move a light by dragging the small white dot located in the center of the light area.**

▶ **Change the direction of a light by moving any of the handle boxes.**

▶ **Resize the light focus by dragging any of the handle boxes.**

▶ **Add additional lights by dragging the light bulb icon located at the bottom of the Preview window. You can have up to 16 lights.**

▶ **Copy an existing light by holding down the Alt key and dragging the light to a new location in the window.**

▶ **Delete a light by dragging the lights center circle into the trash can icon, or by pressing the Delete key.**

Lighting Effects

The Lighting Effects filter lets you produce sophisticated lighting effects on RGB images. You can create multiple lights, set individual light properties, and easily drag lights around in the preview window to test different lighting setups. Access the Lighting Effects filter by choosing Filter > Render > Lighting Effects (see Figure 7-15).

Photoshop Elements provides 16 different prede-fined light styles, and you can create your own and save it for future use. Table 7-1 lists each light style and a brief description.

Figure 7-16 illustrates lighting examples: the original image, default lighting, omni lighting, and a custom lighting setting.

Table 7-1 Lighting Effect Filter Styles

Name	Light Type	Quantity	Intensity	Focus	Color
Blue Omni	Omni	1	Full	Wide	Blue
Circle of Light	Spotlight	4	Full	Wide	Red, Yellow, White & Blue
Crossing	Spotlight	1	Medium	Wide	White
Crossing Down	Spotlight	2	Medium	Wide	White
Default	Spotlight	1	Medium	Wide	White
Five Lights Down	Spotlight	5	Full	Wide	White
Five Lights Up	Spotlight	5	Full	Wide	White
Flashlight	Omni	1	Medium	Wide	Yellow
Flood Light	Spotlight	1	Medium	Wide	White
Parallel Directional	Directional	1	Full	Wide	Blue &
		1	Medium	Wide	White
RGB Lights	Spotlight	3	Medium	Wide	Red, Green & Blue
Soft Direct Lights	Directional	2	Soft	None	White &
	Directional	2	Medium	None	Blue
Soft Omni	Omni	1	Medium	None	White
Soft Spotlight	Spotlight	1	Full	Wide	White
Three Down	Spotlight	3	Medium	Wide	White
Triple Spotlight	Spotlight	3	Medium	Wide	White

Figure 7-16
Be creative with lighting effects

Each light type has many different options. If you select a style that contains multiple lights, you can set the options for each individual light. The On check box obviously turns the light on or off. But why would you want to create a light and then turn it off? You'll find it helpful if you are arranging multiple lights and you want to see specifically what an individual light does. Turning off the extra lights helps you view the effects of a particular light. The Intensity slider lets you determine the light brightness and the Focus slider lets you specify the light width. Click the Color box if you want to change a light color.

The Properties section has more detailed lighting options that are more focused on the image itself:

- ▶ **Gloss: Sets how much light reflects off the surface. Options vary from low (Matte) to high (Shiny).**

- ▶ **Material: Controls how much the light reflects from the lights or the object on which the light is cast. Plastic reflects the light's color and Metallic reflects the object's color.**

- ▶ **Exposure: Increases or decreases the light. Over increases the light and Under decreases the light.**

- ▶ **Ambience: Determines whether the light acts as if it is combined with other lights such as sunlight or fluorescent light.**

- ▶ **Color box: Establishes the ambience light color.**

The Texture Channel has options for adding a texture to the image you're shining the light on.

Sketch Filters

The Sketch effects are another of my favorite categories, as well as another one of the largest, with 14 possible effects designed to apply a variety of different results to your image:

- ▶ **Chrome gives your image a metallic appearance.**

- ▶ **Conté Crayon uses the foreground color for dark areas and the background area for lighter areas and imitates the texture of Conté crayons on an image.**

History of Conté Crayon

Conté Crayon is a brand of crayon made of graphite and clay, usually in black, red, or brown. It originated in the 1850s after being invented by French chemist N.J. Conté.

▶ Graphic Pen uses fine ink lines to enhance image detail. It uses the foreground color for the ink color and the background paper for the paper color.

▶ Halftone Pattern simulates the effect of a halftone process in which image tone is conveyed by photographing an image through a screen, which breaks up the continuous image tones into closely spaced dots.

▶ Note Paper simulates the texture of handmade paper by combining the effects of the Emboss and Grain filters.

▶ Photocopy simulates the effect of photocopying an image.

▶ Plaster molds the image into a 3D plaster effect, and then, using the foreground and background color, colorizes the result. Dark areas are raised; light areas are sunken.

▶ Reticulation makes the image appear clustered in the shadow areas by simulating film shrinking and distorting.

▶ Stamp makes the image appear as if made with a rubber or wood stamp. It uses the color palette's current foreground and background colors.

▶ Torn Edges reconstructs the image as ragged, torn pieces of paper, and then colorizes the image using the foreground and background colors.

▶ Water Paper uses scratch blotches and makes the image appear as if it were painted onto a fibrous, damp paper.

Bas Relief

Chalk and Charcoal

Graphic Pen

Water Paper

Stylize Filters

There are nine different Stylize filters, and they enhance your images by giving a painted or impressionistic effect by displacing pixels and heightening contrast in an image. Choices include Diffuse, Emboss, Extrude, Find Edges, Glowing Edges, Solarize, Tiles, Trace Contour, and Wind. When looking at the samples, notice the one for Glowing Edges was used with a selection. As with all filters, you can apply a filter to a selected area or the entire image, or even to a specific layer. Take a look:

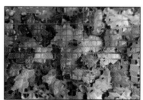

Extrude

Find Edges

Glowing Edges

Texture Filters

The general idea behind the six Texture effects is to give a sense of texture to the canvas. Most of these effects make your image appear as if it were "top coated." You can pick from Craquelure, Grain, Mosaic Tiles, Patchwork, Stained Glass, and Texturizer. Here are a few samples:

 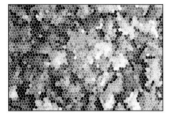

Craquelure   *Stained Glass*

Texturizer   *Patchwork*

Video Filters

The Video filter category is probably the least used category. Like Web pages, television and video don't have the gamut of colors available to other sources. The Video filters category restricts the image colors to those acceptable for television reproduction and smooth moving images captured on video.

Other Filters

The Other filters category is sort of a catch-all or "none of the above" category. But through the Other filters category, you'll find filters to modify masks, offset a selection within an image, and make quick color adjustments. You'll also be able to create your own custom filters.

All image editing is a result of math. Photoshop Elements makes mathematical calculations for almost every command you issue, and filters are no exception. If you are a math wizard and really want a challenge, you can create your own effect filters. Photoshop Elements includes a Custom filter box where you can enter your own values. Click the Filter menu and from the Other category, select Custom. A dialog box with a matrix like the one you see in Figure 7-17 appears.

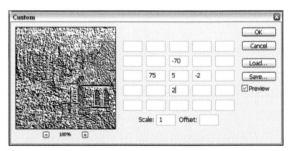

Figure 7-17
Create your own filters.

The Filter matrix allows you to enter the coefficients needed to process pixels for your needed effect. With the Custom filter, you can change the brightness values of each pixel in the image according to a predefined mathematical operation known as *convolution*. Each pixel is reassigned a value based on the values of surrounding pixels.

Begin with the center box. The center box represents a pixel in the image. In this box, you enter the value between –999 and +999 by which you want to multiply the pixels brightness. Next, select the box to the left. This box represents the first pixel to the left of the current pixel in the center box. Enter a value to multiply this pixel. Continue entering values for all the pixels you want to include in the operation. You don't have to enter values in all the text boxes.

Matrix Values

The sum of the values in the matrix should equal 1 to avoid turning the image completely white or black.

The Scale value box is where you enter the value by which to divide the sum of the brightness values of the pixels included in the calculation. For a scale of 1, the values are exactly as you entered them.

For Offset, enter the value to be added to the result of the scale calculation. Figure 7-18 illustrates the original image, and then a second image with the custom filter and a scale and offset values of 1 and 0, and a third image that has the custom filter, but the scale was set to 3 and offset to 5.

Sound difficult? It is. But it's the method you must use if you want to create your own filter. You don't have to reinvent the wheel if you plan on using the filter again. If you only want this look one time and don't plan on using it ever again, just click OK, and Photoshop Elements will apply the filter to your image or selection. If, however, you think you might use this filter again, you can save the settings. Click the Save button and enter a name for the custom filter in the resulting Save dialog box. The next time you want the same filter, you select it after clicking the Load button.

Figure 7-18
Using a custom filter.

Using the Filter Gallery

S O FAR, YOU'VE SEEN THAT to choose a filter, you click the Filter category and pick a filter; then click Edit > Undo if you want to choose a different filter. However, if you don't know which filter you really want, this practice can be time consuming. Fortunately, we're going to take a look at a couple of the tools Photoshop Elements has to help you quickly determine which filter is best for your image.

The Filter Gallery lets you apply filters cumulatively and apply individual filters more than once. Because you can apply more than one filter to an image when you use the Filter Gallery dialog box, you have a lot of control over the way each filter affects your image.

Choose Filter > Filter Gallery to open the Filter Gallery. The Filter Gallery displays a thumbnail of your open image layer where you can view a sample of your image with many filters with its Default and other Preset settings. The Filter Gallery seen in Figure 7-19 may take a moment to load, but you'll find it well worth the wait.

New Effect Layer icon

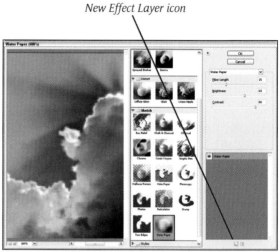

Figure 7-19
Apply filters with the Filter Gallery.

On the left side, you see your current image in a Preview window. Along the bottom edge of the Preview window are zoom controls where you can determine your viewing choice. You can also use your mouse to move (pan) the image around in the Preview window.

In the middle is an expandable and collapsible list of some, but not all, of the different Filter categories. Some categories and filters are available only as individual commands from the Filter menu or the Special Effects section of the Artwork and Effects palette. See the next section about the Artwork and Effects palette.

Open Image

You must have at least one open image before the Filter Gallery becomes available.

Click the triangle next to any category to expand or collapse a category. An expanded category displays an icon representing the individual filters in the selected category.

New Effect Layer

If you want to apply the filter to its own layer, click the New Effect Layer icon located at the bottom-left side of the Filter Gallery window.

When you locate and click the effect you want to try, Photoshop Elements automatically applies that filter with preset options to your image. If the preset filter settings aren't quite what you want, modify any adjustment settings from the area on the right. The available settings change with each different filter. If you want to apply the filter a second time, or add a different filter on top of the existing filter, hold down the Alt key as you choose the next filter; however, it's a good idea to apply each filter on its own effect layer. Table 7-2 lists some of the shortcut keys you can use with the Filter Gallery.

Click OK to accept the filter or click Cancel to back out of the Filter Gallery without applying any filter.

Table 7-2 Filter Gallery Shortcut Keys

To Get This	Do This
Apply a new filter on top of selected	Alt-click on a filter
Open/close all disclosure triangles	Alt-click on a disclosure triangle
To reset the settings	Control then click the Default button
To reset the image	Alt then click the Reset button
Undo/redo	Control+Z
Step forward	Control+Shift+Z
Step backward	Control+Alt+Z

Applying Filters with the Artwork and Effects Palette

Photoshop Elements provides another quick access tool for working with filters. It's called the Artwork and Effects palette, and it's been hanging around in the Palette Bin on the right side of your screen. You can do more than apply filters with this palette, which we'll take a look at in the next several chapters, but for now, let's concentrate on the filter applications.

Take a look at the Artwork and Effects palette seen in Figure 7-20. The five icons along the top represent the different sections the palette works with. The third icon, which looks like gears, is the Apply Effects, Filters, and Layer Styles icon. Click the third icon, and you immediately see some of the filters. There are two drop-down lists, and the second one contains a list of the different layer categories.

Apply Effects button   Filter Category drop-down list   Filters and Layer Styles icon

Figure 7-20
The Artwork and Effects palette.

Select the filter you want and do one of the following:

▶ **Click the Apply button at the bottom of the Artwork and Effects palette.**

▶ **Double-click the filter icon.**

▶ **Drag the filter icon on top of your image.**

As before, some filters automatically apply with no options and others bring up a dialog box relevant to the selected filter.

Working with Plug-Ins

IF THE OVER 100 FILTERS supplied with Photoshop Elements aren't enough, you can add other plug-in filters. Plug-in filters, by themselves, can't do anything, but combine them with Photoshop Elements, and you can create an even wider variety of functions and effects. The concept of plug-in filters originated long ago with Adobe Photoshop, and the success of the feature has many different software companies constantly trying to develop better and more unique filters.

Some are quite pricey, whereas others are free. Typically, you won't find filters available in your local software store, but they abound on the Internet, and in many cases, you can get a trial copy to evaluate.

Most third-party filters are compatible with Photoshop Elements and typically have .8BF as the filename extension, such as SWIRLEYPOP.8BF or BUBBLEJETS.8BF. However, the .8BF extension is not a requirement in Photoshop Elements.

Compatibility

Most Adobe Photoshop plug-ins are compatible with Photoshop Elements.

Look around on the Internet, and I think you'll be quite pleased with what you find. Whether you choose Flaming Pear's SuperBladePro, Alien Skin's Eye Candy, or one of the hundreds of others, you'll find unique special effects in each application. Here are a few places you can begin your search:

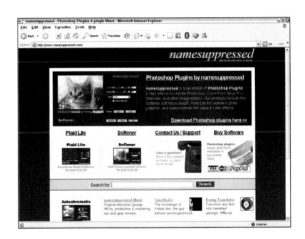

▶ **www.alienskin.com: The creator of the award-winning Eye Candy filters provides a wide variety of photorealistic textures, such as snake and lizard skin, while their Xenofex 2 collection simulates natural phenomena, such as lightning and clouds, or even filters that can transform your photos into Jigsaw puzzles or constellations.**

▶ **www.andromeda.com: Andromeda software provides several excellent filter collections, several of which are aimed at photographic correction and adjustments.**

▶ **www.flamingpear.com**: The Flaming Pear family of filters includes the powerful SuperBladePro and a number of other unusual filters, such as ones that create images of planets or the illusion of flooding.

▶ **www.thepluginsite.com**: This popular site offers free and commercial plug-ins, including their own Colorwasher and Focal Blade. The best part of this Web site is that they provide reviews of a variety of third-party filters and a master index to them.

▶ **www.autofx.com**: Auto FX software carries a variety of plug-in packages with some really unique effects, including edges, wrinkle, tape, and gels.

▶ **www.humansoftware.com**: There are lots of great plug-ins available here, including a wide variety of frames and textures. These are great for working with photographs.

▶ **www.avbros.com**: AV Bros. has some fantastic page curl and puzzle filters. Even if you don't need extra filters, take a look at their Web site and see some of their examples.

▶ **www.namesuppressed.com**: Their products include the Softener soft focus plug-in, Plaid Lite for seamless plaid patterns, and Autochromatic for sepia and color effects.

Figure 7-21
An image after applying one of Harry's Filters (Free from thepluginsite.com).

Installing Plug-in Filters

Each filter manufacturer provides its own method and directions to install its filters. When you install the filters, make a note of their file location because you need to tell Photoshop Elements where you keep those filters on your computer. Photoshop Elements stores instructions to file locations in its Preferences area. Follow these steps to link Photoshop Elements to the plug-ins:

1. Choose Edit > Preferences > Plug-Ins & Scratch Disks. The Preferences dialog box appears.

2. From the Preferences submenu, click the Additional Plug Ins Folder option.

3. Click the Choose button. You'll see a Browse for Folder dialog box like the one in Figure 7-22.

4. Locate and click the folder containing the filters; then click OK twice.

Any new plug-ins are listed under the Filter menu, although you may have to close the Photoshop Elements program and restart it to see the new plug-in.

Figure 7-22
Tell Photoshop Elements where to locate your plug-in filters.

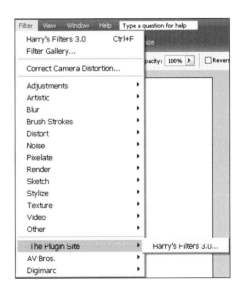

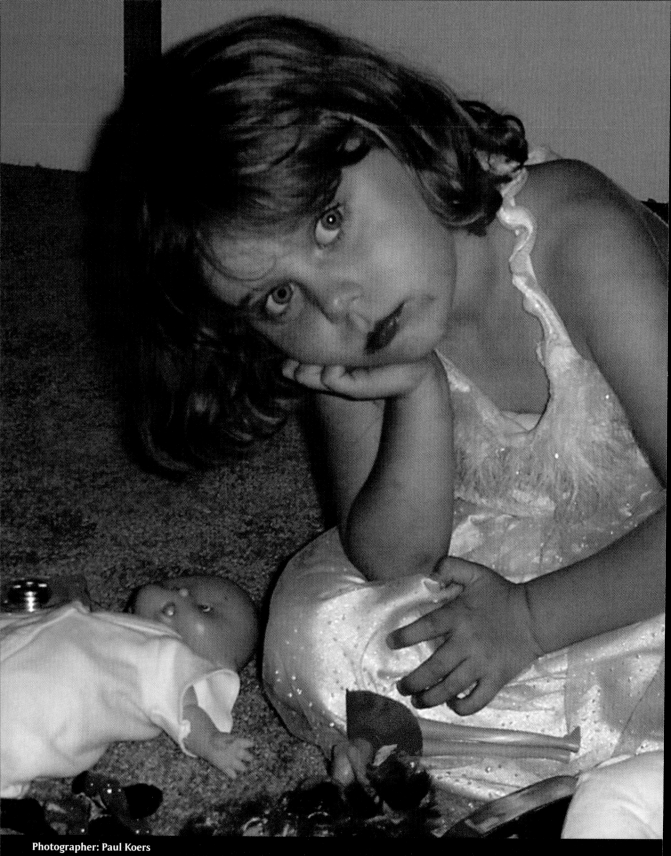

8

Printing and *Sharing*

Photographer:
Paul Koers

PICTURE YOURSELF AS A LITTLE GIRL alone in a room, playing dress-up. Or imagine you are a small boy playing catch all by yourself. There's no one else around. It's quiet…too quiet. That doesn't sound like a lot of fun does it? Children like to share their fun with other children, and while sometimes it's wonderful to keep small delights to yourself, more often than not, it's much better to share the pleasure with others. That's what this chapter is all about—sharing.

You've finally reached the summit. You've snapped, downloaded, corrected, enhanced, resized, and done all kinds of things to your photographs. It's time to share some of the memories your photographs hold. While you probably won't want to share all your photographs with others, there are some that you just can't keep to yourself. Sending pictures to family members or friends makes those images also become priceless treasures to others.

If you plan on printing your photos, you establish *what* you print, as well as *how* you print. You can print items on your own printer, have them printed online by professionals, or print them to the Web in a Web Gallery. You can also design a slide show that you can burn to a CD or e-mail to others.

Printing to Your Printer

L ET'S START WITH THE MOST common printing method—printing to your own color printer. Before you begin any printing operation, you need to tell Photoshop Elements some basic information about your print job, such as the paper size, type, and orientation. You also need to set some color details so that what you see on your monitor is what appears in print. In Chapter 5, you read about color and resolution and why it's important to keep them both in tune with your monitor. They are equally important when preparing to print your images.

Deciding on a Printer

The two main types of printers that most people use are ink jets and laser printers. The technology behind each is distinctly different from the other.

Ink Jet Printers

Ink jet printers are the slowest but most affordable type of printers. They work by shooting tiny sprays of colored wet dyes through microscopic holes in a print head onto pages, one row at a time. Price-wise, ink jet printers are very inexpensive to purchase, many under $100, but the real price of an ink jet printer comes in the replacement cartridges.

Ink jets printers usually come in two flavors: regular and photo-quality. If you're doing photo printing, most of the time you'll get better results with the photo-quality printer. They usually cost a little more but are designed specially for photographs and the high quality required in printing them. When shopping for an ink jet, pay attention to the resolution advertised by the manufacturer, but also take that resolution promise with a grain of salt.

On the other hand, while ink jet printers usually do a beautiful job on photographs, especially on glossy paper, you'll often find ink jet printers produce somewhat fuzzy, jagged text for your printed documents.

Some photo-quality ink jets include extra features, such as a dedicated USB port for connecting your digital camera directly to the printer, built-in media card slots that let you plug in a storage card and hit a button for instant prints, and a special menu for selecting prints. All those features mean you can bypass your computer. But if you use their instant printing features, you don't get the option of first correcting and enhancing your image in Photoshop Elements. Where is the fun in that?

Laser Printers

Cost-wise, you can also purchase a black-and-white laser printer for under $100, but obviously a black-and-white printer won't work if you want a color print. So let's look at color laser printers. Designed for high-volume printing, color laser printers are among the most expensive printers you can purchase. Current prices run from $800 to $2,000 (or more), depending on the features offered, but like most electronics, that price will probably continue to drop. Only a few years ago, the average color laser printer cost around $20,000! Per page cost, however, laser printing is generally less money than an ink jet.

Laser printers don't use a wet ink process; instead, they use a dry toner, similar to a copy machine. The principal behind the laser printer is to apply the toner to the paper through a controlled electrostatic charge. Laser printers print razor sharp text, color charts, and other two-dimensional graphics, and if you need to print images for a layout, they produce acceptable quality. But oddly enough, when it comes to color photographs, most color laser printers can't match an ink jet printer's quality.

Printer Inks

The consumables cost of a printer plays a huge factor in image printing. With an ink jet printer, a color photograph can cost between 6 and 18 cents to print. Many ink jet manufactures include a single ink cartridge containing all three colors. If you print a lot of images with red in them, you'll obviously run out of red ink faster, and even though you have hardly used the green ink, you have to throw it away and replace the entire cartridge. Other manufacturers such as Canon, Epson, and HP sell models with individual cartridges for each color instead of one cartridge for all three colors. The downside is that while you save ink by replacing cartridges one at a time, the individual color cartridges cost a few dollars more, so per page, they end up costing about the same.

Another option is a do-it-yourself refill kit for ink cartridges. Some people think they are great, but most people find them messy, time-consuming, and feel that they produce a lower quality print. If your vendor offers higher capacity cartridges, you might want to take advantage of them as a better alternative. They cost more to purchase, but they contain twice the amount of ink, so they cost less per page.

On the other hand, color laser printers cost about 3 to 8 cents for a color page. Obviously, they are less expensive per page than ink jets, but the cost increases because color lasers have separate toner cartridges for each color, which can cost as much as $250 each. Even with their very high cost, however, in sufficient volume, the cost per page of a color laser's cartridges is still less than for color from an ink jet, because the yields are much higher, ranging from 6,000 to 12,000 pages.

Either way, with ink jet or laser printers, whether you buy the manufacturer's brand of ink cartridge or toner, or one from a third party, it comes down to being a matter of your preference. Some people prefer companies such as Canon, Epson, and HP because they formulate their printers, ink, and paper as a complete system, and they assume that if you buy from a third party, you may not get the results you expect. Others find that the third-party producers are equally good and less pricey.

Selecting Printer Options

You set some of the printer options in the Page Setup dialog box. Either from the Organizer or Editor workspace, choose File > Page Setup; then from the Page Setup box, click the Printer button.

Open Image First

If you are using the Editor workspace, the Page Setup command is unavailable if you don't have an image open.

Select the printer you will use for printing your images and click the Properties button. The printer property options vary, depending on the printer you use. In Figure 8-1, you see the options for a Canon printer while in Figure 8-2 you see the options for an HP PhotoSmart printer. As you notice, the Properties dialog boxes can vary a great deal so you'll have to look for specific printer settings in different locations.

Other Page Setup Options

You'll discover later that you can also access the Page Setup dialog box from several other print functions.

Figure 8-1
Setting Canon printer properties.

Figure 8-2
Setting HP PhotoSmart printer properties.

Determining Paper Size

From the Page Setup box, click the Paper drop-down list and select the paper size you want to use. Again, the options you have available depend on your printer make and model. As an example, if you want to print a 4"×6" print, you will probably want to select a 4×6 paper size. But what if you only have 5×7 photo paper on hand and you want to print a 4×6 photo? That's okay. Select the paper size you will actually use, in this example, the 5×7. When you get to the Print Preview box, that's where you'll determine the actual print size.

Portrait versus Landscape

When printing in portrait orientation, the longest dimension is vertical, while in landscape orientation, the longest dimension is horizontal. Photoshop Elements manages the orientation based on the printer and paper size, and you can also control it further through the Print Preview and Print Photos boxes.

Selecting a Paper Type

You'll find the quality and cost of your print also relies upon the type of paper you use. For best results, use photo quality paper, which is available in a number of sizes, such as 8.5×11 inches, 4×6 inches, 5×7 inches, and so forth. Photo paper costs more per page because the paper itself is more expensive. But hands down, using photo paper instead of regular paper produces a far better print.

Photo paper is available in a variety of finishes, such as glossy or matte. Glossy finishes provide a reflective, vibrant look to your images, while matte paper is specially formulated so that light won't bounce off the photos, which reduces reflection and adds depth. Photo paper resists fading and is smear-proof and water resistant, so your photos never lose their brilliance and can give your images a more professional photolab type of look.

Most people have a variety of sizes at their disposal. The smaller, individual sizes are, per inch, usually more expensive than the full page size papers. But if you just want to print a single picture of your new puppy or your son in his football uniform, you will probably want a single sheet of 3×5 or 4×6 inch paper. If, however, you plan on printing several

copies to hand out to Aunt Martha, Cousin Jack, and Grandma Mary, you should consider using the larger 8.5×11 inch paper for speed and economic reasons, because Photoshop Elements, as you soon discover, makes it easy to print multiple images or multiple copies of an image on a single sheet. You can even print out a page of wallet sizes so that you can give one to each of your friends.

Two other paper aspects you should consider because they also affect print quality are the brightness and the weight. The paper brightness, sometimes referred to as *whiteness*, is the measure of how much light is reflected from the paper. How white it is depends on how evenly it reflects colors. For example, if the paper reflects more blue than red or yellow, it will have a cool hue to it, making it appear even brighter than white, sometimes creating an optical impression because cool white sheets tend to brighten colors. A bright white surface is perfect for high-resolution digital photos, as well as cherished family photos. You'll get realistic skin tones and true photo quality. Don't worry, though, you don't have to stand there and figure out the reflection value yourself. The paper manufacturers list the brightness levels on the packages. Most photo papers have a brightness level between 90 and 104.

Paper weight is measured in pounds or mil. The higher the mil or the heavier the weight, the thicker and sturdier the paper is, making it more durable for framing, albums, and frequent handling than the standard paper you use for printing documents or making copies. Standard copy paper is usually a 20-pound paper and cardstock is around 110 pounds. You'll find a pretty good range in photo papers running from around 45 pound to 88 pound. Keep the paper weight in mind when determining the final use for your image.

To select the correct paper type, follow these steps:

1. From the Page Setup dialog box, click Printer. A different Page Setup dialog box appears. This is the dialog box where you select which printer you want to use.

2. Click the Properties button.

3. Locate the Media Type or Paper Type setting and chose the paper type you plan on using to print your image. In Figure 8-3, I've selected a glossy photo paper.

Figure 8-3
Selecting a paper type.

4. Click OK three times to close all the dialog boxes.

Picking a Print Quality

Picking a print quality is also important. At a low or draft quality, the ink doesn't fill up as much of an area. The advantage is that it's a quick and cheap way to print, but the disadvantage is that you get a very poor quality print and the image can look granulated. If you're just running a test to see how an image looks on paper, you can probably go for a standard quality print, but if it is for your final print of a picture, you'll want the best quality available. To select a print quality:

1. Choose File > Page Setup and then from the Page Setup dialog box, click Printer. A second Page Setup dialog box appears. This is the dialog box where you select which printer you want to use.

2. Click the Properties button.

3. Choose a Print Quality setting.

4. Click OK three times to close all the dialog boxes.

Printing from the Editor

You'll find that printing from the Editor workspace is slightly different than printing through the Organizer workspace. The main difference is the Editor workspace can save you time and paper by allowing you to examine your images and the settings prior to the actual print. Photoshop Elements has a Print Preview feature available when you are in the Editor workspace. The Print Preview dialog box displays information such as the orientation, size, and page edges. Let's take a look. Choose File > Print. The Print Preview dialog box shown in Figure 8-4 appears.

Hide Unwanted Layers

By default, Photoshop Elements prints all visible layers. If you don't want a layer included when you print, hide the layer (see Chapter 3).

Preview pane   *Rotate arrows*   *Border color selection*

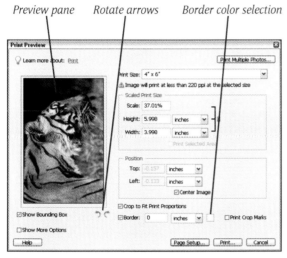

Figure 8-4
Preview before you print.

From here, you can make many selections regarding printing your image:

▶ **Print Size**: Allows you to specify the size of the printed image: Choose Actual Size, Fit on Page, or select one of several preset sizes such as 4×6 or 5×7.

Print Multiple Photographs

Clicking the Print Multiple Photos button launches the Organizer where you can print multiples.

▶ **Scaled Print Size**: Allows you to enter specific values you want in the Scale, Height, and Width text boxes. If you choose a preset size in the Print Size list, you will see the selected size reflected here.

▶ **Print Selected Area**: This option is only available if you preselected a portion of the image before opening the Print Preview dialog box. The preselected area cannot have any feathering.

▶ **Position**: Determines where, on the printable area of the paper, the image should print. Center is the default option. To reposition an image, deselect Center Image and either enter specific values in the top and left text boxes or drag the preview image to a different position.

▶ **Crop to Fit Print Proportions**: This option assures that the photo prints at the size chosen from the Print Size menu. The option is on by default, so if you choose a print size that doesn't match the photo perfectly, Photoshop Elements scales and crops the photo so it fits the paper. Figure 8-5 shows two images, the top image without cropping and the bottom image with the cropping option turned on.

Preview Cropping

Look closely at your image in the Preview pane to make sure nothing is cropped off the image that you don't want cropped.

Figure 8-5
Checking cropping for cutoff edges.

▶ **Border:** When checked, this option prints a border around an image. You specify the width of the border by entering a number and choosing inches, millimeters (mm), or points. You can also click the color selection box to specify a color for the border.

Printing Changes

Changes you make in the Print Preview dialog box, such as scaling or borders, affect only how the image prints, not the actual image.

▶ **Print Crop Marks:** Prints guidelines around all four edges of the photo, making it easier to see where to trim the photo.

▶ **Show Bounding Box:** Displays a box with corner handles around the preview image, which you can use to manually scale the image size.

▶ **Show More Options:** Check this box to expand the Print Preview dialog box so it displays additional options, including printing the file name above the photo or printing the image caption in a 9-point Helvetica type. The extended dialog box also shows drop-down lists for color management. See Chapter 5.

When you are ready to print your image, click the Print button. From the Print dialog box, select the number of copies you want and then click the OK button.

Printing from the Organizer

Printing images from the Organizer workspace is slightly different from the Editor workspace mainly because you can print multiple images each on its own page or multiple images on a single page. Like the Editor workspace, Photoshop Elements includes a place for you to preview your settings before you actually print them, although oddly enough, the folks at Photoshop Elements don't actually call it Print Preview like they do in the Editor workspace.

The best way to print your images is by first selecting what images you want to print. In the Photo Browser, click once on the first image you want; then hold down the Ctrl key and click on each subsequent image. If you don't select photos first, Photoshop Elements asks whether you want to use all photos in the Photo Browser.

Printing Video Files

You can also select to print video files, but only the first frame will print, and because videos are typically low resolution, the quality is likely to be quite poor.

Choose File > Print. You see the Print Photos dialog box in Figure 8-6. You'll need to select a number of print options and then click the Print button to actually begin the printing process.

Figure 8-6
The Organizer's print dialog box.

Basic Print Options

Notice the Print Photos dialog box is broken into three main sections. On the left, you see a gallery of the images you selected for printing. In the middle, you see the print preview with your current settings along with navigation arrows, which allow you to view the different selected images. On the right you see the printing options. As you change print options, the preview section updates to reflect the changes. Let's take a look at those printing options:

1. Select your printer, the type of paper you plan on using, and the paper size. You also need to determine if you want the image printed in portrait or landscape orientation. Check the Borderless check box if you want the printer to print all the way to the edge of the paper instead of leaving a small amount of white border.

Specify Page Printing Options

Optionally, click the Page Setup button to specify page printing options.

2. Select whether you want to print each picture individually or to print on a contact sheet, picture package, or labels. For now, choose Individual Prints. You'll learn more about printing contact sheets, picture packages, and labels later in this chapter.

3. Select the actual print size, how many images go on a sheet of paper, and how many copies you want to print of each photo. You also can uncheck the Crop to Fit option if you don't want Photoshop Elements to scale and crop the photo so it fits to the paper.

Printing Multiple Copies

If you select a print size that allows multiple copies of the individual image on a single page, deselect the One Photo Per Page option and enter a number in the Use Each Photo text box.

Additional Print Options

Click the More Options button. The More Options dialog box appears. Most of these options are the same as you discovered in the Print Preview window in the Editor workspace. You can print the image file name, date, and image caption. You can add a border and specify the thickness and color for the border. You can print the crop marks, and you can also choose Invert Image, which flips the image so you can create a transfer for printing on T-shirts and other similar items.

A very important feature in the More Options dialog box is the Max Print Resolution box (see Figure 8-7). By default, the option is tuned to the lowest setting of 220 PPI, but generally that doesn't provide for a very crisp printed image. If you want a much higher resolution on your image, you'll probably want the maximum, which is 600 DPI. Most importantly, you can select the correct color profile. (Refer to Chapter 5 for more information on PPI, DPI, resolution, and color profiles.)

Figure 8-8
Adding more images to print.

Figure 8-7
Choosing additional printing options.

Adding Additional Images

If you didn't pick up all the images you wanted to print before you opened the Print Photos dialog box, don't despair. You don't have to close the dialog box and possibly lose all the options you've already selected. Photoshop Elements provides a button where you can add additional images to the selection gallery. Simply follow these steps:

1. Click the Add button. Photoshop Elements displays the Add Photos dialog box you see in Figure 8-8. You can use this dialog box to further filter the images you already have selected or to pick additional images.

2. In the Add Photos From section, determine if you want to select images from the entire catalog or just from the current Photo Browser view. You can also further filter the image display, according to its tag or collection.

3. Place a check mark in the box next to any items you want to add to the print selection.

Select All Images

To quickly select all the currently displayed images, click the Select All option.

4. Click the Done button.

Delete From Print

To delete an image from the print selection, click the image and choose Remove.

Producing Contact Sheets

You use contact sheets, sometimes referred to as *index prints*, to review thumbnail size photo images so you can decide which ones you want to be printed full size. They also make excellent visual catalogs of archived photos since they consist of multiple thumbnail size photos printed on a single sheet of paper.

The initial steps for creating contact sheets are the same as for individual prints. First, you select the images you want to print; then choose File > Print. Next, you perform step 1 in the Print Photos dialog box, which consists of selecting your printer, paper type, paper size, and orientation. You'll probably want standard letter size paper for your contact sheets.

Contact Sheet Margins

You cannot change the margins around the contact sheet page setup.

From the Select Type of Print drop-down list, choose Contact Sheet. The preview section shown in Figure 8-9 shows the sheet with 16 thumbnails in a 4×4 layout; however, you can select up to nine columns, although I guarantee you won't be able to see the images in a nine-column format. It's best to stick with three or four columns. The thumbnail size and number of rows adjust according to your choice, and if the number of photos exceeds the capacity of a single page, more pages are added to accommodate them. You can also add text, such as the file name, date, and caption under each image, or add page numbering to the page footer area.

More Options

Click the More Options button to select the color profile.

Figure 8-9
Setting up a contact sheet.

Packaging Your Pictures

Photoshop Elements also provides settings so you can create picture packages, similar to those that school pictures come in. You know the ones where Dad gets a 5×7 for his desk, Grandma gets a 3×5, and each aunt and uncle get a wallet size. The following steps show you how to create a picture package:

1. Select the images you want to print.

2. Choose File > Print, which opens the Print Photos dialog box.

3. Select your printer along with the paper type and size. Most picture packages use regular letter size paper.

4. Check the Borderless check box if you want the printer to print all the way to the edge of the paper instead of leaving a small amount of white border.

5. From the Select Type of Print list, choose Picture Package. The options in step 3 change to allow for Picture Package options.

6. Click the Select a Layout drop-down list and select an option. Twenty different combinations of images sizes are available. Figure 8-10 shows a package with two of the 4×5 prints, two wallet size 2.5×3.5 prints, and four smaller 2×2.5 prints.

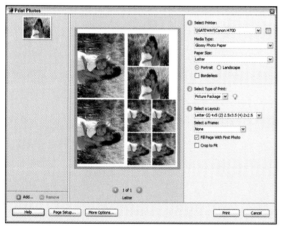

Figure 8-10
Printing a picture package.

Print Orientation

Depending on the layout you choose, Photoshop Elements orients the images to produce the optimum coverage of the printable area. You cannot override the image orientation in a picture package.

7. Optionally, select a frame to place around each image in the package.

8. If you want the entire page to consist of a single image, click Fill Page with First Photo.

Replace Images

To place a different photo in the layout, drag the desired image from the image gallery on top of the preview image.

9. Choose Crop to Fit to crop photos so they fit the layout size perfectly.

Choose a Color Profile

Click the More Options button to select the color profile.

10. Click Print to print the picture package.

Making Labels

Photoshop Elements currently provides four different commercial label sizes you can use to create labels featuring your favorite photo. Photoshop Elements labels are really another form of a picture package, except that instead of plain paper, you use peel and stick label stock and the images are arranged to fit appropriately, according to label stock guidelines.

Like picture packages, you first select the image or images you want and then choose File > Print. Select your printer and paper type. The paper size should be letter. From the Select Type of Print drop-down list, choose Labels and choose a layout. All four options are based on Avery label sizes. Table 8-1 lists the four label numbers and their sizes.

You now see the labels options, such as those shown in Figure 8-11.

Label sizes

Figure 8-11
Printing labels.

Optionally, choose the Crop to Fit option, and if you want the entire page of labels filled with a single photo, choose the Fill Page with First Photo option. For a nice finish to your label, pick a frame from the Select a Frame drop-down list. In Figure 8-12, you see a business card with the Antique Rectangle 2 border around the image.

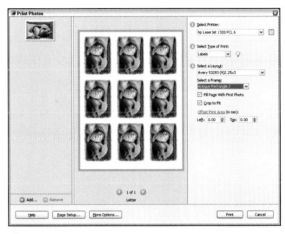

Figure 8-12
Adding a border to surround your labels.

Sometimes, items don't print exactly where you want them, according to the label margins. Before you print on your expensive label paper, first run a test print on plain paper. Lay the paper over your sheet of labels to see if the images and labels align. If the images and labels do not match, you can use the Offset Print Area controls to make adjustments. Negative values shift the printed images either to the left or up, and positive values shift the printed images either to the right or down.

Table 8-1 Avery Label Sizes

Label #	Qty Per Sheet	Size
53265	2	7×4.875
53270	3	3.75×5.875
53271	2	6×4
53283	9	2.25×3

Saving as Your Desktop Wallpaper

YOU PROBABLY ALREADY KNOW how to change your desktop wallpaper using Windows, but just in case, here's a refresher. Right-click a blank area of your desktop and choose Properties. From the Desktop tab, click the Browse button and locate the image you want to use. That's simple enough, right?

There's another way that you can make any photo or even a set of photos the background picture on your computer screen. Simply follow these steps:

1. From the Photo Browser, select the photo or photos you want to use.

2. Choose Edit > Set as Desktop Wallpaper. If you selected more than one photo, the photos are tiled on the screen similar to those you see in Figure 8-13.

Tiled Image Quantities

You'll find that multiple tiled images work best if you have 4, 16, or 36 images.

Figure 8-13
Saving images as desktop wallpaper.

Employing Professional Printing Services

YOU'VE DISCOVERED THROUGHOUT this book how you can manipulate your images and print them yourself to achieve a near professional quality print. But you have other options as well. You can take them to your nearest brick and mortar store, or you can route them through the Internet to a quality online printing service.

It may be a tough decision—do it yourself or have a professional do it? Let's take a look at the pros and cons of sending the images outside your building for printing. Almost all chain drugstores and discount stores have their own photo labs and often they can print your images for less than it costs you to do it. However, typically, your images get printed by a person with a minimal amount of training who generally knows how to operate the equipment, but isn't as skilled in color management, profiles, and other printing options. If you carefully prepare your images before you take them for printing, you should be okay. You can also take your images for processing to a photo specialty store where they generally have professional technicians, but be prepared to pay a little more.

If you send the images to an online service, you usually get a professional print at a very reasonable cost. The disadvantage is that you have to provide the online service company with your credit card information and in today's world of identity theft, many people are reluctant to do that. The solution is to deal with reputable online service centers that provide adequate security measures on their Web sites.

One advantage is that the online services let you share images and order prints easily over the Internet. However, as you see later in this chapter, with Photoshop Elements you can e-mail your images or create your own Web Gallery for your favorite images.

Using the Order Prints Palette

So you've decided to order some prints online. Photoshop Elements makes the process very easy by using the Order Prints palette. You'll find the Order Prints palette in the Organizer workspace. The following steps walk you through the process:

Display the Order Prints Palette

If you don't see the Order Prints palette, choose Window > Order Prints.

1. Before you can order prints, you must first set up a recipient. Click the New button on the Order Prints palette. You see the New Order Prints Recipient dialog box shown in Figure 8-14

2. Enter your (or the recipient's) name, address, and other contact information. Fields marked with an asterisk * are required fields.

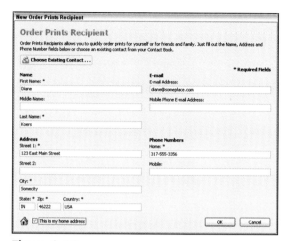

Figure 8-14
Entering recipient information.

Select From Contact Book

Optionally, click the Choose Existing Contact and select a recipient from the Contact Book. See "Managing the Contact Book" later in this chapter.

3. Click OK. Once you set up a recipient (target), his or her name appears in the Order Prints palette.

Edit Recipient

To edit a recipient, select the recipient name and click the Edit button. You cannot edit a target while an order is pending.

4. Select and drag the photos you want printed onto the intended recipient name in the Order Prints palette. Photoshop Elements displays the number of images you want printed, and a Confirm Order button appears next to the recipient name. You can drag images as many times as you want.

5. To remove images from the order, double-click the recipient name, which displays the Order Prints for *name* dialog box, such as the one seen in Figure 8-15. The dialog box contains a thumbnail of your selected images. A zoom control is located at the bottom of the dialog box, and if you want to remove any image, select the image and choose Remove Selected Photo from Order. Click OK and close the Order Prints dialog box.

Figure 8-15
Reviewing images before printing.

6. When you are ready to order the prints, click the Confirm Order button by the recipient's name. The Welcome to Adobe Photoshop Services dialog box appears. The first time you use the service, you must create an account and a password (see Figure 8-16).

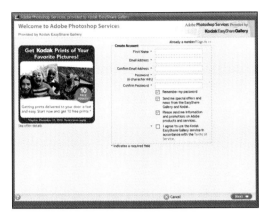

Figure 8-16
Create an Adobe Photoshop Services account.

7. Enter your information. Make sure to read the terms agreement and check the box. If you have already created an account, click the Sign in link and enter your e-mail address and password.

8. Click Next. The Review Order Details dialog box seen in Figure 8-17 appears.

9. Confirm or edit the sizes and quantities you want and click the Checkout button.

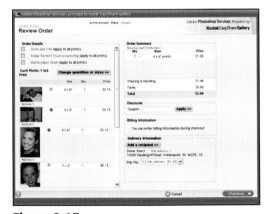

Figure 8-17
Review your order for quantities, shipping method, and pricing.

10. Enter your credit card information and then click Place Order. A printable confirmation screen with your order number appears.

11. Click Upload Photos. Photoshop Elements displays an Upload Progress window, which you can close when the upload finishes. Sit back and wait for the mailman!

Ordering Online Prints from the Editor Workspace

In the previous section, you discovered you could quickly order prints online by simply dragging and dropping images into the Order Prints palette. While that's an easy process, you may have an image in the Editor workspace that you want to order. Choose File > Order Prints. Photoshop Elements launches or switches to the Organizer workspace and launches the Adobe Photoshop Services order form. Create an account or log in if prompted to do so. (See the previous section.) If you have previously ordered through the Adobe Photoshop Services, you aren't prompted to log in (see Figure 8-18).

Choose the size and quantity for each print and then continue with the order process.

Figure 8-18
Review your order for size and quantities.

Creating Web Galleries

Photoshop Elements provides several online photo sharing services where you can post your images to the Internet and invite others to take a look. Some of the services are free, while others are fee based. You upload images to the services server, and the service automatically sends e-mails to whomever you specify, notifying them of the Web Gallery.

Adobe Photoshop Showcase

Let's take a look at how the Adobe Photoshop Showcase, one of the free online services you access from within Photoshop Elements, works. Follow these steps to create your own Photoshop Showcase Gallery:

1. Select the images you want to share. Do not mix video and photographs. You can create a gallery for either, but they cannot be mixed into the same gallery.

2. Click the Share button located on the Shortcuts bar.

3. Choose Share with Adobe Photoshop Showcase and then choose Share Photos (or choose Share Video if you selected video clips). Photoshop Elements launches the Adobe Photoshop Showcase wizard.

4. The first time you share your files, you are prompted to join, which creates your free account (see Figure 8-19). For future visits, you only need to log in. Enter your information and click Next.

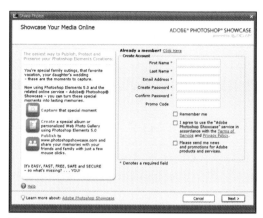

Figure 8-19
Create an account or log-in.

5. Enter a descriptive name for your gallery, such as Susie's Birthday Party or Vacation to Mexico. Then click Next.

6. Click the recipient names you want to notify (see Figure 8-20). If you have addresses in the Photoshop Elements contact book, you can click the Import Addresses button to import them into the Adobe Photoshop Showcase. If you don't have a desired recipient listed, click the Add New Contact link, which displays the Add New Contact screen. You can enter your recipient's name and e-mail address; then click Save.

Make Photographs Public

If you want to share the images publicly with the whole Photoshop Showcase community, click the Everyone check box.

No Guest Information Required

Your guests don't need to register to view your photos and videos.

Figure 8-20
Determine who can view your photo gallery.

7. Click the Next button and Photoshop Elements uploads the selected images to the Adobe Photoshop Showcase. A confirmation box appears and invitational e-mails like the one shown in Figure 8-21 are sent to the selected recipients. The recipient simply clicks the See It Now button to view your photo gallery.

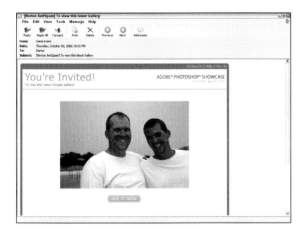

Figure 8-21
The recipient's e-mail.

Delete a Gallery

To delete a gallery, go to www.photoshop-showcase.com. Click My Account and then click My Galleries. Select the gallery you want to delete. Click Settings and choose Delete.

Kodak Easyshare Gallery

The Kodak Easyshare gallery is similar to the Adobe Photoshop Showcase, but it offers the viewer the opportunity to purchase prints, coffee mugs, pillowcases, clothing, teddy bears, mouse pads, and lots of other photo items. The viewer sees the gallery in a slide show format. Figure 8-22 shows a Web Gallery from the Kodak Easyshare Gallery.

Figure 8-22
A Kodak Easyshare Gallery.

To delete a Kodak Easyshare Gallery, follow these steps:

1. Sign in at www.adobe.kodakgallery.com.

2. Click View and Edit Photos.

3. Choose the gallery you want to delete.

4. Click Edit Details and Rearrange.

5. On the left side of the screen, click Delete Album and click Yes to confirm the deletion.

SmugMug

SmugMug is a photo gallery that doesn't have any advertising to distract you, but charges an annual fee. At the time of this writing, the fee was approximately $40 per year for unlimited storage. Like the Kodak Easyshare Gallery, you can order prints and other gifts from SmugMug. Additionally, SmugMug allows you to edit your images, add themes, and view the photos in timelines. Figure 8-23 shows a page from the SmugMug Web site.

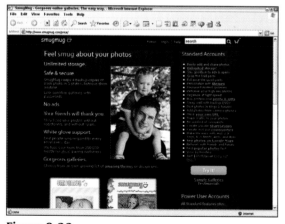

Figure 8-23
SmugMug.

CEIVA Digital Photo Frame

CEIVA is dramatically different from the other sharing services in that the recipient doesn't go directly to a Web site to view your images. CEIVA sells a digital photo frame that updates and displays your photos, via the Internet, and then displays them in a slide show format. The membership to CEIVA is free, but the digital photo frame is around $130.00 (see Figure 8-24).

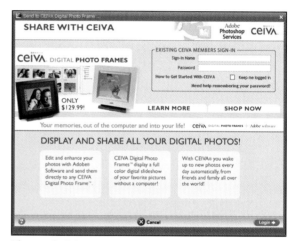

Figure 8-24
The CEIVA digital photo frame.

Designing a Slide Show

THINK OF A SLIDE SHOW as a slow motion movie. In Chapter 4, you discovered that you could view your images at any time in your own personal slide show. But what about your friend Donald, who lives 1,000 miles away? Photoshop Elements slide shows are a unique way to share photos. With Photoshop Elements, you can combine slide shows with music clips, clip art, text, and even voice narration, creating an ultimate multimedia experience.

After you create the slide show, you can save it as an Adobe Portable Document Format (PDF) file or convert it to a Windows Movie Video (WMV) file. Windows usually plays a WMV file using Windows Media Player, which comes with Microsoft Windows. If you choose the PDF format, anyone can view the slide show using the free Adobe Reader program. If your friend Donald has a computer, he probably already has the Adobe Reader program, but if not, anyone can get it for free from www.adobe.com.

Creating a Slide Show

Since slide shows involve a number of images related to a single topic, such as a birthday party or vacation, using the Organizer workspace tends to be the easiest place to collect the images. It's not a requirement, but I recommend you create a collection and drag the images you want to use into that collection. The first step in creating a slide show involves selecting the images you want. The images don't need to be the same size or even the same orientation. In fact, having a variety of dimensions helps keep your slide show interesting to the viewer.

After selecting the images you want, choose Create > Slide Show from the Shortcuts toolbar. The Slide Show Preferences dialog box like the one shown in Figure 8-25 appears.

Figure 8-25
Determining slide show preferences.

You can set your preferences now or click OK to begin organizing the slide show. Even though you can return to the Slide Show Preferences at any time, let's take a look now at the Slide Show Preferences dialog box:

Global versus Individual Slide Options

Options you apply in the Slide Show Preferences box apply to the entire slide show, but you'll see later in this chapter how you can change many options as they apply to an individual image.

▶ **Static Duration**: Determines how long the image stays on the screen.

▶ **Transition**: Specifies how images change from one to the next.

▶ **Transition Duration**: Establishes the transition length of time. Some transitions take longer to achieve, requiring longer transition durations.

▶ **Background Color**: Sets the default color that displays around photos on every slide.

▶ **Apply Pan & Zoom to All Slides**: Applies a random panning, which changes the focus of a photo from one area to another over a period of time, and it applies zooming (magnification) to the slide images. This feature doesn't work with a PDF slide show.

▶ **Include Photo Captions as Text**: Adds any previously attached photo captions to the slide image.

▶ **Include Audio Captions as Narration**: Adds any previously created the audio captions to the slide image.

▶ **Repeat Soundtrack Until Last Slide**: Loops the music until the show is done; however, this feature is also not available with a PDF slide show.

▶ **Crop to Fit Slide**: Crops the photos so they are all the same size. As mentioned earlier, variety is good on a slide show, so I don't recommend that you check this option.

▶ **Preview Playback Options**: Applies a playback quality of High, Medium, or Low. Higher qualities take longer to load, but provide a much better show.

Turn Off Dialog Box

If you don't want to see this dialog box when you create a slide show, remove the check mark from Show This Dialog Each Time a New Slide Show Is Created.

The next screen you see is where you'll do all the work. It's the Slide Show Editor screen that you see in Figure 8-26, and it holds all the tools you need for creating your slide show.

Return to Preferences

To return to the Slide Show Preferences, choose Edit > Slide Show Preferences.

Slide controls   *Palette Bin*

Shortcut toolbar

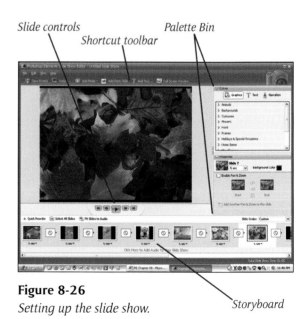

Storyboard

Figure 8-26

Setting up the slide show.

Maximize Editor Window

To get the most out of the Slide Show Editor window, make sure the window is maximized.

Beginning at the top of the window, you'll see a toolbar with commonly used slide show tools. From the toolbar, you can save your slide show (Photoshop Elements calls it a project); determine whether you want the slide show in a PDF or WMV format; add additional photos, audio, and video; add blank slides; add text to annotate a slide; and view the slide show in a full screen preview mode.

Save Often!

To protect yourself, save your slide show project frequently. When you save a slide show, it appears in the Organizer as a thumbnail with a slide show icon. Double-click the thumbnail to reopen the Slide Show Editor window.

On the right side of the screen is the Palette Bin. I'm sure by this time, you're very familiar with using the Palette Bin, but now the Palette Bin contains an Extras palette and a Properties palette.

Under the larger image, you see a series of controls. You use these controls to monitor transitions, audio, and timings you assign to your slide show.

Finally, along the bottom of the screen, you see a storyboard, which displays thumbnail-sized slide show images, arranged in the order they appear in the slide show. See Figure 8-27.

Figure 8-27
A slide show storyboard.

From the storyboard, you can do the following:

▶ **Select a Slide Order:** Click the Slide Order drop-down box and choose from the option list such as date or folder location.

▶ **Manually Rearrange the Slide Order:** From the storyboard, drag a slide to a desired position. As you drag the image, a blue bar appears where the slide will appear.

Reorder Slides All At Once

Click the Quick Reorder button to display a window where you can see all of your slides at the same time, allowing you to quickly drag and drop them into the desired position. Click the Back button when finished.

▶ **Delete a Slide:** Right-click a storyboard slide and choose Delete Slide. Choosing Delete Slide only deletes the slide from the slide show, not the hard drive or the Organizer.

▶ **Set Timings:** Click the timing duration value underneath a slide and then choose a timing option.

▶ **Add Transitions:** Click the box to the right of a slide to add a transition. See more about adding transitions in the next section.

Exit Slide Show Editor

To exit the Slide Show Editor window and return to the Organizer workspace, click the Close box, press Ctrl+Q, or choose File > Exit Slide Show Editor.

Transitioning Slides

A slide transition is a useful special effect that displays the next slide in the presentation. For example, in a Fade transition, the next slide gradually materializes, while in a Blinds transition, the next slide appears with an effect similar to opening Venetian blinds. Not only do transitions provide visual interest, but audiences seem to like transitions as a short breather, giving them a moment to digest what they just viewed.

When you click the transition box at the right of any slide, you see the Properties palette change to accommodate transitions, such as Figure 8-28. When you click the Transition arrow, you see a list of 23 different transition styles, plus an option to let the slide show randomly pick a transition. Some transitions, such as Pinwheel or Fan Wipe, then display an option to set the direction the transition should run.

After you add a transition, the icon to the right of the storyboard thumbnail changes to reflect the transition.

Figure 8-28
Properties palette for transition options.

Editing Slide Properties

If a slide needs slight editing, you can perform minor adjustments from the Properties palette. Select a slide and click the photo in the main preview window. A boundaries box appears around the image, and the Properties palette displays options pertaining to editing the slide. Figure 8-29 shows a selected image and its properties box. You can do any of the following by using the Properties palette:

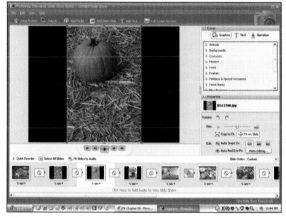

Figure 8-29
Editing Properties palette.

▶ **Rotate**: Click either arrow to rotate the image. Rotating some images causes a huge loss in quality.

▶ **Resize**: Adjust the photo size using the Size slider.

Reposition a Photo

If a photo isn't positioned in a slide just where you want it, use the bounding box to adjust the photo's position.

▶ **Crop to Fit**: Use this option to fill the slide with the image. You can use your mouse to drag the image around so the slide displays different areas of the image.

▶ **Fit on Slide**: Use this option to resize the photo, forcing it to fit proportionally in the slide area, and, if necessary, filling in slide areas around the image with the background color.

▶ **Auto Smart Fix**: Click this option to instantly edit the photo color balance.

▶ **Auto Red Eye Fix**: Click this option to remove photo red eye.

▶ **Special Effects**: Click one of the three buttons to add or remove special effects of Black and White or Sepia. The first button, Normal, removes the Black and White or Sepia effect.

▶ **More Editing**: Click this button to open the image in the Editor workspace. Make any desired corrections, and then save and close the photo. Photoshop Elements returns you to the Slide Show Editor window.

Adding Images

Did you forget a photo you wanted to include in your slide show? That's okay because Photoshop Elements provides a simple way to add additional images to the show. From the toolbar, click Add Media > Select Photos and Videos from Organizer.

In the Add Photos dialog box seen in Figure 8-30, click the check box next to the photo you want to add. You can use this dialog box to further filter the images you already have selected or to pick additional images. Click the Add Selected Photos button and then click Done.

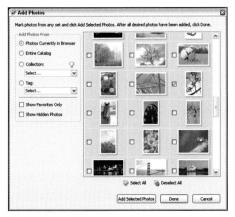

Figure 8-30
Adding additional photographs.

Placing Text

At one time or another, you've probably seen a Microsoft PowerPoint presentation that includes slides with text on them, usually starting with a title slide. While you can place text on any slide, you can also add a blank slide you can use for a title or other purpose. Click the Add Blank Slide button located on the toolbar. Photoshop Elements adds a blank slide to the storyboard, filled with the background color.

Add Blank Slide

Another way to add a blank slide is by choosing Edit > Blank Slide.

Begin by clicking from the storyboard, the slide to which you want to add text. Photoshop Elements provides two methods of adding text:

▶ **From the Extras palette, click the Text button.** The Text palette displays a variety of predefined font styles you can use on your slide. If you see one you like, drag the text icon onto your slide. Photoshop Elements places a text box object styled in the text you selected. Double-click the text object to type your text.

▶ **Click the Add Text button on the toolbar.** An Edit Text box appears where you type the text you want; then click OK. By default, Photoshop Elements uses a Tahoma font, in a 36-point, white color until you add text using the Extras palette. Then the last used style becomes the default font for the current slide slow.

There's a reason Photoshop Elements changes the default font. Studies have shown that too many different fonts in a presentation can be distracting, and for general good style you shouldn't mix too many different fonts. However, that doesn't mean you can't change fonts! It really depends on your slide show's overall message. Notice that the Properties palette changes to reflect text options. From here, you can click any text object and change the properties for only that text object.

You can change the font type, size, style, alignment, color, or even add shadow effects to your text. There is also an option for opacity. If you want the slide contents to be visible through the text, set the text to a lower opacity percentage. See the text example in Figure 8-31.

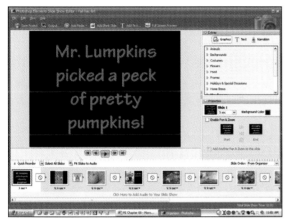

Figure 8-31
Placing text on a slide.

After you type your text, if you decide you want it wrapped differently, use the handles around the text box to resize it. Dragging the size handle doesn't resize the text size, only the layout.

Delete Text

To delete the text, right-click the text box and select Delete or just select the text and press the Delete key.

Including Clip Art and Narrations

Photoshop Elements includes a wide variety of clip art that you can add to your slides. Most of the time, you won't want clip art on an image, as it generally distracts from the photograph, but it can be quite an attraction on title or text slides.

Narration, on the other hand, helps you explain a thought behind an image. In order to add narration to your slides, however, you must have a microphone attached to your computer. Earlier in the chapter, you discovered you can add voice captions. Narrations can also serve as voice captioning.

Let's take a look at adding these items to your slides.

1. For clip art, select the slide you want to place the graphic on and then click the Graphics button in the Extras palette. A list of graphic categories appear, such as those seen in Figure 8-32.

2. Click the arrow next to any category to expand or collapse the category.

3. Select the graphic you want and drag it onto the slide preview.

After adding the graphic, you can resize it by dragging a handle around the bounding box, move it by dragging it to a different location, or delete the graphic by pressing the Delete key.

Figure 8-32
Adding clip art.

You can add a narration to a specific slide by selecting the slide and choosing the Narration button on the Extras palette. If you have a microphone hooked up to your system, you can use the controls to record your own narration, or you can click the Use an Existing Audio File icon to locate a prerecorded narration for the slide. Available formats include .MP3, .WAV, .WMA, and .AC3 audio files. If you choose to record your own narration, click the Record button and speak into the microphone. The Record button turns into a Stop button, which you click when you finish your narration recording. Other controls include the volume level, playing back the recording, and deleting the recording.

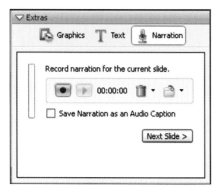

Making Beautiful Music Together

If you are like most of us, you probably observed on television or the Internet, the slide show depicting the horrific events of September 11th, 2001, viewed to the tune of Enya singing "Only Time." That was a classic example of music seriously enhancing the impact of the slide show.

Adding Music

Photoshop Elements also provides the opportunity to enhance your slide show by importing music from your Organizer catalog or from any location on your computer. Just follow these steps:

1. Click the Add Media button on the toolbar.

2. Choose Audio from Folder. If you already have the music added to your Organizer, choose Audio from Organizer. The Choose Your Audio Files dialog box in Figure 8-33 appears.

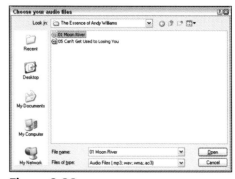

Figure 8-33
Select the audio file you want to use.

3. Navigate to and select the audio file you want to use and click the Open button. The music file name appears under the storyboard.

Trim handles

Add Audio to Organizer

When you select an audio clip from the folder, Photoshop Elements automatically adds it to the Organizer.

Pacing the Music

After you add an audio file, take a look at the Properties palette. The Properties dialog box displays the audio file name and length. You can add additional music to lengthen the music time if you need it, or you can shorten the length of the current music.

The default timing for each slide was five seconds, but clicking the timing duration value underneath a slide allows you to select a specific timing for each slide. One other option is to click the Fit Slides to Audio button (at the top of the storyboard), which takes the total music length and divides it up evenly between the slides in your slide show. For example, as you see in Figure 8-34, the music clip is 2 minutes and 48 seconds (168 seconds total) in length, and there are 12 slides, so by clicking the Fit Slides to Audio option, each slide timing is 14 seconds.

Now, 14 seconds may not seem like a long time for a single picture in a slide show, but it really is. In fact, it's too long. An audience would soon walk away from a slide show if the images displayed lasted 14 seconds each. So there are two options: either add more slides to the presentation or shorten the music time.

Figure 8-34
Manage the audio file length.

From the Properties palette, you can control the music length. At the beginning and the end of the Trim Audio bar, you can shorten the song from the beginning, the end, or both. Drag the trim handles at the left to shorten the music from the beginning or drag the right side trim handles to shorten it from the end. In most situations, it's best to trim from the end, but that really depends on the music track you selected.

Display Audio Settings

If the Properties palette doesn't show the audio settings, click the music file name under the storyboard.

As you drag the timing arrows, the music duration indicator changes to reflect the new timing. To see the effect on your slides, click the Fit Slides to Audio button to refresh the slide timings. A good average timing is between 5 and 8 seconds.

Let's take a look at one other option about working with music files. If you don't want the music to begin until it gets to a particular slide, slide 3, for example, drag the music file bar under the storyboard, to the right until it begins under the slide where you want it to start.

Selecting Slide Show Output

You've worked very hard to get your slide show just right, and now it's time to share it. When you click the Output button on the Shortcuts toolbar, Photoshop Elements provides several different output types: Save as a File, Burn to Disk, E-mail Slide Show, or Send to TV.

Let's review a couple of the output methods. Figure 8-35 shows the Save as a File options.

Figure 8-35
Determine the output method for your slide show.

▶ **Save as a File**: This option saves your slide show in either a PDF format or a WMV format. You can select a slide size, which you determine by your intended viewers' screen resolution. The resolution also determines the file size. For example, in a two-minute slide show with 14 slides and music attached, when saved as a WMV file at a 800 x 600 resolution, the file size is around 4.30 MB. The same slide show saved as a PDF file in an 800×600 resolution is 3.31 MB and in a medium 1024×768 resolution is 4.84 MB. You should know that most of today's monitors run at a 1024×768 or higher resolution. If you select a PDF format, there are two other options: Loop, which automatically replays the show over and over, and Manual Advance, which prohibits the show from automatically advancing from slide to slide. The viewer must click the mouse to view the next slide.

Transitions Change as a PDF File

When saved as a PDF file, some transitions appear different than originally created.

▶ **Burn to Disc:** This option saves your slide show as a WMV file on a DVD or Video CD (also known as a VCD). While the DVD burn uses a process that provides much better quality, you can only burn directly to the CD if you have Adobe Premier Elements, an accessory program to Adobe Photoshop Elements. Burning directly to a VCD gives a lower resolution than using a DVD, but is readily available if you have a CD burner on your computer. You also have an option to put other Photoshop Elements slide shows on the CD as well. Slide shows burned to a VCD can be played on any computer with a CD drive (see Figure 8-36).

Save as WMV

Another good option is to save the file as a WMV in the size you want and then use Windows to manually burn it to a CD.

▶ **E-mail Slide Show:** Saves the slide show as a .PDF or .WMV and then prompts you for recipient information. See the next section "Sharing Images via E-mail" for more information.

▶ **Send to TV:** This option, seen in Figure 8-37, creates a WMV file that, along with your Windows XP Media Center Edition computer, can output to your television. You can choose settings such as Standard Definition, Wide Screen, or High Definition.

Figure 8-36
Create a DVD or VCD for your slide show.

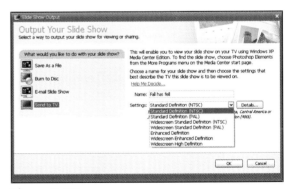

Figure 8-37
Using the power of a Media Center PC with your television.

Sharing Images via E-mail

I F YOU'RE USING PHOTOSHOP ELEMENTS, then it's obvious you have a computer. If you have a computer, then it's most likely you have e-mail. It seems like everybody is sharing things via e-mail: funny stories, inspirational thoughts, birthday wishes, and business communications.

Photoshop Elements provides several methods of sharing your photos via e-mail, all of which preserve tag and metadata information. You can send the images as an attachment, or you can send them via Photo Mail, which embeds the photographs into the body of your e-mail message. Photo Mail also allows you to select from mail accessories such as backgrounds, frames, and borders. You can use Photo Mail with Outlook, Outlook Express, and Adobe E-mail Service, but you can't use Photo Mail if you don't use one of those three services.

Setting E-mail Preferences

Before you can send e-mail through Photoshop Elements, you must specify your e-mail program. E-mailing an image through Photoshop Elements works best with Microsoft Outlook or Outlook Express, but you can also use the Adobe E-mail Service if you're using a Web-based e-mail, such as Yahoo! mail. A fourth option lets you save the images on your hard drive and manually attach them by using any method with which you are already familiar.

To set the e-mail preferences, choose Edit > Preferences > Sharing. Photoshop Elements displays the Preferences dialog box you see in Figure 8-38. Click the E-mail Client drop-down list and choose the method you prefer. Depending on which option you select, you may be prompted for more information. For example, if you select Adobe E-mail Service, you need to enter your name and e-mail address. Before you can actually send images through the Adobe E-mail Service, a test message is sent to your e-mail address to verify the legitimacy of the address. If you choose Save to Hard Disk and Attach File(s) Yourself, you need to select a folder you want to use as a default location for saving the files.

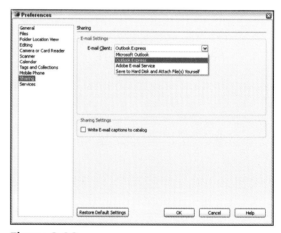

Figure 8-38
Select your e-mail client.

Managing the Contact Book

When you send e-mail through Photoshop Elements, you can use the Photoshop Elements contact book to specify who you want to receive the images. Open the contact book by choosing Edit > Contact Book. The following steps walk you through managing your contact book:

▶ **Add a Contact: Click the New Contact button, which displays the New Contact dialog box shown in Figure 8-39. Enter the recipient information and click the OK button.**

Figure 8-39

Add a contact to your contact list.

▶ **Edit a Contact: Select the contact you want to edit and click the Edit button. Photoshop Elements displays the Edit Contact dialog box where you can change any information.**

Double-Click Contact to Edit

Optionally, double-click a contact, which also displays the Edit Contact dialog box.

▶ **Delete a Contact: Select the contact you want to delete and click the Delete button. Click OK at the confirmation message.**

▶ **Import a Contact List: If you want to import addresses you already have stored in Outlook or Outlook Express, click the Import button and, from the resulting Choose Contact Source dialog box, select vCard Files, Microsoft Outlook, or Outlook Express.**

▶ **Sort a Contact List: Click any column heading to sort in A to Z alphabetical order. Click again to sort in reverse alphabetical order (Z to A). In Figure 8-40, the contacts are sorted by name.**

Figure 8-40

Sort contacts by any column heading.

E-mailing Photos

From the Organizer workspace, select the photographs you want to send. Choose one of three methods to launch the e-mail. From the Shortcut toolbar, choose Send > E-mail, or from the menu choose File > E-mail, or simply press the Ctrl+Shift+E shortcut key combination. The Attach to E-mail dialog box shown in Figure 8-41 appears.

Figure 8-41
E-mailing your photos from Photoshop Elements.

The left side of the dialog box shows the selected items. Click the Add button to add additional photographs. Next, you select the recipients from your contact book, although you cannot select any recipients and later enter the e-mail addresses manually.

Now select a format for the images, typically Individual attachments, which send each photo as an individual attachment or Photo Mail. With the Individual Attachments options, you also need to specify the image size and quality. If you choose Simple Slide Show, Photoshop Elements combines the images into one slide show and sends it as a PDF file. If you choose the Simple Slide Show option, you also need to specify a file name for the PDF file.

Non-JPG Images

If you have non-JPG images selected, Photoshop Elements converts them to JPG images unless you deselect the Convert Photos to JPG option.

Type an optional message in the Message box and then click the Next button. The option you see next depends on the format you selected:

▶ **Individual Attachments:** Launches your e-mail program and shows you the e-mail message.

▶ **Simple Slide Show:** Displays a confirmation message about the attachment. Click OK.

▶ **Photo Mail:** Launches the Stationery and Layouts wizard, where you can select additional options for your e-mail (see Figure 8-42). Open any of the seven stationery categories by clicking the category name. Select a stationery and then click Next Step. In step 2, you can change the photo size, select layouts, fonts, borders, or add captions. Click Next, and Photoshop Elements launches your e-mail program.

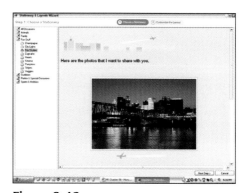

Figure 8-42
Choose an optional stationery background for your images.

Sharing Images on a Mobile Phone

YOU CAN ALSO SEND IMAGES to a cell phone, as long as any recipients are using a service and a plan that allows them to receive images. Sending images to a cellular phone is very similar to sending them via regular e-mail except that in the contact list, you must have their cell phone e-mail address already listed. Select the images you want to send and from the Shortcuts toolbar, choose Share > E-mail to Mobile Phone. You see the Send to Mobile Phone dialog box shown in Figure 8-43. Select the recipient, a desired file size, and an optional message, and then click Next. Photoshop Elements sends the images using your default e-mail program.

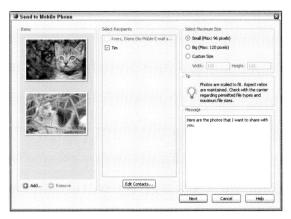

Figure 8-43
Sending images to a mobile phone.

9

Creating a Photo
Panorama

PICTURE YOURSELF STANDING ATOP A HILL, overlooking a great city. You turn your head from side to side trying to take in the wide view of the majestic beauty, hoping you'll never forget the moment. Of course, you take pictures…lots of pictures trying to capture the image. Your eyes see it as a panorama because you can view the entire width of the scene. Unfortunately, most camera lenses just can't capture the same as the human eye.

A panorama is described as a wide view of a physical space. The word originated to describe paintings of an Irish painter named Robert Barker. Today, we see lots of things in a panoramic mode. Theme parks often construct theaters to show movies in a 360-degree setting, and most major cities now have an IMAX theater where you watch movies in an *almost* 360-degree setting.

In the photography world, panoramic photography is a style that strives to create images with exceptionally wide fields of view. Some people used to say they had a wide-angle lens and while there is no formal definition for the point at which wide-angle leaves off and panoramic begins, truly panoramic image are thought to capture a field of view comparable to, or greater than, that of the human eye. The resulting images offer an unobstructed or complete view of an area, usually taking the form of a wide strip.

Preparing for a Panorama

EVEN IF YOU DON'T HAVE an expensive panoramic camera, you, too, with the help of Photoshop Elements can create panorama images. You need several pictures of the scene (which we'll discuss shortly) and the Photomerge™ Panorama feature available in Photoshop Elements. The Photomerge™ Panorama feature is a photo stitching process that joins multiple photographs with slightly overlapping fields of view in order to create a larger, panoramic image once assembled. The software interpolates or recalculates the final image where the component images are not in precise alignment.

When you take your photographs, you need to plan ahead if at all possible. Your source photographs play a large role in your panoramic composition. Most methods require that the images have all been taken from the same point in space. You don't have to be perfect when you take your shots. The Photomerge™ Panorama can help with some correction, but you do need to take the best images you can. Here are a few guidelines to help you take the best shots for your panorama:

▶ When shooting the images you intend to blend into a panorama, it's a good idea to avoid moving people and subjects very close to the camera in the areas where the images will be blended together.

▶ Take lots of shots with a liberal overlap of the photographed area. The overlap will enable Photoshop Elements to choose the best position for the blending between the frames. Overlap images should overlap approximately 15% to 40%. Any more or less can make irregular blends in the merged images.

▶ Use a consistent focal length. Avoid using the zoom feature of your camera while taking your pictures.

▶ Keep your camera level and steady. Use a tripod, if you can, to help maintain camera alignment and viewpoint.

▶ Stay in the same position. Try not to change your location as you take a series of photographs, so that the pictures are from the same viewpoint.

▶ Avoid using any special distortion lenses.

▶ Maintain the same exposure. Don't use a flash in some pictures and not in others.

FreeStockPhotos.com

Using Photomerge™ Panorama

TYPICALLY, CREATING A PANORAMA involves joining anywhere from two to ten images. While most panoramas are based on a wide horizontal view, Photoshop Elements can also create a vertical panoramic image. The basic premise is that you tell Photoshop Elements what pictures to use and Photoshop Elements does the rest! It's almost that simple. Let's take a look at how to create a panorama.

Begin by optionally opening the photographs you want to use in the panorama. Only images that have been saved can be used in creating the composite. Then from the Editor or the Organizer, choose File > New > Photomerge Panorama. The Photomerge opening dialog box seen in Figure 9-1 appears.

Which Workspace?

You can create a panorama from either the Editor or the Organizer workspace, although I personally find it easier to begin in the Editor workspace since that's where I'll end up for final panorama editing.

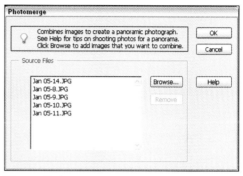

Figure 9-1
Select the images you want to merge.

If you opened the images before you started the Photomerge, you should see them listed in the dialog box. If any are listed that you don't want in the merge, click the image name and then click the Remove button. If you want to add images, click the Browse button to locate the photographs. Click OK when the list contains the images you want to use. Photoshop Elements opens and processes the image and then displays the Photomerge working dialog box seen in Figure 9-2.

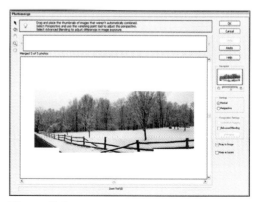

Figure 9-2
A preliminary panoramic image.

A dialog box notifies you if the process couldn't figure out where a particular image fit into the merge.

From the Photomerge working dialog box, you'll see a toolbar on the left, (which you can use to manipulate the merge); you'll notice a lightbox along the top for storing unused images; and on the right you'll see options for viewing and editing the merge. The tools include:

▶ **Select (shortcut key A):** Use the Select tool to move an image in the merge or to drag an image to or from the lightbox.

▶ **Rotate (shortcut key R):** Click the Rotate tool and click the image you want to rotate. Drag the mouse to rotate the image.

▶ **Vanishing (shortcut key V):** Use the Vanishing tool to change the vanishing point image.

▶ **Zoom (shortcut key Z):** Use the Zoom tool to zoom in to a specific area of your image. Hold down the Alt key to zoom out.

▶ **Move (shortcut key H):** Use the Hand to navigate around the image.

Other Navigation Tools

On the right side of the dialog box, you'll also find a Navigation window and a zoom slider.

Moving Images

While the Photomerge function does a great job assembling the panorama, sometimes it misses a common area. Take a look at Figure 9-3. While zoomed in, you can see that in two different places the fence posts don't quite line up.

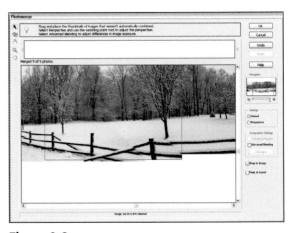

Figure 9-3
An image with misalignments.

You use the Select tool to click the image that needs adjustment. A red border appears around the image, and the selected image name appears along the bottom. You can use the mouse to drag the image to a new location, but a better option for minor adjustments to the individual image placements is pressing an arrow key. In this example, we need to move the image up just a little. Each key press moves the image one pixel at a time. It's important to examine the image closely for these inconsistencies and correct them now. They really show up later in the final merge.

Rotate Image

Sometimes, an image needs just a little bit of rotation. Select the Rotate tool and adjust the image as needed.

Change the Perspective

While the concept of perspective is based on mathematics, perspective drawings typically have an (often implied) horizon line. This line, directly opposite the viewer's eye, represents objects infinitely far away. In this example, the fence line serves as the horizon line. You have some control on the perspective. Click the perspective option, and Photoshop Elements redraws the image improving the perspective (see Figure 9-4). You can more clearly see the curved edges of each segment of the panorama. This is due to the image warping needed to present such a wide angle of view. The image takes on a shape of a bow tie. You'll soon discover how you can correct the bow tie distortion.

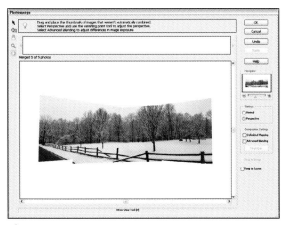

Figure 9-4
Changing your perspective.

Any Photoshop Elements panoramic scene has one vanishing point, which is a point in a perspective drawing to which parallel lines appear to converge. By default, Photoshop Elements uses the middle image as the default vanishing point image. You can, however, control the vanishing point.

While in the perspective mode, select the Vanishing Point tool and click the image you want as the vanishing point. Figure 9-5 shows the last image being used as the vanishing point. Notice how you see less of the road and feel like you turned to the right in the view.

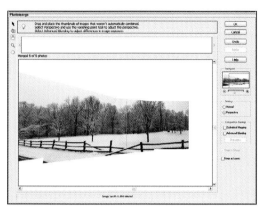

Figure 9-5
Adjusting the vanishing point.

Once you apply perspective correction to a panorama, the nonvanishing point images become linked to the vanishing point image. Clicking the Normal button breaks the link and reflattens the images.

Adjusting Distortion and Color

After you apply the perspective correction, you may often notice the distortion that occurs, usually in the form of a bow tie. Photoshop Elements includes several composition options to reduce the distortion without losing the perspective:

▶ **Cylindrical Mapping: While I'm not quite sure exactly how it works, selecting this option helps reduce the bowed distortion. The Cylindrical Mapping option is only available if the Perspective option is selected.**

▶ **Advanced Blending: Selecting this option helps blend the image colors and tones to minimize the color inconsistencies that can occur if your images have exposure differences. It works by blending broader colors and tones over a large area and blending the detailed colors and tones over a smaller area.**

You won't notice the changes until you click the Preview button. You can only see the corrections in Preview mode and in the final panoramic image. The Preview window (see Figure 9-6) displays a noneditable version of your panorama. Click Exit Preview to return to the editing mode.

Figure 9-6
Previewing distortion and color repairs.

When you are finished, click the OK button. Photoshop Elements generates the panorama and places it in the Editor workspace as a single layered image.

Keep as Layers

If you click the Keep as Layers button, Photoshop Elements generates the panorama and displays each image on its own layer. Be careful. Using this option makes it very easy to disturb the panoramic placement and options you just worked so hard to get together.

Finishing the Panorama

NOW THAT YOU SEE THE IMAGE in the Editor window, you'll notice there are some transparency areas showing through around the edges. Again, this is due to the warping and aligning needed to create the panorama. You need to choose the Crop tool and crop the image so that none of the transparency shows through (see Figure 9-7).

You can finish the image by adjusting lighting, or color, or even applying filters. Figure 9-8 shows the finished image.

Figure 9-8
A beautiful snowy scene.

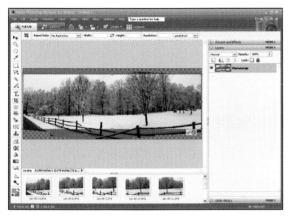

Figure 9-7
Crop the image to remove transparent areas.

Here's another example of a Photoshop Elements' Photomerge Panorama.

Photographer: Griffing Partington

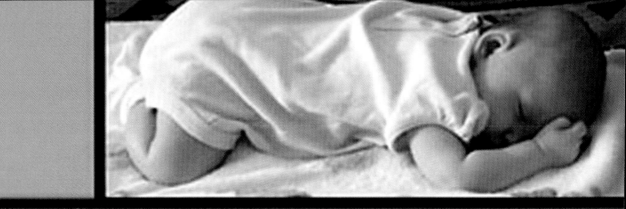

Body
Parts

LAUNDRY INSTRUCTIONS

MADE IN U.S.A.
OF SUGAR AND SPICE
AND EVERYTHING NICE

HAND WASH
WARM WATER
GENTLY TOWEL DRY
100% GIRL

Creation by Lois Van Ackern

10

Creating Scrapbooks, Cards, and Other Fun Creations

PICTURE YOURSELF SITTING ON THE SOFA, reminiscing about a special event in your life: a prom, a wedding, a vacation, a birth, or the home run you hit at the company softball game. You open your photo album and look though all the photographs and other memorabilia of that time and relive the day as though it were just yesterday. You come across the first card you ever received from your special someone and touch the front of the card as a gentle reminder and laugh at the funny message inside.

You can recreate and recapture some of those moments by creating items such as scrapbook pages, greeting cards, postage stamps, and photo albums. Before we begin, you need to know there's no right or wrong creation. Each page is unique according to your subject, your personal taste, and the story you want to tell. Some creations will be very simple, while others can be quite elaborate. In this chapter, you'll learn more about the tools you need to add backgrounds, mats, embellishments, text, and other items you might want to appear on a scrapbook page, card, label, or photo album. I'll give you the basics—the rest is up to your imagination.

You're going to *love* this chapter!

Photo Creations Types

Photo Creations are the finishing touches you can apply to your photographs. In fact, in Chapter 4, you discovered how to create an interactive slide show with some of your images. Slide shows are just one of the many different types of Photo Creations.

Besides just printing your images or posting them to an online Web site, with Photoshop Elements, you can create electronic photo albums, scrapbooks, greeting cards, CD/DVD labels and jackets, and photo layouts. These items are called *photo creations*, and they can be printed on your own printer, or you can have them professionally printed, although a few creations can only be ordered through online services.

Photoshop Elements provides a dialog box to make the creation setup nice and easy. For most creations, you basically specify the type of creation you want, and then select from available sizes, layouts, and themes. Photoshop Elements opens the creation in the Editor workspace so you can customize it to your heart's desire. Let's take a look at some of the Photo Creation types available within Photoshop Elements:

▶ **Photo Book Pages:** Photo books are a series of images, typically containing related images one to a page, with backgrounds and embellishments, which you save as a Photoshop Elements creation using a PSE extension. You can then print each page on your printer, or you can upload the file to Adobe Photoshop Services for online ordering (see Figure 10-1).

Figure 10-1
Creating a photo book.

▶ **Photo Layouts:** You use photo layouts when creating items such as scrapbook pages and photo collages. You'll see how to create photo layouts later in this chapter.

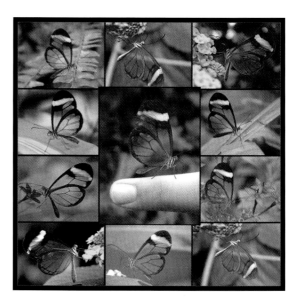

▶ **Greeting Cards**: Create greeting cards with or without your favorite photographs.

▶ **Album Pages**: Album pages are similar to photo books in that you create a layout and theme for your images and then print them, e-mail them, or order prints online; however, album pages generally have multiple images per page.

▶ **CD and DVD Jackets or Labels**: Photoshop Elements lets you create and print CD or DVD inserts that fit inside the case, such as the one you see in Figure 10-2. You can also design CD and DVD disk labels that you can print on adhesive labels. You can usually find the CD or DVD adhesive labels at any office supply store.

Figure 10-2
Creating a CD jacket insert.

▶ **Photo Galleries**: Photo galleries are slide shows you can publish to the Adobe Photoshop Services online sharing site, to your own FTP site, or you can burn them to a CD. The slide shows can be static with multiple images per slide, or they can be animated or interactive.

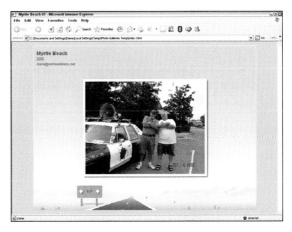

Figure 10-3
A photo gallery as viewed in a Web browser.

▶ **Flipbooks:** You probably created flip-books when you were younger. A flip book is a book with a series of pictures that vary gradually from one page to the next, so that when the pages are turned rapidly, the pictures appear to be animated by simulating motion or some other change. Photoshop Elements saves the flipbook as a Windows Movie File (WMV). If you take photos using the burst mode on your digital camera, a flip book is a good tool for displaying them. Figure 10-4 shows a flipbook creation made from photographs taken at an air show.

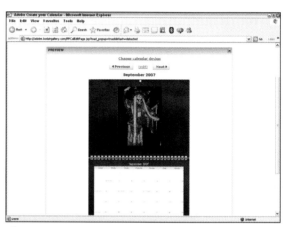

Figure 10-5
Create customized photo calendars.

Figure 10-4
Create mini movies with flipbooks.

▶ **PhotoStamps®:** PhotoStamps are really fun. You select your favorite photograph, and the folks at PhotoStamps.com convert it into a postage stamp (see Figure 10-6). The stamps are real postage and are officially authorized by the USPS. The stamps aren't cheap, though. A sheet of twenty .39 cent stamps costs $17.99.

▶ **Photo Calendar:** Order personalized calendars for the New Year with your photographs on each page. You can select 13 images, one for each month and one for a cover, and using the Create button, order the calendar from the Adobe Photoshop Services Web site. You get to select a background, as you see in Figure 10-5, and you can select which image you want for each month. Available for around $20.00, photo calendars make great gifts!

Figure 10-6
Mail your cards and letters with style!

Using the Artwork and Effects Palette

FOR MOST OF THIS BOOK, we've ignored a palette that's been hiding in the Palette Bin. It's the Artwork and Effects palette shown in Figure 10-7, which provides an easy-to-get-to area from which you can select and apply graphics, themes with built-in decorations, special effects, and text styles to your images. There are five buttons running along the top of the Artwork and Effects palette, each filled with a variety of items to enhance your creations and photographs. Each category displays thumbnail examples of the graphic or effect.

Add to Favorites

When you see a feature you would like to quickly access in the future, click the icon and then click the Add to Favorites icon.

Add to Favorites

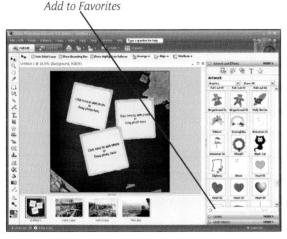

Figure 10-7
The Artwork and Effects palette.

▶ **Frames, Background, Graphics, and Shapes:** With this button, you can choose from a huge variety of elements you can place on your photos and creations. There are four categories (Frames, Backgrounds, Graphics, and Shapes), and each category has numerous subcategories. For example, there are 14 different Background subcategories, such as Baby, Nature, Sports, School, and Travel. The Frames category has 11 different subcategories, including Colorful, Professional, Soft Edges, and Vintage. Graphics have 21 different categories and Shapes have 17 categories.

▶ **Apply a New Theme:** Think of themes as layout templates with backgrounds, frames, and other elements already assigned. Photoshop Elements includes 20 different themes from which you can select.

▶ **Apply Effects, Filters, and Layer Styles:** In Chapter 7, you used this option on the Artwork and Effects palette as a means to apply filters to your images. You can also apply special photo effects and choose from 14 different styles where you can add enhancements like bevels, drop shadows, and inner glows.

▶ **Add Text:** Use this to apply any of 11 different preset effects, such as embossing, shadows, or glows to your text.

▶ **Favorites:** This option provides a location where you can save preferred designs, themes, styles, and effects so they are easily located.

Scrapbooking the Digital Way

ANSEL ADAMS ONCE SAID: "A true photograph need not be explained, nor can it be contained in words." And we've been told that a picture is worth a thousand words. Photoshop Elements has certainly proved both statements to be true over and over again. But, sometimes you just have to spell it out and want to tell a story about your pictures. Whether you create traditional or digital scrapbooks, you can combine the story and the photographs you've so painstakingly taken and then corrected and enhanced. Scrapbooking, which has been around as long as there have been photos, is the practice of combining photos, memorabilia, and stories in a scrapbook style album.

Digital scrapbooking is the newest, hottest trend in the scrapbooking world. With digital scrapbooking, you can merge your passion for preserving precious memories with your love for working on the computer. Whether you add to or replace altogether your traditional scrapbook supplies and tools, you can use your computer, digital graphics, and Photoshop Elements in this exploding art form.

There's a lot to learn, so just take it a little at a time and don't expect perfection right away. Every layout you create will turn out better than the one before. And if you are really unhappy with the first layouts you do, you can always go back and redo them and change the unwanted parts. That's something that's much harder to do with traditional scrapbooking!

(Creation by Lois Van Ackern)

Why Digital Scrapbooking?

Scrapbooking has really come a long way from the days when your grandmother used to do it! With traditional scrapbooking, you end up with paper scattered throughout your house, ink and glue all over your hands, and you make many trips, spending hundreds of dollars (or more) buying expensive paper and supplies. And what about the times you spend hours working on a layout, only to decide that you really wish you'd used a different color scheme or design? Sigh…you probably had to start all over again.

Digital scrapbooking provides you with complete freedom of design since you aren't limited to the supplies you have on hand. You'll find it affordable, convenient, efficient, and flexible.

Affordability

It is easy to see why digital scrapbooking is versatile and economical. As a digital scrapbooker, you don't have to purchase anything to start your scrapbook because you already have your computer and Photoshop Elements.

For traditional scrapbooking, you often buy a lot of different items because you aren't sure which things are going to work for the look you want to achieve. You end up spending a lot of money and then not even using half of what you buy. However, with digital scrapbooking, once you have your backgrounds and graphics, which you can create yourself, find for free on the Internet, or purchase from other scrapbookers, you can use them over and over again, totally unlike the stickers or background papers you buy. You'll never run out of letters and other items.

You also always have just the right colors of whatever you need when you use Photoshop Elements because you can change the color of anything instantly. You can design a layout and then print out as many as you need in just minutes, so you can make identical scrapbooks for everyone in your family if you want to. With digital scrapbooking, your only consumables are your paper and ink if you plan to print your layouts.

Convenience

There are very few full-time scrapbookers. Most scrapbookers work on their creations in their spare time. With traditional scrapbooking, unless you are fortunate enough to have a room devoted exclusively to scrapbooking, you end up with papers and supplies strewn all about a room or over the dining room table. You find yourself constantly having to take out the supplies, work for a while, and then put them all back.

Whenever you have five minutes free, you can work on your digital scrapbooking project without dragging out any supplies. This gives you a chance to tweak your layout, save it, and then come back to it whenever you have another few minutes free. No mess to drag out and put away.

Efficiency

When you work with digital scrapbooking, you never have to compromise your layout because you don't have the right color of materials. You can use Photoshop Elements to create your own perfect color. With over 16 million colors to choose from, one of them is bound to be right for your layout.

Flexibility

Digital scrapbooking allows you to be very creative and adventuresome when working with your designs. With traditional scrapbooking, you take your scissors and glue and manipulate your photograph into the shape and size you want. But once you've cut the image, you're stuck with the new smaller size and shape. Not so with digital scrapbooking. Since you don't use the original photographs in the layout page, you can let your creative side flow with virtually no risk to your precious photographs.

If you don't like something you did, or you make a mistake, use the Undo or Delete commands and try something else.

(Creation by Lois Van Ackern)

General Design Rules

The elements and principles of design are the building blocks used to create any work of art. You'll find many of the same guidelines used by professional photographers are used when designing scrapbook pages. Since design is a visual language and your goal is to tell a story with your visual images, everything you do to create the page should be done with a purpose. Let every item on the page guide you (or whomever is looking at the page) to remember and feel the story behind the page. Design your page for interest and when you compose a scrapbook page, take a look at more than just the subject.

Become aware of shape, form, color, and light—all of which combine to make your page more interesting. Some designer theories say those are the four main elements of design; others say there are seven elements to design; and still others break the number of elements down into even more, smaller categories. Whichever theory you follow, how you apply the basic principals of design determines how successful you are when creating your

scrapbook page. As we take a look as some of these design principals, just remember, they all work together.

▶ **Subject:** Carefully arrange the page so it has one main topic or subject. Don't confuse the viewer with multiple topics on the same page. Relating the design elements to the idea being expressed reinforces the page unity.

▶ **Color:** In Chapter 5 you read about the color wheel and how different colors can project particular emotions, such as red suggesting danger and passion. When creating your scrapbook pages, your choice of color combinations can greatly influence the story you are telling. Color works best when you use strong contrasts, such as dark accents on a light background and light accents on a dark background. Color gradients are good too because they produce linear perspective and add movement.

▶ **Lines:** Lines represent order and give the eye explicit directions about where to look and how to interpret what it sees. Lines are used to group related objects together and divide unrelated objects. Most often lines are emotionally and physically functional rather than decorative. For example, horizontal lines tend to portray calmness, stability, and tranquility. Vertical lines provide a feeling of balance, formality, and alertness, and slanted lines suggest movement and action. Decide which part of your page is the most important and direct attention to it by judicious use of lines. Do not scatter lines about at random. Remember that margins are an invisible line.

▶ **Shape:** A shape is a defined area of geometric form. The main problem is to arrange all of the different sizes and shaped items into larger and more important shapes, and then to relate them to the rest of the design. If you use background shapes, keep them simple and large. Any shape that overlaps another seems to be in front of it, and warm colors seem to be in front of cool ones. Anything that adds depth or the appearance of depth will enhance the display. And remember that size is simply the relationship of the area occupied by one shape to that of another.

▶ **Balance:** In scrapbook page design, balance is a critical element. Where you place your items can impact the emotions felt by those viewing your page. Balance, however, doesn't mean everything is level and even. You could have a page where the central focus is centered and stable (symmetrical), or you could also have a design that is off-centered, which creates a sense of movement (asymmetrical). Another type of balance is radial where the design has a pattern around the page, such as elements in all four corners, or a design that radiates from the center or swirls around the page. The main idea is that you can look at the scrapbook page and feel the story you're telling.

▶ **Texture:** Texture is the surface quality of a shape—rough, smooth, soft, hard, glossy, and so forth. Texture can be physical or visual. Surfaces can look or feel smooth, rough, soft, cool, or warm. Natural appearing fabric patterns are especially good for backgrounds because you can sense how they would feel to the touch. Matte and shiny finishes also add texture.

▶ **Center:** Called the *Rule of Visual Center*, this guideline states that the most natural direction of your eyes when looking at a page is to focus first on an area on the page that's slightly to the right of and just above the actual center of the page. Designers say that placing an item exactly in the center of a page makes a demand upon the viewers' eyes to stay at that point, resulting in a dull and uninteresting page. By placing the most important element or photo at this visual center, you're directing the viewer to use that as the starting point.

▶ **Thirds:** One of the basic rules used by photographers is the *Rule of Thirds,* where you imagine that your picture area is divided horizontally and vertically into thirds. Any of the four points where the lines intersect forms a good line for a subject. Graphic designers use this same rule to make their designs more interesting. As important as the Rule of Thirds is, it's still just a guide to taking more interesting pictures and creating more attractive designs, so don't feel you have to use it all the time.

▶ **Space:** Less is more. How many times have we heard that statement? When you design a scrapbook page, you don't have to fill every inch of the page with some sort of decoration. Sure, most pages are busy, but some blank space is a good thing to have. These blank spaces, often referred to as *negative space* or *white space*, are simply areas on your page that aren't filled with different elements. Blank space helps the balance of the page and enables the viewer to experience more of the idea behind the page—a memory. The blank space doesn't have to be black or white, but should be only one color.

One more thing about design rules. It's all right to break them now and then. Once in a while, you have to bend the rules a little to emphasize your point!

Scrapbooking Components

So, besides your computer and Photoshop Elements, what do you need to begin scrapbooking? Most scrapbook pages use several types of elements, including backgrounds, text, photographs, mats, and embellishments. With the exception of the photographs, you can create all of these elements with Photoshop Elements, but if you don't feel that ambitious, you can use elements created by other digital scrapbook artists, many of which are free or available for a small charge.

Figure 10-8 shows a sample of a very simple scrapbook page. Let's take a look at each type of element:

Figure 10-8
Not all scrapbook pages have to contain every element.

(Creation by Keri Schueller of ScrapGirls)

> **This section will introduce you to the many different types of elements you use when creating scrapbook pages. Later in this chapter, you'll learn more about *how* to create some of these elements.**

Photographs

Scrapbook pages don't *have* to have photographs, although most of them do. When planning your scrapbook page layout, determine which photographs you intend to use. Some pages contain multiple images, some contain a single image, and some contain a single image, but also include smaller cutouts based on the original image like the one you see in Figure 10-9.

Figure 10-9
Select the photographs that best tell your story.

Here are a few tips to keep in mind when working with your photographs:

▶ **Choose a few pictures of a single event. Pick out the best photos. Get rid of the blurry photos and the photos that do not help tell the story or don't show anyone's face clearly.**

▶ **You should have three to five photos of the event. A general rule of thumb in design is to use an odd number of images if you use multiple images (although this is not a requirement, just a tip).**

▶ **Try to select the one great photo that should be the focal point of the page.**

Backgrounds

A scrapbook page background plays a crucial part in the overall layout of your page. It's the largest element you use and typically the other components are modeled, color-wise, after the background. Backgrounds can be solid, textured, gradients, patterned, or created from photos. Figure 10-10 illustrates a few different background examples, but the choices are really limitless. You can choose from the ones provided with Photoshop Elements, or you can create your own.

Figure 10-10
All of these backgrounds are included with Photoshop Elements.

Frames

Use frames as matting to make your photos, journaling, and memorabilia stand out on the page. You can coordinate matting colors and textures with your photographs and memorabilia. For example, use a solid color mat to blend in with the layout or a patterned mat to make it stand out. Figure 10-11 shows two scrapbook pages, one with frames and one without frames.

Figure 10-11
Use mats to enhance the other elements on your scrapbook page.

Titles

Another optional feature is a title for your page. Scrapbook page titles can help describe the moment or occasion. Typically, you create any text, including titles, on a vector layer, which you'll learn about shortly. Figure 10-12 shows a scrapbook page with a title. You can use a single font or "mix them up." You can run the title across the page, vertically along the side, or have it repeat along all four sides. The choice is yours.

Figure 10-12
Titles help tell part of your story.

(Creation by Lois Van Ackern)

Journaling

Another type of text element is *journaling*. Journaling refers to text on a scrapbook page giving details about the photographs. The art of telling a story in print is what separates scrapbooks from photo albums. It is probably the most important part of memory albums. Your scrapbook page won't be complete until you tell the story behind the photos.

Some journaling consists of stories, quotes, or sayings to enhance the page (see Figure 10-13). Personal journaling lets you connect the page viewer with the actual event. Personal journaling records more than just titles, dates, and names. You can describe your reactions to what was happening, tell what the subject was doing and why, share how you feel when you look at the photos, or point out what you notice now that you didn't when the photo was taken. Recollections may seem trivial at the time—the weather, what you ate, a travel situation, something funny that happened, for example—but these details will prove fascinating to those who view your scrapbook pages years from now.

Figure 10-13
Use journaling to bring the viewer into the image event.

(Creation by Lois Van Ackern)

One journaling trick is to pull your five senses into your writing. Sight, touch, sound, smell, and taste—using your senses to describe things when you journal creates an interesting read as you pique the interest of your viewers and invite them to join in your world.

Embellishments

Use embellishments or decorations to personalize and further enhance your scrapbook pages by highlighting photos, drawing attention to journaling, or helping to set a theme. Nearly anything can work as an embellishment. In scrapbook pages, you might see buttons, rivets, shapes, tags, blocks, lines, or Photoshop Elements shapes. You can create the decorations yourself in Photoshop Elements, or you can purchase them online.

The page you see in Figure 10-14 illustrates quite a few different types of embellishments.

Figure 10-14
Use embellishments freely.

(Creation by Angie Briggs of ScrapGirls)

Fonts

Fonts, the typefaces used in text, are one of the most important pieces of digital scrapbooking. The title and journaling you place must be readable, but still be creative. There are thousands of fonts available, but the ones you have available depend on the different software programs you have on your system. Many fonts come with Windows, but others are often provided with various software. Many, many fonts are available on the Internet, often for free. Once you get a font, you must install it on your computer before you use it. Figure 10-15 displays some sample fonts that you could use in your scrapbook pages.

Figure 10-15
All the fonts listed here came with Windows or were free off the Internet.

In the nonscrappers' world, such as in a letter or memo, mixing more than two fonts in a document is typically a "no-no," and you should *never* mix fonts in a single sentence. But in scrapbooking, you can place great emphasis on your statements by mixing your fonts. Go ahead…get creative.

Layers

In Chapter 3, you learned how you can use layers to enhance your photographs, particularly with adjustment layers. The flexibility of digital scrapbooking comes from using layers. You create a layer for each element on your scrapbook page so you can easily reposition, delete, angle, resize, or recolor the elements individually. In Figure 10-16, you see the scrapbook page consists of nine layers, with the text being on a vector layer and everything else on raster layers.

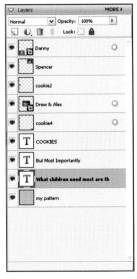

Figure 10-16
*Using layers makes
element manipulation easier.*

Starting a Scrapbook Page

Now that you understand the concepts behind a scrapbook page, it's time to put your creative cap on and put it to work. Remember that the examples you see in this chapter are just that, examples. Use your imagination!

Disk Space

Scrapbook pages generally use a resolution of 180 to 200 DPI. Scrapbook pages tend to get quite large, especially with a high resolution and a large page size. Make sure you have *plenty* of hard disk storage space or the ability to write to CDs before you begin. I've seen individual scrapbook pages anywhere from 10 MB in size up to 150 MB in size!

Begin by gathering the items you want to memorize. Open the photographs you want to include. Scan in memorabilia such as maps, ticket stubs, ribbons, stamps, or anything that is meaningful to the page you're creating. You'll find lots of scrapbooking items such as backgrounds, frames, and embellishments included with Photoshop Elements. You can also use Photoshop Elements to create your own embellishments, but remember you'll find lots of free scrapbooking stuff online. You'll also see some freebies and demos on the CD included with this book. And, of course, gather your photographs.

Using the Creations Button

You could start with a new blank Photoshop Elements canvas and create the page from scratch. But Photoshop Elements includes a *great* feature where you can get your scrapbook page started quickly and easily. From either the Editor or the Organizer workspace, click the Create button on the Shortcuts bar and select Photo Layout. You see the New Photo Layout dialog box shown in Figure 10-17.

Preselect Photos

Optionally, from the Organizer, select the images you want to use on the page before you click the Create button.

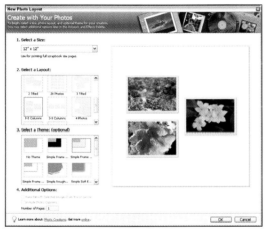

Figure 10-17
Use the Create feature to quickly start a project.

1. From the Select a Size drop-down list, choose the size you want. Most scrapbook pages are at a 12"×12" size, although if you're going to print the page, consider that most printers don't handle that size so you may want to choose 8.5"×11".

2. From the Select a Layout area, scroll through the options until you find a layout that somewhat fits what you have in mind, as far as the number of photos and the placement. If you don't find what you want, choose an option close to it. You can modify the layout later to better fit your needs.

Size Considerations

You need to consider whether you will print it yourself upon completion, have a professional printer print it, or just keep it only for computer viewing. If you plan on printing it and placing it in a scrapbook album, plan your page size accordingly. Some scrapbookers print at an 8"×8" or 8.5"×11" size, but most prefer a 12"×12" layout. While you can enlarge or reduce the canvas at any time, there's a possibility that resizing could distort your entire layout.

3. From the Select a Theme area, select a theme that meets your needs (Figure 10-18). If you don't like any of the options, choose No Theme, and you can design your own later.

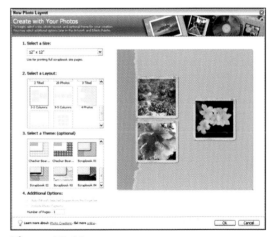

Figure 10-18
Optionally, choose a theme.

Theme Choices

Theme choices may vary depending on your page size.

4. If you preselected images from the Organizer, leave the Auto Fill box checked, and Photoshop Elements will automatically place your images on the page. Uncheck the box if you want to place the images manually.

5. Again, if you preselected images from the Organizer, you can include any photo captions. Most of the time you will not want this option selected.

6. Click OK, and Photoshop Elements will begin your creation. The scrapbook page opens in the Editor workspace so you can continue working on it.

Save Often

Don't forget to save your project often. Save the file as a PSD file at least until you finish.

Placing Images

Placeholders appear on the image according to the layout you suggested. You have a number of options for working with the placeholders and the images you want to place in them. You can drag your photograph from the Photo Bin into the frame, or you can click a placeholder, which displays the Open dialog box from which you can select your photograph.

When Photoshop Elements places your photo into the placeholder, notice the adjustment bar seen in Figure 10-19 that appears above the image placeholder. Drag the slider to enlarge or shrink the photo so it fits into the frame the way you want. Also, you can drag the image around in the frame to position the subject where you want. Click the Apply check mark when you are finished.

Replace Images

If you decide you want a different image, simply drag a different image into the placeholder. The new image replaces the old image.

Adjustment bar

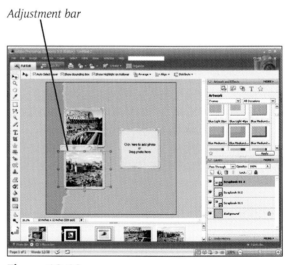

Figure 10-19
Adjust your photograph size.

Notice that the Layers palette shows a layer for the background and a layer for each image placeholder.

Naming Layers

Scrapbook pages tend to have lots of layers, and it really helps you position elements if you name your layers according to their content. Right-click any layer and choose Rename Layer.

Some photographs lend themselves to a different shape than provided with the placeholders. One option is to select the placeholder and resize the frame. This also resizes the photograph to the same size. Another option is to make the frame fit the entire photograph. Right-click the placeholder and choose Fit Frame to Photo.

Rotate Frames

To rotate any frame, select the placeholder and drag the rotation handle so the image is the angle you like.

As you view Figure 10-20, notice how one image is larger, and the other two images are moved and rotated.

Figure 10-20
Modify image placement.

Changing Elements

If you're not pleased with your background, you can easily change it. From the Artwork and Effects palette, choose the Artwork icon and select Backgrounds as the category. Select a subcategory and when you find an option you like, click the icon and choose Apply. In Figure 10-21, I changed from a tan scrapbook background to a green textured background.

Figure 10-21
Change backgrounds.

Other Background Options

If you have an image you'd like to use as a background, select the background layer and drag the background image onto your scrap page. If you want to reduce the layer opacity, right-click the background layer icon and choose Layer from Background. You can then modify the layer opacity.

If you would like to change the frames (matting) behind your photographs, from the Artwork section, select Frames and choose a different frame. Drag the frame icon until it is over the image you want to reframe. Repeat for any additional images. This gives you the flexibility to have different frames for different images.

Adding Text

Now you're ready to tell your story. It can be a short story, just a word or two, or it can be lengthy. To begin with, think about what you really want to say. Who will view it? Is there something you want the viewer to know that the picture can't tell them? Scrapbook journaling is a very personal process, and each person has their own style. In Chapter 2, you discovered the Horizontal and Vertical type tools. Those are the same tools you will use to add text to your scrap page.

Select the desired text tool and then select a font type, size, color, and alignment. Take a guess if you don't know what you want. You can change it later if you need to. Click the mouse where you want the text to begin and type away. As with the images, Photoshop Elements places each individual text object on its own layer. The layer name reflects the actual text.

To edit the text or text attributes, right-click the text object and choose Edit Text. Photoshop Elements highlights the text, and you can make any desired changes. Click the Apply button when you are finished.

For depth and accent to your text, choose a Layer Style, such as bevels or drop shadows, and drag the icon to your text object. You can also apply any of the text styles from the Text icon in the Artwork and Effects palette. In Figure 10-22, both text objects have a bevel style applied, and the year has a deep drop shadow.

Embellishing the Story

When someone is telling a story and they add a little extra to it, they are said to be *embellishing* the story. You can add a little extra to your scrap page story by adding embellishing elements. The embellishments can be simple from small gold

Figure 10-22
Tell your story.

dots to fancy like leaves, ribbons, trinkets, and the like. Like other elements, you can select them from the Arts and Effects palette, or if the embellishments are in their own file, you can drag them into the scrap page.

Experiment with adding embellishments and adding different styles. A well placed drop shadow makes an item appear three-dimensional (see Figure 10-23).

Figure 10-23
Add elements for emphasis.

Installing Additional Elements

YOU'RE GOING TO BE SO HOOKED on scrapbooking that you'll find yourself searching all over the Internet for the thousands of free brushes, backgrounds, textures, and patterns. Oh yeah, also fonts, embellishments, and images. The question then becomes how do you tell Photoshop Elements that you have all these wonderful items?

Installing Fonts

Let's start with fonts. Fonts are controlled by Windows, not Photoshop Elements, so they must be installed through the Control Panel. All you need to know is where you currently have the fonts—did you put them in a download folder, on a CD, or on your desktop? Click the Start button and open your Control Panel.

If your Control Panel looks like the one you see in Figure 10-24, click Switch to Classic View.

Once you are in Classic view, double-click the Fonts icon. A Fonts window opens displaying all your current fonts. Choose File > Install New Font, which brings up the Add Fonts dialog box. Using the Folders and Drives areas, locate the folder where your fonts are located. You will see the font names listed in the top box, as shown in Figure 10-25. Select the fonts you want to install and then click OK. Your computer does the rest for you. Simply close the Fonts window and, if necessary, the Control Panel window when you are finished. Whenever you use your text tool, your new fonts are available.

Switch to Classic View

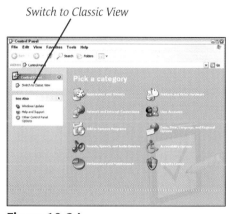

Figure 10-24
Changing the Control Panel view.

Fonts Are Universal

The fonts you install are not just available for Photoshop Elements, but for all Windows applications.

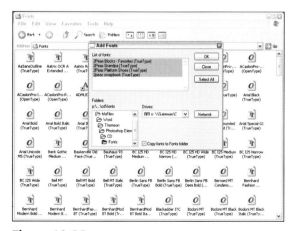

Figure 10-25
Installing new fonts.

Installing Additional Presets

As you've probably noticed, Photoshop Elements installs with a number of different brushes, textures, shapes, gradients, and styles, such as bevels and shadows. When designers create these types of files, certain rules must be followed, and each type of brush, shape, gradient, and so forth must follow a particular file naming convention. For example, Photoshop Elements sees patterns as a file with a PAT extension, such as Holiday.PAT. Most pattern files actually contain more than one pattern and usually they are somewhat related, such as Holiday Stripes.PAT.

Photoshop Elements stores these standard files, along with any new ones you create or download, in an area called *Presets*. Table 10-1 lists some of the different Preset categories and a sample file name illustrating the appropriate file extension for each file type.

Photoshop Elements includes other presets, but these are the main ones you'll use while scrapbooking. When you purchase or download new presets you need to tell Photoshop Elements about them. Some purchased elements include their own installation program, but most do not so here's how to load them. It involves two main processes: copying the file to the proper folder and loading the file into Photoshop Elements.

1. Locate and right-click the file you want to install (i.e., PASTELS.GRD) and choose Copy. It won't look like anything happened, but it did. Windows is storing that computer file in memory.

Close Photoshop Elements

For best results, close Photoshop Elements before installing new presets.

2. Open your local hard drive from the My Computer windows and then locate and open a folder named Program Files. You should see lots of folders listed, similar to what you see in Figure 10-26. Your folder names will vary, depending on the software you have installed on your computer. (If, after opening Program Files, you see a notice similar to Click Here to Show Files, go ahead and click the option.)

Table 10-1 Preset File Naming

Description	File Extension	Sample File Name
Patterns	.PAT	NATURE PATTERNS.PAT
Brushes	.ABR	WET MEDIA BRUSHES.ABR
Custom Shapes	.CSH	ARROWS.CSH
Gradients	.GRD	PASTELS.GRD
Styles (i.e., Bevels & Shadows)	.ASL	DROP SHADOWS.ASL

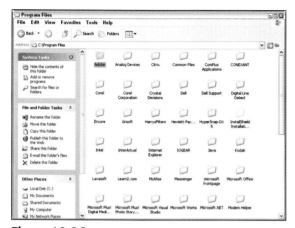

Figure 10-26
Locating the Program Files folder.

3. Double-click the folder called *Adobe* and then double-click the folder called *Photoshop Elements 5.0.*

Default Installation

The default program path is C:\Program Files\Adobe\Photoshop Element 5.0. If you installed your program in a different location, navigate to it instead.

4. Double-click the folder called *Presets* and then open the folder with the style of preset you are installing, such as Patterns.

5. In the resulting window, choose Edit > Paste. Windows copies the file to the proper location. Now you must tell Photoshop Elements about the file.

6. Open Photoshop Elements and choose Edit > Preset Manager. The Preset Manager dialog box opens.

7. Select the Preset type you're installing, such as Patterns or Brushes, and then click the Load button. The Load dialog box opens. (See Figure 10-27.)

Figure 10-27
Install the preset into Photoshop Elements.

8. Locate and select the preset you want and click Load. The new elements appear in the Preset window and are also available by category if you click the More button. Click Done when you are finished loading new presets.

Jump to Default

Photoshop Elements should open right to the Presets folder. If not, navigate to the appropriate folder where you copied the preset file.

Greeting Cards

ONCE YOU HAVE THE BASIC concepts of scrapbooking, you can apply the same measure to creating greeting cards. Create Christmas cards, birthday cards, get well cards, thank you cards, or just an I'm thinking of you card. You manage greeting cards in the same way as a scrapbook page. Begin by clicking the Create button and choosing Greeting Card. The New Greeting Card dialog box seen in Figure 10-28 appears.

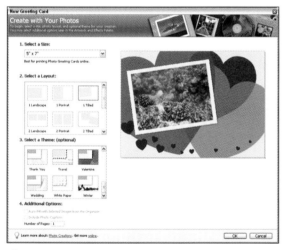

Figure 10-28
Create custom greeting cards.

Select a size, a layout, and an optional theme and click OK. As with scrapbook pages, you can change the background and add text and embellishments.

If you want to create a card without photographs, select the photo placeholder and press the Delete key. Photoshop Elements confirms you want to delete the selected layer.

(Creation by Smart Art Cards)

Create your own personalized two-page greeting cards. Design the front the way you want and then add your message on the second page. To print a two-page card, print the first page on your card stock and then place the card back into your printer to print the second page on the card inside. See your printer manual for placement instructions.

Isn't it fun making creations with Photoshop Elements? You've discovered that scrapbooking digitally frees you from being confined to just working with memory albums and the elements that you can find in your local scrapbook store. You've also discovered that you can create your own personalized greeting cards, making sure the recipient hears just the message you want. The possibilities are endless.

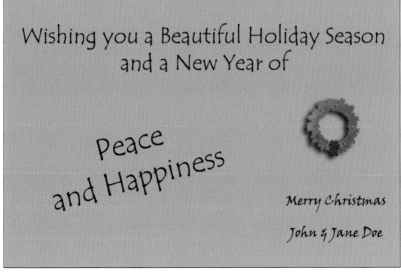

Index

License Agreement/Notice of Limited Warranty